# FREEDOM

## *from* FEAR

Only victories cure

D. L.

# FREEDOM *from* FEAR

## Overcoming Anxiety, Phobias, and Panic

HOWARD LIEBGOLD, M.D.

**CITADEL PRESS**
Kensington Publishing Corp.
www.kensingtonbooks.com

CITADEL PRESS BOOKS are published by

Kensington Publishing Corp.
850 Third Avenue
New York, NY 10022

All Kensington titles, imprints, and distributed lines are available at special quantity discounts for bulk purchases for sales promotions, premiums, fund-raising, educational, or institutional use. Special book excerpts or customized printings can also be created to fit specific needs. For details, write or phone the office of the Kensington special sales manager: Kensington Publishing Corp., 850 Third Avenue, New York, NY 10022, attn: Special Sales Department; phone 1-800-221-2647.

CITADEL PRESS and the Citadel logo are Reg. U.S. Pat. & TM Off.

First printing: December 2004

10  9  8  7  6  5  4  3  2  1

Printed in the United States of America

Library of Congress Control Number: 2004106180

ISBN 0-8065-2591-6

THIS BOOK is dedicated to my son Mark, an undiagnosed agora-phobic, who could stand the pain no longer and took his own life at age twenty-one.

After my own phobic cure I decided to dedicate my professional life to helping others overcome these devastating afflictions. I founded the Mixed Anxiety Phobease classes for adults and children and conducted countless lectures and workshops to prevent others from committing suicide and to convey one simple message of hope: You don't have to be anxious for the rest of your life and you don't have to kill yourself to end your suffering because *all phobias and obsessions are truly curable*.

# Contents

# Acknowledgments

I WOULD LIKE to thank my wonderful wife, Carol, who co-facilitated innumerable Phobease classes and workshops and encouraged me to write this book. She also originated and now conducts the ongoing Phobease support group.

Special thanks to the following:

Stephanie Chambers, my stepdaughter, who typed many of my earlier manuscripts. After her phobic cure she has continued to promote and teach many Phobease workshops and classes.

All those recovered phobic patients who subsequently volunteered to co-facilitate Phobease classes, especially Yvonne and Dale Bullock. Their willingness to share their wondrous accomplishments inspires others to combat their fears.

Lou Anne Dibble and Beverly Finn who initiated Phobease classes in many hospitals, and have continued to teach at several locales. Their creativity is incorporated in all classes and workshops.

My children, Gregg and Michele, both recovered phobics, for creating, conducting, and maintaining the Phobease web site (angelnet. com). Their diligent efforts have taken the Phobease doctrines to the far corners of the earth.

The more than 15,000 phobic and obsessive children and adults who have courageously faced their fears in Phobease classes, workshops, and home courses.

All the therapists who have utilized Phobease materials to effectively treat their clients.

Dena Fischer for putting up with my lousy handwriting and typing this manuscript.

My very special agent Amy Rennert for her efforts to promote this book. She believed in my mission.

Finally, a very special thanks to Joyce Kaplan, MFCC of Terrap, who saved and gave me back my life by teaching me how to overcome thirty-one years of phobic desperation. Her teachings and legacy are manifest in every patient that attends Phobease.

I love you all.

# Introduction

FEAR AND ANXIETY are epidemic in our society. It is estimated that anxiety disorders have doubled in the past four decades. According to the latest National Co-Morbidity Study, forty-six million Americans will suffer a significant anxiety disorder during their lifetime. Even that figure is underestimated since the study omitted people over fifty-five years of age and those diagnosed with obsessive compulsive disorder (OCD).

In essence, one of every five Americans will be affected. The cost is staggering. According to the Anxiety Disorders Association of America (ADAA), $42 billion is spent yearly and much of it, more than half, is wasted on non-psychotherapeutic endeavors. The average phobic will waste more than $10,000 on unnecessary laboratory tests or office visits, visiting six to ten practitioners. The average phobic will go six to twelve years before being adequately diagnosed and treated. Painfully, 70 percent of anxious patients will never be properly diagnosed and they are overwhelming the nation's medical resources. Because anxiety symptoms mimic a host of medical conditions, anxious patients are three to five times more likely to consult a physician; they are six times more likely to be hospitalized. Forty-three to 60 percent of anxious patients will become depressed or self-medicate with alcohol or drugs. Three to 5 percent will commit suicide.

The intent of this book is to convey hope to all anxiety sufferers that their condition is treatable and curable. It will act as a guide to assess the appropriateness of past and current therapies. It is not intended to replace professional psychotherapy. Phobease is never in competition with existing therapies, rather it is a supplement to any ongoing program. By the same token, there is much research to suggest that manualized treatment, utilizing books such as this one, can effectively treat anxiety disorders. Over 15,000 successful Phobease graduates can't be wrong. Indeed, all phobias and obsessions are curable. (Did I mention that before?)

I always tell my classes that to cure an anxiety disorder you must begin on page one. In the prologue I will discuss how I developed my own phobia. More important, I will discuss the three major mistakes I made that allowed me to maintain and perpetuate my disorder for thirty-one years. Chances are you have made the same ones or you wouldn't be reading this book.

Chapter 1 is about understanding anxiety disorders: It will abolish your shame and guilt about your condition when you learn the origin, physiology, and evolutionary benefits of anxiety. This chapter is so important you ought to read it twice.

In chapter 2 you will find more than forty tools and strategies you can use immediately to minimize or abolish anxiety today.

In chapter 3, "Desensitizing to Phobias and Obsessions," you'll learn how to creep up on any fear: the gradual safe, incremental but safe, planned and safe, and finally controlled and definitely safe (did I mention safe?) way to confront *any* fear, a process defined as desensitizing or getting familiar with your fear.

Chapter 4, "Phoboc Potpourri," is dedicated to conditions that require specialized treatment. It includes imagined ugliness, fear of blushing, bowel accidents, choking and gagging, vomiting, hoarding, illness phobias, shy or bashful bladder, suicide, self-mutilation, and hair pulling.

Chapters 5 and 6 focus on cognitive therapy: how to stop scaring, demeaning, and depressing yourself and how to stop bashing yourself over the head so you can fall in love with yourself.

Chapters 7 and 8 offer life skills for wounded birds: assertiveness, mastering the art of conversation, arguing, and speaking in public.

Chapter 9 tackles self-esteem, where it went and how to get it back.

Chapter 10 examines codependency and how to overcome any psychological disorder.

Chapter 11 tells you how to be happy though phoboc.

At the end of chapters 1–11 there are short but important home-work assignments. There are no shortcuts. Phobease only works if you do. Each chapter assignment leads you down a path that will allow you to surmount your fear and live the expansive life you so desire. Some people say some of the assignments are "hard." Is a few minutes of "hard" worth years of unrestricted, fear-free life? I can tell you personally, *it is*.

Finally, a word about my teaching and writing style: When I was growing up there was a magnificent singer named Kate Smith. Besides a wonderful voice, she was famous for the clarity of her diction—you could understand *every* word she sang. I wish I could say that about some modern-day artists. Nevertheless, I always strive for simplicity and clarity. If you are looking for a complex, scientific treatise on obtuse psychological theories to explain your disorder, I suggest you put this book down and look elsewhere. I brag to my children's classes, age six to fourteen years, that I teach at a twelve-year-old level. When I teach my adult classes, I teach at a twelve-year-old level, and when I teach physicians, psychotherapists, and psychiatrists, you guessed it, I teach at a twelve-year-old level. I also warn my participants if there is something important, I will repeat it "47 to 94 times." If you complain that this text is too simple and too repetitive, I will take it as a compliment. While knowledge alone can never cure anxiety disorders, lack of knowledge will maintain and perpetuate them. You need a specific body of information to cure and this book will provide that. Good luck on your quest for that fear-free expansive life.

# FREEDOM
## *from* FEAR

# Prologue: My Story

I AM A PHYSICIAN, a board-certified specialist in rehabilitation. I was chief of the Kaiser Foundation Rehabilitation Center for twenty-five years and in 1991 was elected California Rehabilitation Physician of the Year. I conducted the acupuncture clinic for twenty years, the chronic pain and temporo-mandibular joint clinic for eighteen years.

I hope you are impressed with all these accomplishments. But I forgot to mention something else. For thirty-one of my thirty-eight professional years I had a zealously guarded secret. I was a severe claustrophobic. So severe that at the height of my phobia I was only safe at home and at the hospital. The only place I felt worthwhile was at the hospital. It was not uncommon for me to spend 100 hours a week there. "I was always in!"

It all began my junior year at the University of California at Los Angeles. I was a pre-med major, under great stress to make grades. No one in my family had gone beyond high school. The family business was a failing hardware store and thus the only hope for a better future was to do well academically. I simply decided in my freshman year to study harder than anyone else at the university. I studied six to eight hours every day, including weekends. I made Phi Eta Sigma and Phi Beta Kappa, both scholastic achievement societies.

Then one day I walked into my third-year Shakespeare class with no idea that events in the next few minutes would devastate my life for the next thirty-one years. Moments after I sat down my heart began to pound, I was breathing rapidly, my hands were sweaty and cold, my mouth became numb. I experienced severe abdominal cramping and discomfort and severe bowel urgency, as if I were going to have a bowel movement. I felt if I didn't leave that room I would die. I was terrified. I literally ran from the room. Incredibly I entered that room

1

a normal human being and left a severe claustrophobic. Actually, that's a lie. I wasn't normal. I was extremely shy in high school and shyness is a phobic manifestation. I was awesomely sensitive and overly responsible—more indications of a phobic predisposition. My hands shook if I lit a girl's cigarette—a form of scriptophobia—an inability to write without trembling if being observed. I was born to have an anxiety disorder. Unknowingly, I was a walking phobic time bomb. That bomb exploded that morning in class.

Unfortunately, for the next thirty-one years I never ventured anywhere without worrying about having another of those anxiety attacks.

I calmed down for my next class but made three crucial mistakes that guaranteed the persistence of my anxious symptoms. Instead of going to the student health service, I chose not to tell anyone. I was afraid they would think I was crazy and would notify medical schools about my condition, thus wasting three years of scholastic work. I decided not to tell anyone. Second, I went to the bathroom prior to entering my next class just to make sure I didn't have a bowel accident, and third, I sat on an aisle seat closest to the door so I could leave easily. I followed those same patterns for the next thirty-one years, guaranteeing the persistence and maintenance of my phobic fears. Everything I was doing was rehearsing my fears.

Unfortunately, once a phobia begins it has a life of its own. It increases in scope—a phenomenon I would later find out is called "generalization." It began in a classroom but soon spread to restaurants, theaters, buses, freeways, bridges, parties, courtrooms, and planes—any situation wherein I did not have an immediate escape or access to a bathroom.

Phobics have "target" organs: bodily systems that express their anxiety. Some have cardiorespiratory symptoms: chest pain, rapid heart rates and shortness of breath, concerns about heart attacks, and strokes. Others have cerebral symptoms—dizziness, light-headedness, feelings of detachment and dissociation—they worry about brain tumors, multiple sclerosis, or going insane.

My target organs were my stomach and bowel. When I got anxious, I felt severe abdominal pain and nausea and a sense of bowel urgency. My greatest fears were that I would vomit in public or have a bowel accident. Again, for the next thirty-one years I chose behaviors to avoid these two fears and again reinforced and perpetuated them. I never ate before lectures and ate only turkey breast and mashed potatoes with white gravy before social events because they would look less offensive if I threw up. I avoided red sauces, thinking that would look like blood. Eating turkey and mashed potatoes, I would learn, were subtle neutralizations that only reinforced my phobic fear.

My world began to shrink. Anything I did was accomplished at a high level of anxiety. I had great difficulty going anywhere away from home—agoraphobia. Nevertheless, I married but never told my wife about my phobia. I was accepted to the prestigious University of California at San Francisco medical school and performed well.

Medical school in those days was conducted like a Marine boot camp. The first morning a Nobel Prize laureate welcomed us and informed us that there were five students waiting out there for one of us to stumble. If that happened, we would be summarily flunked out of school. We were given a 300-page reading assignment that night and informed there would be a test the next morning. I went home, threw up, and studied until 5:00 A.M., then took a three-question test that was not graded—surprise. Things never changed. The homework was daily and lengthy. I was rooming with four other freshman medical students and all we did was study. It was a competition to see who could stay up the longest. The one who went to bed before 3:00 A.M. was probably first.

The first semester included one primary class—human anatomy. Four students were randomly assigned to one cadaver and virtually dissected it from head to toe. *Gray's Human Anatomy* was our eight-pound, 1,400-page bible that was to be learned from cover to cover. Every waking school moment, weekends too, were devoted to that study. It didn't take too much imagination to realize the importance of test scores in that class. There would be a midterm and a final that comprised 80 percent of the grade. It was rumored that the bottom 5 percent would flunk out.

The midterm was announced: a three-hour, fifty-question practicum. Each of the twenty cadavers would have areas marked with arrows or colored strings indicating parts to be identified anatomically. There were rumors circulating that in the past, cutthroat students would move the arrows or strings so that those who followed would answer incorrectly. It was part of the lore but added to the prevailing stress.

One way I coped with stress was to be comedic. I have, to this day, a perverse sense of humor. I would be the one on the cadaver team telling sacrilegious jokes—not about the cadaver—but medical school, professors, and the absurdity of our academic burden. That was my reputation—comic. As such, I wasn't taken too seriously and from a phobic standpoint, that was good. I could fade into the woodwork—nobody would notice. As test day approached, study hours increased. It wasn't uncommon to study the entire night, staggering off to school the next morning and catching a few winks when the lights went out for slide projections. The night before the test no one slept. My roommate decided to do some additional studying from a German anatomy text and was asking the questions that weren't covered in our English texts. We concluded he was a genius and would score higher than anyone in the class.

Test day arrived. We were lined up one by one to enter the anatomy lab. The mood was as somber as a funeral. No one spoke. Professors and assistants carefully observed the test takers to make sure no one cheated. Touching the exhibits was forbidden. At the conclusion the participants acted as if they had been let out of solitary confinement—indeed we had. We gravitated to our favorite beer pub and spent our yearly allowance. We reviewed various questions, shaking heads in disbelief when the answers given didn't coincide with our own. It was a consensus that indeed we had all flunked.

Two weeks later, midterm scores were posted outside the dean's office. Eighty eager students descended en masse to the grading spectacle. When I was eight or ten people from the wall, I heard someone say, "Who is Liebgold?" "I dunno" someone else answered. When it was my turn, I looked at the posted list of eighty names arranged in order of score. At the top was "Liebgold, H." I knew then I belonged. My roommate? He scored in the middle of the pack. He was overprepared. He closed his German text and studied only English for the rest of the semester.

My cover was blown. Phobic or not I could no longer hide behind a veil of anonymity. Professors dropped by our table to compliment me, our anatomy assistant shared in my accomplishment and beamed that "one of hers" had taken top grade.

The pride I felt didn't change my phobic concern. I was preoccupied with the fear of having a panic attack and being deemed as weak, ineffective, and blemished. I continually fed my claustrophobic fears by sitting on an aisle seat near the exit and never went to a class without first going to the restroom.

People always ask how I could have been anxious for so many years. I wasn't anxious all that time—I avoided any anxiety-provoking situations. You see, I could nicely hide behind my academic responsibilities. I didn't have to go many places because I was either studying or on call. Phobics can always find a way to avoid discomforts. Later, I had three children, another wonderful way for agoraphobics to hide. Initially, just taking care of them, and later taking them to parks—open areas with lots of restrooms. Even as a physician, I was relatively unencumbered. Only in meetings would I experience anxiety, but if I got too anxious I would pretend my beeper had gone off. I would go to the nearest phone and complete an imaginary consultation. I would then leave to go see a "patient"—my secret safe for another day.

But my level of anxiety gradually escalated since I was continuously fearful that I would be found out. I finally admitted I needed help. Even though I was a Kaiser physician and eligible for free psychiatric care, I opted to go elsewhere for therapy so no peers would see me going into the Kaiser psychiatric unit.

We had only a brief introduction into psychiatry in my medical training. It was all Freudian and psychoanalysis was held in very high regard. I was a doctor and had the money; surely psychoanalysis would cure me. I found a therapist who would see me at night after work. I didn't tell my wife about my phobia, but since I almost never left the hospital before 7:00 P.M., I could attend therapy unnoticed. I went for eleven months, spent close to $17,000, and at the end of therapy, though I felt a little better, my phobia was unchanged. I didn't know then that Freud, the father of psychiatry, was a travel phobic and couldn't attend his own mother's funeral. I also didn't know that psychoanalysis, or even psychodynamic talk therapy, was not an appropriate primary treatment for phobias and obsessions. This is not psychiatry bashing—the techniques in use today were simply not available then.

Several other times in those thirty-one years when I was in crisis I again sought outside psychiatric care. The most devastating event came when my oldest son, a brilliant student, in the top 0.05 percent in SAT scores, a straight-A student throughout high school and college, took his own life. He was an undiagnosed agoraphobic who was also receiving inappropriate psychotherapy. He had dropped out of school because of increasing anxieties and took a fatal dose of poison. I had barely heard the term "agoraphobia" and couldn't appreciate the depths of his avoidant pain.

I was devastated. The outcome of all my psychiatric ventures was the same. They helped to deal with the acute crisis, that is, death and divorce, but my phobias remained unchanged. I concluded that I would never be cured. I would realize later that all phobics share this same depressing myth.

I decided to follow my son's path and took up a new hobby—pistol shooting. My intent was to commit suicide to finally be free from the incessant pain. I had obsessed on suicide in the past. Once in a third-year medical class I drew a picture of the Golden Gate Bridge with an arrow leading to the water. My dilemma was that if I killed myself, my death had to appear accidental. Absurdly, like most phobics, I was concerned about what people would think (the famous WPTs we'll talk about later). As such, I purchased a .22 caliber target pistol. If you buy a .357 magnum and put that in your mouth, everyone would know your intent. I decided to make a beautiful wooden carrying case for the pistol. No one would waste their time on such a project if they were going to kill themselves—"it surely must have been an unfortunate accident."

I always look back and wonder why I didn't pull the trigger. Incredibly, it wasn't lack of courage or a sense of parental responsibility. I was afraid I might miss, become paralyzed, and end up a patient in my own rehab center, unable to run from my claustrophobic fears. And so I carried on—one difficult day at a time.

Things came to a head in 1983. My surviving son wanted to go to the 1984 Olympic games in Los Angeles. To a claustrophobic, afraid of crowds, the Olympics would be a living hell. They were talking about two million visitors; the freeways would be so crowded they would become parking lots—things claustrophobics love to hear. Even that year's telephone directory had a picture of a packed Olympic stadium on the front cover. Every time I saw that picture I knew I could not handle the crowd. Every newspaper carried articles about the expected transportation difficulties. My only hope was that one article reported that so many people were applying for tickets to the opening event that there was only 1 chance in 4,500 to obtain tickets. I told my son in advance that I would mail in the application but I doubted we would get tickets. Whew!

In October 1983, I received a congratulatory letter from the Olympic committee stating that I had, indeed, won two tickets to the July 1984 Olympic Games Opening Ceremony. Nine months in advance I had a severe panic attack because I knew I would not be able to handle the situation.

I was still in a very high level of anxiety the next day when I was presented two subpoenas at work. As chief at a large rehabilitation center, my patients, who had been catastrophically injured, often filed lawsuits. Again, courts were very confining and difficult for me. I always felt trapped in them. In twenty-five years I never received *two* subpoenas in one day. These were big cases involving big companies for millions of dollars. *Big* and *millions* increased my anxiety greatly. I barely could get through the day. I had a surreal feeling of weightlessness and detachment. I thought I might explode. My mind was racing—how could I get out of these obligations? I was frantic. I couldn't see a way out. Should I use that target pistol now? I was never closer to ending my life.

I don't know whether you believe in God or a universal spirit, but my God, who because of my perverse sense of humor resembles Mel Brooks, said, "Howie, you better watch the 10 o'clock news."

That night there was a segment on our local TV news about a group in nearby Lafayette who claimed phenomenal success with phobias. They mentioned the name of the organization but it was an abbreviation and I didn't know how to spell it. There is a famous Chinese proverb "When a student is ready, a teacher will appear." I was very ready.

Fortunately, there was a follow-up article the next morning in our local newspaper—TERRAP—short for territorial apprehension, that is, agoraphobia. (I'm going to have terrible trouble writing this next sentence as the tears are flowing, as they always do when I recall this moment.) I called first thing in the morning and scheduled an intake interview for that afternoon. For the first time in thirty-one years I was told what I had were panic attacks and agoraphobia and that they were curable. I had never heard those words before.

I enrolled in their sixteen-week class but read all the course materials and the three recommended supplemental texts the first weekend! I could not sleep. For the first time there was hope and a path. Four weeks later I was 95 percent better. Four weeks, that is eight hours of instruction, I was 95 percent better. In four weeks I was sitting in a movie theater watching *The Natural*, tears cascading down my cheeks, not because Robert Redford had just hit a home run, but because for the first time in thirty-one years (many, many more tears) I was sitting in the middle of a row, not in an aisle seat, without anxiety.

Incredibly, for thirty-one years I was eight hours away from being helped. Not eleven months of psychoanalysis—eight hours of teaching. All those years bordering on the brink of suicide and alcoholism—although doctors don't become alcoholics, we become wine connoisseurs. (However, the glass got bigger and the brew got fresher and I knew if I continued I would be an alcoholic. I didn't care—I had found at least one way to get that fist out of my stomach.) That day, I stopped "wine tasting" and decided to sell my pistol, the one with the exquisite case. I knew I didn't need them anymore. The therapy was working. There was more than hope, there was success and the promise of a cure. (That last word always does it—a few more tears.)

I came home and wrote a fairy tale—"The Phoboo"—about a young man named Howie and how he slew his Boo monster. The manuscript, like this one, was soaked in tears. I have never been able to read or discuss these events, or that story, even twenty years later, without the torrential outpouring of tears. (I couldn't even proofread it dry.) I had gotten my life back.

In the next weeks I systematically attacked every phobic fear I had. Victory after victory piled up. I took rapid transit, I rode elevators, I flew, I dated for the first time in the three years since my divorce. I ate in restaurants, ate Mexican food, went to shows. I gave talks without fear, I gave depositions, I gave court testimony. I have now gone on over thirty-five cruises and traveled to fifty countries—none before my cure. I couldn't go on cruise ships because they close their doors and sail away from port. Airplanes, too, have that same routine. Closing doors meant I was trapped and that simply was not tolerable. I lived my very constrictive but safe existence for thirty-one years. I never thought I would ever wake up in the morning without apprehension, knowing I could handle whatever came along that day. It was called peace of mind.

In July of 1984 I attended the Olympic games in Los Angeles, sat thirty-five seats from the aisle with my son, with two million visitors, with freeways jammed bumper to bumper WITHOUT ANXIETY. I don't have to mention the tears I shed that day, but three reservoirs overflowed and the two-year drought was resolved.

I realized that I had a new mission. I would devote my entire professional life to teaching others how to overcome their fears and obsessions. I realized that what I was doing all those years was learning about how to cure anxiety disorders. I had become the world's authority on the topic, because now, twenty years and 15,000 patients later, I always brag to my classes, I never met a patient who had a symptom I didn't have. In thirty-one years, I had them all. Now I know those years weren't wasted.

I had always been told I had a unique gift for organizing and teaching and I now applied those skills to create my own Phobease classes. I am a voracious reader and while I was going through my phobic cure I read every article on anxiety, phobia, and obsessions written in the previous ten years. I combined that with my personal phobic experiences and a multitude of human growth development seminars and created the first Phobease class in October 1984. Armed with an array of unique props—rubber brains, rubber monsters, a brain bag, squirt guns, squeak hammers, marshmallows, magic wands, and T-shirts with pertinent messages—I entered the foray. I used these props to drive home the Phobease principles.

What's unique about Phobease is it treats the entire anxiety spectrum in large mixed-anxiety classes. So whether you worry excessively, have panic attacks, phobias, obsessions, or post traumatic stress disorders, the Phobease principles will work for you. I view phobics as wounded birds, limited in social skills. So what is needed in order to cure any anxiety disorders is life skills training added to a conventional curriculum—assertiveness, conversational and arguing skills, and even dance lessons.

At the first class, sixteen frightened patients sat in a circle and used a 32-page photocopied manual. While it may not be reassuring to hear how one frightened doctor cured his phobia, twenty years later, 160 pages added to the manual, and 15,000 successful graduates should be enough to convince you, if you do the Phobease work, you will cure! Fifteen thousand patients should be able to tell you that all phobias and obsessions are curable. Please believe.

# 1

# What You Need to Know to Cure Your Anxiety Disorders

*Ingredients:*

1 Dr. Fear tie
1 grocery bag inscribed "Brain in Bag"
1 large rubber brain
1 large rubber monster hand puppet
1 bag large marshmallows
3 squirt guns—small, medium, large
3 juggling balls
1 bent magic wand
1 big sign: "Face the Fear _____ ? _____ and It Will
  Disappear"

*Directions:*

Display prominently on a large table in front of seventy terrified phobic children and adults.

## The Three Most Important Things
## You Need to Know

### 1. All phobias and obsessions, including yours, are curable.

Fifteen thousand successful Phobease class graduates cannot be wrong. If you do the work, you will cure. Do you want to know something else? *They are easy to cure!*

### 2. You were born to have an anxiety disorder.

There is a huge genetic contribution. It runs in families. It is not lack of courage, willpower, or moral fortitude and it is not the result of poor parenting. You were born with an anxious predisposition or a biological sensitivity that led to your anxiety disorders.

### 3. You are not trained.

I don't look at anxiety disorders as terrible psychiatric problems. Rather, no one has trained you in how to effectively manage your anxiety. Almost daily, I receive phone calls from patients who have been in therapy for years. Five minutes later I realize they have virtually no insight or useful knowledge about their condition and do not know what they have to do to cure. By the time you have completed chapter 3 you will be trained.

## Scope

Anxiety and fear are epidemic in our society. Nine of ten people have mild restrictive fears. Two of three people are uncomfortable speaking publicly. Prior to September 11, 2001, one-third of all people were uncomfortable flying, and now two-thirds are uncomfortable. Twenty-five million people won't fly at all. Fear has crippled the American airline industry. One in ten of us, myself included, have severe restricted phobias and one in twenty-five have obsessive compulsive disorders (OCD).

The painful part of anxiety disorders is that we will waste $10,000 on unnecessary medical visits and tests. I spent three times that much. We will see six to ten practitioners and go six to twelve years without being appropriately treated. Seventy percent of us will never be diagnosed. I went thirty-one years before I was diagnosed correctly. During that time, the most bothersome statement I read was "If you face the fear it will disappear." Well, for thirty-one years I faced my demons every morning. Upon awakening I would review the day's events to see where I might be trapped, have a panic attack, and be found out. For thirty-one years I was forced to endure the anxiety caused by public presentations, shows, and restaurants. Hundreds of times I found myself at high levels of anxiety, hanging on by the skin of my teeth, while I repeatedly faced my fear—and it got worse! Why? Because there was a word missing from that "face the fear" phrase. The word was "correctly." Face your fear correctly and it will truly disappear. I was facing it incorrectly all those years. I did the exact opposite of what I needed to do to cure.

## Can You Juggle?

For thirty-one years I did everything wrong. I always ask my classes, "Can you juggle three balls or more?" I can and proceed to demonstrate my skill, but in a class of fifty it is rare for more than one or two people to raise their hands. I ask, "How come you others can't juggle? Is it because you are stupid and uncoordinated? Is it because you have never been trained?" With prompting, they agree they have not been trained.

The reason you have had your phobias or obsessions for years, the reason you are reading this book, is that no one trained you in how to effectively manage your anxiety. The reason I had phobic symptoms for thirty-one years is that I was untrained. Well, I'll teach you how to juggle: throw one ball a little higher than your head and catch it in the other hand. Then, start with one ball in each hand. When the ball reaches its apex, throw the second ball inside of the first. Finally, with two balls in one hand and one in the other, complete the juggling process by throwing each ball inside the apex of the other. Practice two million times to get an automatic muscle program called an "engram," and you are a juggler.

This book will take you on a specific path that will teach you to cure your anxiety disorder. There is nothing vague about the process. You don't even have to know how your problem began. You will never be forced to do anything you are not ready to do. Phobease is not in competition with your present therapy, but most people can cure their phobia or obsession without a therapist. The American Psychiatric Association (APA) and the Anxiety Disorders Association of America (ADAA) have recommended that the preferred therapeutic regimen is psycho-educational, cognitive behavioral, and experiential desensitization. How's that for a mouthful? If you have not been treated with such a program you have not been treated appropriately. By the time you finish this book, you will be "trained." You will know precisely what you need to know and how to use it correctly in order to cure your specific anxiety disorder.

## Three Myths

All phobic and obsessive patients share three devastating myths:

1.  *"I'm the only one who has this."* Ptooey! You and forty-six million Americans will suffer an anxiety disorder in their lifetime—virtually one in four adults and 13 percent of children. The problem with such a myth is that it isolates you. "I don't dare discuss it with anyone because it's so rare they probably wouldn't understand and would think poorly of me." I never shared my disorder with anyone for fear they would know I was blemished and defective.

2.  *"I am crazy or will go crazy."* As a matter of fact, phobics don't go crazy, but we worry that we will. Indeed, one of the most annoying aspects of these disorders is that we are amazingly sane. "This disease doesn't make sense. I should be able to solve this rationally and logically, but I can't. I've read innumerable books and visited the Internet ad infinitum and I'm no closer to a cure." I used to envy four-year-olds who were sitting in an inside seat. I always thought it would be nice to

get a brain enema. Flush the phobic thoughts out of my brain and I could start over with a clean slate. You will find out later that you can't stop thinking of things and that approach is unproductive. The problem with myth number 2 is that it scares us and adds to our daily stress level. So far, I'm isolated and frightened.

3. *"My case is so severe, so unique, so chronic, that I am incurable."* Ptooey again! The result of this myth is depression, a feeling of helplessness and despair, and utter lack of hope. Sixty percent of patients with anxiety disorders get depressed. After thirty-one years of symptoms, multiple therapists, and many medication trials, my phobia persisted. It did not take a rocket scientist to come to a very depressing conclusion. I was going to be like that for the rest of my life. Can you imagine my surprise when I finally received the appropriate treatment and in four weeks, just eight hours of instruction, I was 95 percent better? I knew then the fallacy of the third myth. Indeed, all phobias and obsessions, irrespective of their duration, are curable.

## The Anxiety Spectrum

As I began to treat large numbers of patients, I realized that anxiety is a spectrum and a continuum. The average phobic has twelve to fifteen separate issues. Regardless of their disorder, the dynamics of the disease and the people who got it were the same. Incredibly, that meant that no matter the prevailing diagnosis, the Phobease treatment was applicable. In essence then, every word in this book applies to your anxiety disorder—*every word!*

At one end of the spectrum is a condition called generalized anxiety disorder (GAD). For every anxiety disorder there is a prominent target symptom. It is the target symptom that generates anxiety. For GAD the target symptom is *worry*. I am talking about industrial-strength, incessant worry. It is so persistent that to qualify for the diagnosis you must have had it for more than six months. People with this disorder find themselves in a constant state of severe anxiety from the moment they awaken to the time they fall asleep. They worry about important things like their children getting killed or their parents dying, but in the next moment can be intensely concerned about the menu for next weekend's dinner.

The next condition in the spectrum is panic attacks. These are defined as the acute onset (peaking within ten minutes) of abject terror. Dramatic physical changes and intense psychological fears of impending doom overwhelm the patient. The events are so terrifying that patients may endlessly ruminate about how they can avoid having subsequent attacks. My first attack occurred in a third-year Shakespeare class and I spent the next thirty-one years trying to avoid the next one. The target symptom in panic attacks is fear of physical (somatic) sensations. Patients are afraid of having their heart burst out of their chest, having a heart attack, a stroke, cancer, multiple sclerosis, fainting, vomiting, brain tumors, and especially dying. They focus on and exaggerate the implication of any bodily sensation.

Farther along the spectrum are phobias. Phobias are exaggerated restrictive fears. The target symptoms are fear of things or events. Initially, phobic fears were defined as irrational. Nothing could be further from the truth. All fear responses are rational. The problem with us phobics is our perception. If you perceive an event as life threatening, your exaggerated fear response will be appropriate. I resented that irrational label. I knew as a physician, board-certified specialist, chief of rehabilitation, and 1991 California Physician of the Year that I was not irrational. What I didn't know was that I was born, predisposed, to develop an anxiety disorder. I wished I had known that.

Next on the continuum is obsessive compulsive disorder (OCD). An obsession is an anxiety-producing thought, image, or urge. It is intrusive, persistent, and repetitive. It creates anxiety because it is often unacceptable to the person experiencing it. This is called "ego-dystonic"—against your will. You will find that your anxiety-producing thoughts are the opposite of your moral beliefs. Thus if you are a righteous citizen, an obsessive thought might be a fear of yelling out an obscenity in church. Fastidious people might fear contamination from dirt or germs. Nonviolent people might obsess about punching, stabbing, or otherwise hurting others.

Compulsions are behaviors adopted to allay the anxiety caused by obsessive thoughts. For contamination, I might wash, bathe, or clean excessively. For blasphemous thoughts I might pray endlessly for forgiveness. The target symptoms in OCD are thoughts.

Inching along the spectrum we come to post traumatic stress disorder (PTSD). Having been exposed to or viewed a life-threatening event, either man-made—wars, hijackings, car jackings, rapes, or beatings—or natural—hurricanes, tornadoes, or earthquakes—the characteristic symptoms are anxiety, hyper-vigilance, flashbacks, sleep difficulties, and nightmares. The target symptoms in PTSD are memories.

Finally, at the end of the spectrum are impulsive or addictive behaviors. The target symptoms with these disorders are urges. Impulsive disorders are a result of an inability to resist those urges. Trichotillomania (hair pulling), skin picking, nail biting, self-mutilation, hoarding, and eating disorders are seen in 4 to 8 percent of patients with anxiety disorders.

Interestingly, the average patient with an anxiety disorder will have components of the *entire* anxiety spectrum. Eighty percent will worry and ruminate excessively (GAD). Phobics frequently have panic attacks and vice versa. I have never treated an obsessive-compulsive patient who didn't have phobic fears. Successful management demands recognition of all the components and treatment directed at their respective target symptoms.

## Phobocs

To avoid having to constantly mention all of the disorders, I have formulated a new word: "phobocs." The first part, "phob," includes GAD, panic, and phobias, while the "ocs" part includes the remaining part of the spectrum: OCD, PTSD, and impulsive disorders. One word—one disorder, and a treatment approach that works for all.

## 220 Phobias and Obsessions

There are 220 recognized phobias and obsessions and several hundred unofficial ones. There are thus plenty to choose from to get each individual's twelve to fifteen personal ones. Fear of public speaking is the number one phobia in the world listed on the Internet. When you speak you are under a microscope. You could be negatively evaluated or screw up for the whole world to see. Comedians know the risk of performing. If you do a poor routine, you "bomb" or "die," but do a good one and you "kill," "slay," or "murder" them. The number two phobia is fear of death. Literally speaking, most people would rather die than give a speech or would prefer to be in the coffin rather than give the eulogy. Fear of disease and flying round out the top four. Claustrophobia, fear of enclosed spaces, is fifth. Sixth is agoraphobia, literally fear of the open market, but really being in situations where you don't have easy access to safety. Finally, a fear of having panic itself comprises seventh place.

The most common phobic category is social phobia—an intense fear of being embarrassed in a social setting. It includes fear of vomiting, being watched, fainting, passing gas, blushing, trembling, or sweating. It includes a fear of being found less than, defective or incompetent, screwing up, not knowing what to say, and not being liked or accepted. Next are the simple phobias: fear of dogs, cats, bugs, spiders, snakes, bats, shots, doctors, and dentists are common, but I have seen patients who have feared butterflies, balloons, worms, and grasshoppers.

## Obsessions

The most common obsession is fear of contamination from germs, viruses, chemicals, or dirt. Now, why would we be so concerned about germs? If you were born with an anxious perception you might pay attention to articles reporting that when you flush a toilet, a mist of urine will descend on your toothbrush if it is located within seven feet. Thanks for that information. Perhaps you read that your kitchen sponge contains five billion germs and is dirtier than your toilet. Some recommend washing your sponge in your weekly dishwasher cycle. I grew up where a rag hung on the kitchen faucet. If the dog threw up, we wiped it up with that rag, rinsed it out, and hung it back up. Today, many kitchen products and toys have antibacterials in them.

Of course, you never heard of bioterrorism, anthrax, small pox, ebola virus, hanta virus, flesh-eating *E. coli*, West Nile virus, and now SARS—help! The second most common obsession is fear of harming oneself or others. Third is fear of disease. Other common ones are fear of making mistakes or offending others, committing suicide, gaining weight, bodily secretions, and concerns about normalcy of bodily functions—especially urine or stool. Scrupulosity is the fear of committing blasphemy or going to hell. More themes are unacceptable sexual thoughts or urges, imagined ugliness (body dysmorphic disorder), superstitions, and extreme perfectionism. Hoarding, hair pulling, skin picking, and self-mutilation are common manifestations of what are labeled obsessive compulsive spectrum disorders.

## Compulsions

The most common compulsions—behaviors performed to allay the anxiety caused by obsessions—are washing, checking, and counting. If contamination is the number one obsession it follows that excessive washing and cleaning would relieve the anxieties concerning the fear of germs. When it entails three hours of daily showering or bathing in Lysol, it qualifies as excessive. Repeated checking may involve doors, windows, stoves, garage doors, or appliances. It might include checking for lumps, nodes, blood pressure, or pulse. Perfectionists might repeatedly check for mistakes before handing in a work project or school paper. Frequently, "perfection paralysis" sets in and projects are not submitted for fear of an overlooked mistake. Counting compulsions complete "the big three." These might include an intense need to count telephone poles, window panes, ceiling tiles, or people or cars passing by. Although the task may seem illogical, one feels compelled to do it lest something bad will happen. Other compulsions are eye-blinking rituals, excessive apologizing or reassurance seeking, praying, chanting, or reciting magical phrases, as well as repeating tasks, rubbing, touching, or tapping, and needing things to be done until they are done right. Superstitious rituals are often performed to avoid some vague catastrophic occurrence. These rituals consume enormous amounts of time and energy.

## Dr. Fear

My nickname, my license plates, and the tie I wear to the first class all
say "Dr. Fear." In Phobease the word fear stands for:

**F:** False
**E:** Exaggerations
**A:** Appearing
**R:** Real

Later we'll find as we learn some tools that Dr. stands for dispute and
reframe. It is extremely important to note that *all* fears are exaggerations of normal concerns. We are not crazy; this is a dangerous world.
Phobocs always want to be reassured that things are safe. I tell them,
"If you want to be safe, don't be born!" That's usually met with an
audible groan. Safety is an illusion. There can never be a guarantee of
safety. Even our perceptions about the topic are distorted. We view
flying as dangerous. I'm going to cure your flying phobia right now.
Do you know how many people were killed on American commercial
airlines in 1998 and 2002? None, nada, zilch, zero. But during those
same two years, 100,000 people were killed in highway accidents, so
don't drive to the airport—stay home. Unfortunately, in those two
years, 16,000 people died in home accidents—so get out of the house.
Take a walk. Alas, 12,000 pedestrians were killed those two years. So,
the next time you hear the airplane door closing say, "Thank God,
now I'm safe." You are safer on an airplane than virtually anywhere
else in the United States. So how come if you have an airplane phobia,
you're not cured? We'll learn later that words, knowledge, rational
logic, and even facts cannot cure phoboc fears. Only experiential victories—purposeful exposures to the thing one fears—cure phobic and
obsessional fears. I will devote an entire chapter teaching you how to
get them.

I have a perverse hobby of collecting annoying ways to die, events
such as a wheel falling off an airplane, crashing through the roof of a
house, and killing the bedroom occupants. There was an incident in
Germany where a train derailed. The front wheels of the locomotive
broke free and rolled a mile and a half into town, crashed through

the wall, and, you guessed it, killed the bedroom occupants. We are not even safe in our own bedrooms. Annoyingly, there is a risk to living. Until you are willing to recognize and accept that risk you will never be free to live your expansive dreams.

## Phobease Class Format

The class format parallels the chapters in this book. It begins with education as to the origin, physiology, and biochemistry of anxiety. It is important to understand that your condition is primarily genetic. You were born predisposed to develop an anxiety disorder. That knowledge allows you to dispel any shame and guilt you may have concerning your disorder. As you have read, they are not a sign of insanity or a lack of courage, or a sign of weakness, immaturity, or neuroses—they are genetic and curable. I wish I had known that during my phobic years.

The second part of the Phobease approach is cognitive behavior therapy (CBT). Cognition is the sum total of your mental skills. It is the totality of your knowledge, social upbringing, your personal expe riences, and coping skills that you bring to resolving psychological challenges. CBT is a discipline that helps you identify those thoughts and beliefs that foster your anxiety and create unhappiness and depression. In essence, all phobocs know how to scare the hell out of ourselves with what we say to ourselves. Cognitive restructuring teaches you how to challenge and change those destructive or scary beliefs.

Finally, the most important part of any effective anxiety program is experiential desensitization. In real English that means learning how to safely and gradually creep up on any fear. "Experiential" means you can't just think, imagine, or read your way to a cure. You must expe rience it in real life. The *only* way to cure any phobia or obsession is through repeated experiential victories. A victory is the *purposeful* exposure to the thing you fear. *There are no shortcuts—the only way out is through*. So, if you have not had a psycho-educational, cognitive behavioral, experiential desensitization therapy program—you have not been appropriately treated. In the future, if you are seeking fur ther therapy, you simply ask, "Do you do cognitive behavior therapy?"

Then you'll be able to evaluate the therapist's approach in light of what you learned in this book.

## Avoidance

The disease of all phobias and obsessions is avoidance. The first time you avoid something because of fear is when the disease begins. And once it begins, it has a life of its own and it keeps getting worse. Avoidance is rehearsing fear. Avoidance is magnifying fear. Every time you avoid, you are practicing negative reinforcement, a psychological phenomenon that unknowingly strengthens your fear. The cure? Non-avoidance.

Have you ever waded into a cold swimming pool? You get up to your mid-thighs and decide the next step deeper will be very uncomfortable. So you get out of the pool and warm up. But the next time you go in the pool it is just as cold. Finally, you decide enough of this nonsense, you dive in, swim vigorously for a few strokes, and in a short time your body gets used to the invigorating temperature. That process is called habituation. That is the exact process you will copy when you are ready to cure your anxiety disorder. Up until now, every time you got anxious, you left the cold pool and warmed up, and every time you did that, you got to keep your phobia for another day, another week, and another lifetime. What all of us have to eventually find out is that if we stay in an anxiety situation and use the tools we will learn, the body will habituate and the anxiety will go away and we will have started on a pathway to cure.

One of my fifteen or so phobias was shopping malls. When I got anxious, I would hurriedly leave and guess what? My anxiety would go away—rapidly! What a wonderful lesson—as soon as you get anxious, run, do not walk, to the nearest exit and you will see a rapid diminution of your discomfort. But then you get to keep your phobia for another disgusting day, terrifying week, and depressing lifetime. For thirty-one years I did the exact opposite of what I needed to cure. I constantly exited the cold pool, warmed up in the comfort of absent anxiety, and never habituated. I never found out that if I stayed, the anxiety and my phobia would go away.

People always ask me how I could have been anxious for thirty-one years? I wasn't anxious for thirty-one years. I avoided for thirty-one years. I could find an excuse to get out of anything. I never had a panic attack in an exotic foreign country—I never went to any. I never had an anxiety attack on a cruise ship—because I never boarded one. Unbeknown to me, every time I never went, I was reinforcing my fear. I only went places where I was safe, where I could be in control, drive my own car, and be able to leave the scene at the first symptom of anxiety. I left that pool more times than I could tell you, thus constantly rehearsing and reinforcing my fear.

Once a phobia or obsession begins, untreated, it gets worse. It begins a process called "generalization." Simply, it increases in scope and intensity. What started for me in a classroom spread to theaters, restaurants, planes, bridges, conference rooms, and courtrooms. Over time, my life became more and more constricted. At the height of my phobia, I was "warm" and safe only in my home and at the hospital. I became a very "dedicated" physician. I didn't know that if I did the exact opposite, practiced dedicated non-avoidance, I would lose my demons in weeks. Stay in the cold pool and cure.

## What Has Evolution Got to Do with It?

Why have fear? There is a science called neuro-ethology that explains neural and biochemical events from an evolutionary standpoint. It appears that every species from guppies to man can be divided into conservative and bold categories. A simple experiment demonstrates this nicely. A group of bold and conservative guppies were placed in a small rubber pool with one hungry bass. There was ample floating vegetation for the conservative guppies to hide behind. Now the bold guppies demonstrated their bravado by venturing out to assess whether the bass was a threat. Twenty-four hours later, there were no bold guppies left. There is obvious survival benefit to being fearful. I'm sure that bold cavemen ventured out to see whether the local visitor was a vegetarian brontosaurus or a meat-eating tyrannosaurus while the phobocs stayed in the cave decorating the walls for future generations. I assume many bold cavemen failed to return.

Thus we are evolutionarily designed to be fearful in order to survive. More important, survival systems tend to be exquisitely sensitive. They are set on a hair trigger—a term that applies to target shooting. The amount of force to move the trigger is set so low that barely touching it discharges the weapon. If you had to pull the trigger hard it would jerk the barrel off target and you wouldn't hit the bull's eye. We have a smoke alarm in our kitchen that goes off at the slightest provocation. That's the kind of fire alarm you want. It wouldn't be too practical if it only sounded a warning when the flames are fifteen feet high. A lightly tanning piece of toast sets it off. That's the same way the body guarantees survival. Our survival mechanisms are overly sensitive.

You can choke on saliva or water, but you can't choke to death on liquids. Nevertheless, they perpetuate the same life-saving cough reflex. You can choke on a chicken or fish bone but you can't choke to death on them. To choke to death, for those of you who have that fear, you must be deeply intoxicated to suppress the cough reflex and then swallow a piece of meat two inches by three inches to cover the entire larynx. One piece of popcorn or a normal bite size mass won't do it.

In your brain you have two small pea-sized structures called amygdalae. These are your storehouses for survival information—your command centers. If at any time you perceive (accurately or not) that you are in danger, the amygdalae will hijack all of your brain processes to mobilize it for mortal combat. They will entreat a huge outpouring of survival hormones that you will experience as fear and anxiety. The response is instantaneous. It doesn't ponder or weigh alternatives. It simply explodes in an all-out effort to save your life.

## Fight or Flight

We are all familiar with the "fight or flight" mechanism. When the body faces mortal threat, a powerful drug is secreted called adrenaline. Instantly, the body is transformed into an incredible fighting machine, capable of superhuman feats. You have read stories of the seventy-year-old grandmother who goes out in the yard to find her grandson pinned under a car that has slipped off its jacks. Grandma runs over and lifts the car and the grandson crawls out. Now you need a force of 700 pounds to lift the corner of a car but when CNN comes out the next day to investigate the story, Grandma can only generate 100 pounds. So where did the other 600 pounds of force come from? It was the secretion of the powerful hormone, adrenaline. It is a drug designed to help you fight a saber-tooth tiger—those prehistoric 1,000-pound pussycats.

Whenever you feel anxious, you have squirted adrenaline. That means that every symptom you experience when anxious is *normal* preparation for mortal combat. More important, that means that adrenaline is a normal body function and *no normal bodily function leads to death or disease*. Anxiety does not lead to heart attacks, strokes, or insanity; it just makes you uncomfortable and by now you are an expert at discomfort. Innumerable studies of panic have shown that the chest pain and heart discomfort you feel when anxious is not due to a lack of blood getting to the heart (cardiac ischemia) but rather more blood flowing into the muscles of the chest. I always ask my classes, "How many people have had panic attacks?" Virtually everyone, including myself, raises their hand. I then ask, "How many people have died of their panic attacks?" Everybody utters that nervous giggle because they're thinking, "Not yet, but what about the next one?" That's when I hold up that famous package of marshmallows and proclaim "Anxiety attacks are no more dangerous than dropping these marshmallows on your bare feet." I point out, further, that these are the big marshmallows and not the minis. Panic attacks are not a physiological threat. Pulse rates and respiration are in the mild exercise range. Since 90 percent of people experience anxiety, if it were deadly, you would have to climb over a mountain of bodies just to get to the neighborhood market. We don't die from anxiety and panic and we never will.

Every symptom you experience when anxious can be explained as a useful preparation for mortal combat. Your hands sweat for the same reason baseball players spit on their hands before holding the bat, so you can grasp your assailant more securely and choke them. Your stomach hurts because if you're fighting for your life you don't need to digest yesterday's hamburger. The blood is shunted away from the bowel to the heart and muscles because they are needed to fight better. The heart pounds because more blood is pumping to the fighting muscles. Why do you have a feeling of bowel and bladder urgency? The body wants them empty in mortal combat. If your opponent slices open your bowel you won't soil yourself and cause infection. You may get numb and feel detached and dissociated. This results from the secretion of another substance called endorphins. Endorphins are 200 times more powerful than morphine. Their secretion creates a wonderful state for a warrior: imperviousness to pain. Fueled by adrenaline, every anxious bodily symptom is preparation for mortal combat—a great drug for fighting the saber-toothed tiger—but not for driving onto a freeway, speaking in public, or dealing with any of your phoboc situations.

## Fight, Flight, and Freeze

While we are quite familiar with "fighting" and "flighting," there is another response to the perception of mortal threat: freezing. Animals, when threatened, become motionless because flight might provoke a sudden attack. There are a number of freezing responses that have survival benefits. When called on to speak, it is common to experience a temporary paralysis of the vocal chords so that no sound can be uttered. From an evolutionary standpoint, that would be useful. Crying out would reveal your position to your enemy. In very shy children, there is a condition called selective mutism: an inability to speak in certain social situations. I believe this is an adaptive survival response of a larynx "frozen" by fear.

There are two things animals can't do under mortal threat: urinate and fornicate. A condition called paruresis (paralysis of urination), shy or bashful bladder, occurs when people cannot urinate in certain social environments. Similarly, impotency is common with extreme performance anxiety. These are all examples of target organ freezing due to adrenaline. You relieve the anxiety and you cure these disorders.

### Adrenaline: The Ten-Minute Drug

Adrenaline, one of the most powerful drugs in the body, incredibly, lasts for only about ten minutes. If your child was having an asthmatic attack and you brought him into the emergency room when I was working, I would give him an injection of 1/10,000 milligrams of adrenaline and the attack would immediately cease. But, if it wasn't cured, the symptoms might recur shortly and the injection might have to be repeated. That's because of the short duration of the action of adrenaline.

So, let me ask you a question. If I asked you to stay drunk for an entire weekend, what would you have to do? Obviously, keep drinking, because if you stopped, you'd sober up. So, here's a more challenging question. How can you stay anxious for an entire weekend with a drug that only works for ten minutes? This is where I take out the first small squirt gun. With each negative or scary statement I make, I squirt some water into a resonant tin plate. "What's happening to me?" (squirt). "Maybe there's some disease that the doctors haven't found" (squirt). "Why is God punishing me?" (squirt). I get out a bigger gun and continue with much more forceful squirts. "What if I never get over this?" (squirt). "What if it gets worse and I can't leave home?" (squirt). "What if I lose my job?" (squirt). And by now I've got the water blaster—a huge gun that squirts a torrent of water. "What if I become homeless?" (whoosh). "What if I lose my license?" (whoosh). "What if my wife leaves me?" (whoosh whoosh whoosh).

Every negative or scary thought, statement, belief, or dream is accompanied by a shot of the most powerful drug in your body: adrenaline. It is not a voodoo god in New York creating your anxiety—it's you! You will soon learn how to stop it. Look at the following list of symptoms caused by the secretion of adrenaline and circle those that you have experienced. These were all mine.

| | |
|---|---|
| blurred or distorted vision | diarrhea |
| can't swallow | disassociation (separated from |
| chest pain | your body) |
| choking sensation | dizziness |
| clenched teeth | dry mouth |
| cold hands and feet | faintness |
| depersonalization | fast startle |
| detachment (dream-like state) | fatigability |

fear of doing the uncontrollable
fear of dying
fear of going crazy
fear of vomiting
feeling of impending doom
feeling of unreality
fidgetiness
flushing
headache
holding breath
hot or cold flashes
hyperventilation (over-breathing)
irritable bowel
jumpiness
lightheadedness
loss of appetite
loss of balance
lump in the throat
muscle aches
muscle tension
muscle weakness
nausea
numbness
pallor
palpitations
rapid heart rate
restlessness
sexual dysfunction
shakiness
shallow breathing
shortness of breath
skin problems (itching, burning)
smothering sensation
stomach pains
sweating
tight chest
tingling in arms, face, legs
trembling
tunnel vision
unsteady feeling—knees shake
urinary frequency
urinary or bowel urgency
vomiting
weakness

Did you circle all fifty-nine? All of these symptoms are the result of the secretion of a normal reaction to threat. However, if you look carefully, many of these could mimic significant disease. You see, doctors are symptom trained. For that reason, anxious patients with somatic symptoms are often exposed to a multitude of unnecessary medical tests and procedures. Led astray by their symptoms, 70 percent of anxious patients are not diagnosed correctly.

## The Brain in the Bag

I hold up my life-size rubber brain and ask, "What is the world's record for brain jumping? How high can the human brain jump?" The audience is usually stumped. As a matter of fact, the human brain has no legs and thus can't jump. I then perform a famous Phobease ritual. I throw the brain into a large grocery bag and I turn it around to reveal a large printed "Brain in the Bag" sign. Since it has no legs, the brain can't jump up and see out of its prison. It can't tell what's outside the bag. It is a high-speed computer that makes 100 million computations per second but cannot distinguish between truth and fiction. You are its master. *It believes everything you tell it.* I yell into the bag: "I'm in New York, there are 3,000 people in the audience, and it's snowing outside." In truth, I'm in Vallejo, California, there are seventy in the class, and it's 68 degrees and sunny outside. When you tell your brain that something is scary and life threatening, it believes you. It does not challenge it, but reacts immediately and mobilizes the body defenses with a massive outpouring of adrenaline.

Now there are two things your brain doesn't want to do. It is the basis for *all* phobias and obsessions. *It doesn't want to die or be embarrassed.* If at any time you perceive a threat to your survival or your ego, you'll get the massive secretion of adrenaline and the host of anxious symptoms that accompany the outpouring.

Incredibly, while the brain makes 100 million computations per second, it can focus on only one thing at a time. What it focuses on are thoughts with the highest energy. It focuses on things that make you anxious because anxiety signals mortal threat. If someone bursts into your office shouting, "Someone in the hall is shooting people with an AK-47," would you:

1. Take the opportunity to create that night's dinner menu? *or*
2. Focus on survival: barricade the door, call 911, ask if anyone has a weapon?

Of course, you would focus on the latter. When something frightens us, we ruminate constantly, the brain is totally consumed with the topic. In time, our entire being becomes concerned with avoiding anxiety. We are thus in constant preparation for the mortal combat that never comes. It is enervating and exhausting and creates a state of chronic fatigue. That in itself is frightening. We digest poorly, we sleep poorly, constantly on vigil for that imagined saber-toothed tiger that never materializes.

## The Boo Voice

Everyone has a Boo (scare) voice. Its job is to peruse your environment twenty-four hours a day to find what it is you don't want to find. It acts like a salacious fiend whose job is to demean, deprecate, depress, and devastate your life. It is a devious, taunting bully. I demonstrate the Boo by placing a large rubber puppet monster on my right shoulder. While the puppet monster adds a bit of levity to the moment, I then tell the audience, *"Your ability to cure your phobia or obsession is 100 percent dependent on how well you recognize and deal with your Boo."* It is so important, you will be asked to name yours. If you were born phoboc, you will never be lonely; you'll always have your Boo to talk to. Whenever you are stressed, vulnerable, depressed, or tired, you will hear from your Boo.

When I began teaching my children's Phobease class, I described the scare voice as the phoboc voice. Children didn't relate too well to that term. However, I found out that most five-year-olds had a friend who would hide behind a bush and jump out and yell, "Boo," so I began to use the Boo in children's class and they understood it. Thereafter, I used it in my adult classes and they, too, understood. I even use the Boo in my professional therapists' workshops and they understand it too because they had the same five-year-old friends.

### Boo Characteristics

The following information is so important, I always tell my classes, "It will be on your final." (There is no final exam, but if there were, all of this material would be on it.) The Boo has three characteristics:

1. It *always* lies.
2. It *always* exaggerates.
3. It *always* catastrophizes.

Thus, if you recognize a Boo message, and you will very shortly, you will know whatever it said or implied is a lie, an exaggeration, and an implied catastrophe. It is the Boo that is destroying your life. Everything you'll learn in this course will help you to deal effectively with your Boo.

## The Boo Has Only Two Weapons

1. *The WPTs:* What will people think. Phobocs, and especially social phobocs, are very concerned with what people think of us. We tend to be people pleasers, and thus we are very sensitive to any perceived rejection. From an early age, we read people very carefully. Every sigh, raised eyebrow, scowl, and frown is interpreted as a personal affront. Up until age twenty, we are desperately trying to fit in and the WPTs are extremely powerful influences. By age forty, we realize what people think is not important. By age sixty, we realize people weren't even thinking about us—but we feel so bad about ourselves that we project that negativity on to other people. We will subsequently learn how to deal with the WPTs.

2. *The what ifs:* The imagined catastrophes generated by this heinous villain. The Boo constantly asks frightening "What if" questions: "What if both wings fall off the airplane?" I'll tell you what happens. The plane noses down at 16,000 miles per hour and in twenty seconds, you'll be dead. (Note: if at any time you die during a Phobease course, you don't have to do that week's homework.) I want you to remember that whenever you're concerned about your own safety. Here's something truly important: *never, ever, answer a "what if" question.* When you do, you pay the emotional price, in adrenaline, as if that event were actually happening now! *All worries are "what if" questions in disguise.*

The Boo plays the game of "gotcha." Remember in school, how someone would point to your chest and tell you you've got dirt on your blouse, you'd look down and they'd run their finger up your nose? The next day, and the Boo is good at this too, they'd alter the message a little so you'd fall for it again. "No kidding, you've got blood on your shirt." You look down and you get that demeaning finger up your nose. Whenever you respond to a Boo "what if," you have "looked down" and the Boo gets to run that famous finger up your chagrined face. You're at war with the Boo. It's a war of points.

Every time the Boo gets a gotcha point, you get a shot of adrenaline and you get to keep your phobia for another day, week, and that infamous lifetime. Don't look down, don't answer "what if" questions and you stop the adrenaline secretion. You get the point and the Boo begins to lose its power over you. If the Boo says "What if the wings fall off and you look out the plane window, the Boo gets a point, you get that proverbial shot of adrenaline, a finger up the nose, and a lifelong phobic disorder.

### All the Boo Can Do Is Go "Boo"

As powerful as the Boo appears to you now, in reality, it has only one tool—adrenaline, a substance you now know quite well. Adrenaline is a *normal* body secretion and never leads to death or disease; that it is no more dangerous than marshmallows on your bare feet, and it lasts only a few minutes. If I stay in the situation, the body will habituate and the anxiety will go away. Thus, in reality (I learned this in the kids' classes) all the Boo can do is go "boo." Now, if you were walking down a dark street and I jumped out of a doorway and screamed, "boo," you would probably be startled and might squirt a little adrenaline. But if I stood there and kept shouting, "boo," you would accommodate rapidly, yawn a few times, and eventually ignore my ranting. That's it. It can't kill you, make you go crazy, make your dog die, or cause you to develop cancer in twenty years. It can't do anything but go, "boo," squirt adrenaline and make you uncomfortable. By now, I am sure you are probably an expert on discomfort. Soon you will learn forty or more tools and strategies to further vanquish your tormenting impotent Boo.

### Booland

Every phoboc has his or her own Booland. It is our own private haunted house. It is our own disaster movie, full of our most feared consequences, that we play when facing our fear-provoking phobias and obsessions. *We always respond to our Booland rather than to the actual event.* I was phobic about crossing bridges. I would get high levels of anxiety just approaching the bridge, while thousands of people crossed it daily without giving it a second thought. People would reassure me that the bridge was perfectly safe. With my perverse sense of humor, I would always think to myself, "Hooray, I'm cured, why didn't someone tell me that before?" Nonsense. The script I played, my bridge Booland, went like this: "What if" (you know now the Boo is about to speak) "you had a panic attack on the bridge, lost control of your car, crashed head-on into an oncoming car, and killed all its occupants? What if you were arrested, brought before the judge who said, 'If you knew you were going to have a panic attack then why the hell were you on the bridge?' Then he takes away your medical license and sentences you to life imprisonment?" Meanwhile, thousands of nonphobics are singing opera arias as they drive, nonplussed, across that very same bridge. It is never the actual event we are responding to, but our scenario: written, directed, and produced by your favorite Boo.

## Phoboc Personality: Who Gets Phobias and Obsessions?

I hope you have your seatbelt securely fastened to keep you from falling out of your chair. highly intelligent, imaginative, creative, sensitive, caring, sympathetic, empathetic, diligent, awesomely responsible and accomplishing human beings are the ones who get anxiety disorders. We have to be highly intelligent and creative to scare the hell out of ourselves with our imagined disaster scenarios. Phobocs are good, kind human beings. We make devoted husbands and wives, innovative lovers, loyal citizens, and conscientious workers, but we are born with an annoying biological quirk that makes us vulnerable to developing anxiety disorders. That is our burden to bear. Buddha said, "Life is suffering and your goal is to overcome." You will use this same personality characteristic to eventually overwhelm your Boo and claim that expansive life you have always dreamed about.

### Born Phoboc

How did you get to be phoboc? You were born, genetically predisposed, biochemically predestined, to develop an anxiety disorder. A wealth of research data documents this. If you give an injection of sodium lactate, a normal occurring blood chemical, to people who have had panic attacks, they develop panic attacks. If you give the same substance to normals (is there such a thing?), nothing happens. If you give one breath of concentrated carbon dioxide to patients who have had panic attacks, they develop panic symptoms. With normals nothing happens. There is a polypeptide found in our brains called cholocystokinin. Inject that into panic patients and they develop panic symptoms while normals show no response. Incredibly, when you introduce these challenges to family members of panic patients, even though they have never had panic attacks themselves, they develop panic symptoms. *These disorders run in families. If you have one, your brother or sister may have one, too. It is quite likely that Mom or Dad or both suffered similarly. Your anxiety disorder is not the result of poor parenting—it is genetic.*

## Conclusion

We are born biologically and biochemically sensitive. In actuality, we display a higher incidence of allergies and asthma, we are sensitive to light (photophobia), sensitive to sound (hyperaccusis), sensitive to smells. We are exquisitely sensitive to chemicals and to drugs and their side effects. I am the cheapest drunk on the block. A half a glass of wine and I am soused. If I drink a cup of tea at 3:00 in the afternoon, I won't sleep for three nights—a slight exaggeration—but the point is that we are biologically wired that way. One chemical that we are very sensitive to is our own scare juice: adrenaline.

People often ask if they have a chemical imbalance. Yes, you do, but you have created that imbalance. Adrenaline, as you now know, is a hormone that prepares you for mortal combat. You don't want a calming drug circulating in your body at the same time that you are fighting for your life. So when you squirt adrenaline you suppress serotonin (your calmative drug). Almost every drug that helps depression, anxieties, and obsessions tends to raise the level of serotonin. Thus our anxiety has created our imbalance and curing the anxiety will restore it.

There have been further genetic studies on monozygotic (identical) twins. If one twin has OCD, the other twin has a 67 to 83 percent chance of having it as well. However, in the normal population, OCD occurs in only 2 to 4 percent of people. Eighty-three percent would be a twenty to forty times greater occurrence. Let's make it more profound. In similar twin studies, if one twin has anorexia nervosa (voluntary starvation), the identical twin has that same 67 to 83 percent chance of having that disorder. However, in the normal population, the incidence is only 0.5 percent. Therefore, 83 percent would represent a 160 times greater genetic risk. There is no question that there is a huge genetic contribution to the development of anxiety disorders. So, dismiss your shame and guilt. *You were born to have an anxiety disorder*.

## Depression and Addictions

An estimated 30 to 60 percent of anxious patients will become depressed. Much of this happens because after multiple failed treatments, we embrace that third myth: "My case is so severe, so chronic, so unique, that I am incurable." The lack of appropriate treatment and the failure even to diagnose anxiety disorders in over 70 percent of patients adds further to the problem. Physicians are often focused on the predominant physical symptoms caused by chronic adrenaline secretion, and they order tests to elucidate their origin. Anxiety can and does mimic a host of possible serious medical conditions. As stated previously, physicians are symptom oriented. They are trained to pursue and treat such symptoms and obviously, too frequently, overlook their anxious origin. As a result, we phobocs may drift further from conventional medicine in our quest for understanding and a cure. Often we accept a host of expensive and unproven approaches. When they fail, it adds further to our despair and depression. As frustrated patients, we may seek our own forms of self-medication, which explains the high incidence of addiction in anxious patients.

## "Trained" Phobocs

The goal in Phobease is to produce a highly trained "Boo" killer—a patient therapist. Phobocs are always looking for a safe place and a safe person to support them. At the end of this course, you will be that safe person and everywhere you go in the world you bring the tools and strategies that will keep you anxiety-free. You don't need anyone to cure you but yourself. Therapists can be effective and supportive coaches, but ultimately you will find that only you can affect the cure.

We use the word "trained" as a mnemonic, where each letter stands for an important Phobease doctrine:

**T:** *Thought stoppage.* A basic tool you use when you identify a Boo message. You say, "stop" and immediately employ an anti-anxiety measure.

**R:** *Relaxation.* You will learn a calmative breathing technique similar to that used in Akido. It is utilized at the first sign of anxiety and always after invoking "thought stoppage." You will be asked to practice relaxation exercises daily.

**A:** *Activity.* Exercise burns adrenaline and makes the heart more resistant to its effects. We will ask you to start a progressive exercise program: a few minutes a day to start, working up to thirty to forty-five minutes seven days per week.

**I:** *Imagined desensitization.* The safest place to begin creeping up on your fears is in your imagination. You will soon learn how to construct a gradual approach (hierarchy) to combat any fear.

**N:** *Nutrition.* There is no magical nutritional formula. One should eat a balanced diet with several snacks per day to avoid low blood sugar (hypoglycemia). When your blood sugar gets low, the body secretes adrenaline to raise that level back to normal. Any time you secrete adrenaline for any reason, you will feel anxious and may feel you are going to have a panic attack. Therefore, include a small amount of protein in each meal to avoid large swings in sugar levels caused by carbohydrate overloads. *Don't drink your stress.* Caffeine has almost the same formula as adrenaline. Reduce or eliminate caffeine from your diet. Read your labels. Phobocs don't need eight cups of coffee, Mountain Dew, Surge, or highly caffeinated lattes.

**E:** *Eliminate stimulating drugs.* These include nicotine, cocaine, ephedra, amphetamines, and marijuana. These have all been implicated in precipitating panic attacks. Unfortunately, large amounts of theobromines in chocolate can do the same thing.

**D:** *Desensitization hierarchies.* A safe, incremental, safe, controlled, safe, way of gradually creeping up on any fear. (Did I mention safe?) I devote a whole chapter to this topic because it is the basis for curing any phobia and obsession.

## Calmative Breathing

The first night of the phobia group I attended, they showed us how to breathe. I thought, "I just paid $1,000 to learn something I've been doing for fifty-two years! Give me a refund!" As a matter of fact, "breathing" has been a relaxation cornerstone of many of the Eastern disciplines for thousands of years.

Phobease breathing is slow, deep, abdominal breathing. Breathe in through your nose, hold it for a count of four, and exhale slowly through pursed lips until you have expelled all of the air in your lungs. You can tell if you are doing it correctly by first practicing it lying down, with this book on your stomach. At the height of inhalation, the book should have moved upward toward the ceiling. This is the same diaphragmatic breathing practiced by singers and lecturers. In through the nose, hold it, one, two, three, four, and exhale through pursed lips—not very dynamic. Wrong! Everything you do has a specific physiological effect to reduce anxiety:

1. *Breathing through the nose.* This slows down the process and counteracts rapid shallow breathing.

2. *Holding for a count of four.* Anxious phobocs tend to over-breathe and worse than that, breathe fast and very shallow from their upper chest (hyperventilation). When you do that, you alkalinize the blood and that reduces the ability of your red blood cells to give up oxygen. Your brain, which is 1 percent of your total body weight, consumes 20 percent of its oxygen. If it doesn't get enough oxygen, it secretes adrenaline,

you feel anxious, and the hyperventilation is exaggerated. Counting to four is a mild form of breath holding that restores the blood to a normal pH, allows improved release of oxygen from the red blood cells, and improves oxygenation of the brain. Wow, all that just by counting to four.

3. *Exhaling through pursed lips.* This prolongs and slows exhalation. Eastern disciplines have long known that exhalation is the calming phase. When you exhale, you secrete a drug called acetylcholine that counteracts adrenaline. Thus, the longer you exhale, the more you can neutralize your stress hormone: adrenaline. Finally, anxious patients are often frightened because in the height of their panic they often feel chest tightness and cannot take a deep breath. Of course not, their lungs are already full from the shallow over-breathing. Focusing on prolonged exhalation empties the lungs; the fifteen pounds of atmospheric air pressure will take care of refilling them.

Thus, what sounded like a simplistic exercise has a profound ability to immediately reduce anxiety. At the very first sign of anxiety, say, "Stop" and take a calmative breath. You can repeat this process several times if need be. You can enhance the effect by doing a fast body check with that first breath. Unclench your fists and jaw and do a total body contraction and then relax completely. You want to mimic a rag doll and try to go totally limp as you continue your calmative breathing. Relaxation is a learnable skill that must be practiced. At first, even when you are not anxious, practice the technique several times a day, use it prior to any situation that might cause you anxiety. It's instantly available, cheap, fast, and effective. It was worth the whole $1,000 course tuition.

## Relaxation

You can't be relaxed and tense at the same time. Thus, it is important to master the art of relaxation. Purchase a Phobease relaxation tape (see appendix A). Listen to the tape at least once daily, more if you are facing anxiety-producing stressful situations. The tape is a combination of Jacobsen's Progressive Relaxation and autogenic muscle relaxation. It takes less than fifteen minutes to complete. Experiment to find the most effective relaxation time for you.

Interestingly, some patients initially get more anxious when they start to relax. Phobocs have been chronically tense for so long that it feels normal. Sometimes we feel if we relax, bad things might happen. It's like a deer being trailed by a mountain lion. If the deer lets its guard down, the lion will attack. If that happens to you, shut off the tape, do some calmative breathing, and start the tape again. In a short time, your body will adapt to its newly relaxed state.

## Medications

Bad news. We are always looking for that magic potion, but there will never be a medication that cures anxiety disorders. Some more bad news: there will never be a drug to make you a concert pianist, a world-class golfer, or a black belt in karate. Perhaps, even worse, there will never be a pill that will allow you to juggle three or more balls. To accomplish any of these things requires learning some basic skills, getting a coach or teacher, and practicing until you have mastered the challenge. Curing phobias and obsessions demands the same approach. There are no shortcuts.

According to the APA (American Psychiatric Association), the primary initial treatment of anxiety disorders should be CBT, not medications. They have suggested that the only indication for medications is when the patient is too anxious or too depressed to do the work required by CBT.

There are several drawbacks to using medications. Twenty-five percent of phobocs won't take medications. They are afraid of physical or psychological dependency. Sometimes they fill the prescription but end up flushing the pills down the toilet. Fifteen to 25 percent discontinue anxiolytic medications because of intolerable side effects. We are exquisitely sensitive to the side effects of many drugs. Interestingly, 25 percent of patients show no benefit from the currently available medications. That means that only 25 to 40 percent of patients get long-term useful benefits.

Treated with medications alone, 80 percent of patients will relapse after discontinuation of the drug. That figure is reversed if patients are treated with CBT. That is expected since it is the long-term skills learned through CBT that protect trained individuals against relapse. The most frequently prescribed medications affect serotonin levels. Higher serotonin serum concentrations have an associated anti-anxiety and anti-depressant effect.

**selective serotonin re-uptake inhibitors (SSRIs)**   These are a group of medications that raise serotonin levels by blocking their removal from serum. They have a strong safety profile, are non-addictive, and are generally well tolerated. They have proven useful in a large number of anxiety, obsessive, and depressive disorders. Prozac, Paxil, Lurox, and Zoloft are current examples. They have a slow onset of action, taking four to eight weeks to achieve effective therapeutic effects.

**serotonin re-uptake inhibitors (SRIs)**   Anafranil (chlomipramine) was one of the earliest representatives. It was virtually the first drug available that demonstrated effectiveness in modifying obsessive-compulsive disorders.

**benzodiazepines**   These are a series of drugs that have a rapid anti-anxiety effect. Valium, Xanax, and Klonopin are commonly used representatives. They are often used temporarily to acutely allay anxiety until the slower-acting SSRIs take effect. Unlike the SSRIs, they have an addictive potential and chronic high dosage use may result in habituation and withdrawal difficulties.

**beta blockers**   These medications specifically block the cardiovascular effects of adrenaline. They are used most often to allay performance anxieties, particularly public speaking or instrument solos. Inderal is the drug of choice.

**others**   Finally, there are a whole host of available drugs and drug combinations that can often reduce disturbing patient symptoms. Newer drugs are eagerly sought as new and unique pathways are discovered.

Medications help many patients to help themselves. By reducing anxiety, patients are more likely to tolerate the challenges of exposure therapy, which is an important component in effective CBT programs.

Approximately one-third of patients who participate in Phobease classes are on anti-anxiety medications. They always ask what the prospects are for getting off their medications. If you have had several severe bouts of major depression or a strong family history of depression, it is likely that you'll be advised to remain on drug treatment permanently. However, most patients, if they cure with a combination of CBT and medication, can be slowly and safely weaned off their drugs. Sometimes, they have to cure twice. Your Boo says, "Sure you cured on meds, but you couldn't do it without them." The Boo is wrong. The tools and strategies allow rapid re-introduction to phobic and obsessive challenges without medications.

## Formulas

The formula for creating a phoboc is:

1. Find a genetically vulnerable human being.

2. Introduce an anxiety-producing thought, image, or urge that the person buys as a truth or possible truth.

3. Observe the person who then avoids, represses, suppresses, and tries to prove or disprove that thought. This approach provides the negative reinforcement that starts the patients on the downward cycle toward their restrictive phobia or obsession. Once started, as you know, the phobia or obsession has a life of its own and if untreated, will generalize (expand).

The cure formula:

1. *Face your "specific" fear.* The big word is specific. When you study hierarchy formulations you will understand the significance of that term.

2. *Experience the fear.* Here I go again, *ptooey.* Every phoboc hates to hear that requirement. We want the magic wand treatment (I always hold up a damaged magic star wand and apologize

that it is no longer working). There is no magic but there is a precise path that you will find shortly.

What every phoboc has to find out, experientially, is that anxiety is not dangerous; that all anxiety goes away; that it is just the result of a normal body secretion and no more dangerous than marshmallows on your bare feet. You have a flying phobia. If you take three Xanax, two Valiums, and five martinis prior to the flight and fly to New York in a coma, you don't get credit for a phoboc victory because you didn't experience the fear. That's an issue with taking any medication, alcohol, or street drugs that diminish your fear. Cure demands the confidence you gain by *experiencing your full fear* and effectively dealing with it. There are no exceptions and no shortcuts. (Have I mentioned that before?)

3. *Habituate and master your fears.* The body doesn't like being anxious. If you stay in the situation, the body sets up a series of chemical changes that return you to your normal state. Like the cold pool example, the body adapts to the stressor. That adaptation is called habituation. If you repeatedly and purposely place yourself in stressful situations, the body becomes more efficient at habituating; your initial anxious response is lessened, and the duration of anxiety is markedly reduced. Eventually, your body will stop reacting with adrenaline and you will have *mastered* that event.

While the disease is purely intellectual in that we scare ourselves with what we say to ourselves, the cure is automatic. You *face* your fear on purpose, you *stay* and experience the anxiety, you *habituate* repeatedly, and eventually you *master* your fear. People say, "It can't be that simple." The wonderful news is that it is!

People always ask me if I'm cured. I always say, "I just got back from my thirty-fifth cruise—none before my cure. I have now visited over fifty foreign countries—none before my cure." To a fellow who couldn't go twelve miles without anxiety, that is a cure. Then they always ask the next question. "Do you still have phobic and obsessive thoughts?" "All the time, but they no longer cause anxiety." So that's my definition of cured: *It is not the absence of phobic or obsessive thoughts but the effective management of your anxiety so you can live an expansive life.*

## Chapter 1 Highlights

1. You were born to have an anxiety disorder—it's genetic and runs in families.

2. Anxiety is preparation for mortal combat and is no more dangerous than marshmallows dropped on your bare feet.

3. Adrenaline, a normal body secretion, never leads to heart attacks, strokes, or insanity—just discomfort.

4. Your Boo always lies, exaggerates, and catastrophizes. It is a salacious bully whose goal is to destroy your life.

5. Anxiety always goes away.

6. Adrenaline effects last only ten minutes—stay in that cold pool.

7. Phobocs tend to be highly intelligent, creative, imaginative, responsible, and empathetic—good human beings.

8. The disease of phobias is avoidance—the cure is non-avoidance.

9. The only weapons the Boo has are the "WPTs" and the "What ifs." The only tool it has is adrenaline.

10. Everyone has their own personal haunted house, their Booland. We respond to that and not to the actual event.

11. Two things your brain doesn't want to do: die or be embarrassed.

12. *All phobias and obsessions are curable.*

## Chapter 1 Assignment

**Listen to a relaxation tape fifteen to thirty minutes daily.**
Purchase a commercially available tape or record your own. If you are unable to do either of these suggestions, just find a relaxed place and breathe in through your nose, exhale through pursed lips, and say the word "peace" or "calm" slowly. Repeat that for fifteen minutes.

**Do daily diary. Write about your phobic progress
and phoboc victories.**

List any distinguishable changes in your behavior. Record the times you
used Thought Stoppage or used your breathing to reduce your fear.

**Exercise daily.**

Start slowly and gradually build to twenty to thirty minutes of continuous activity. Exercise burns up adrenaline and makes you more resistant
to its effects. It teaches you to become comfortable with rapid heart
and breathing rates, which are normal by-products of exercise.

**Discontinue stimulating drugs, especially caffeine, nicotine,
and alcohol.**

**Make a fear list.**

1. Make a list of what situations and things cause you trouble. Write
   down everything that causes you to have fear symptoms (i.e., everything that you don't like to do or feel uncomfortable doing). All of
   these may have a phobic base.

   1. _____   7. _____
   2. _____   8. _____
   3. _____   9. _____
   4. _____   10. _____
   5. _____   11. _____
   6. _____   12. _____

2. Write down the goals that you would like to accomplish. What
   could you do if you had no fear? Be specific.

   1. _____
   2. _____

3. _____

4. _____

5. _____

6. _____

7. _____

8. _____

3. Identify what triggers your anxiety attacks. What things: words, pictures, thoughts, and/or situations. For instance: chemicals or a picture of insects, or talking to authority figures, or asking someone out for a date. List them:

1. _____     6. _____

2. _____     7. _____

3. _____     8. _____

4. _____     9. _____

5. _____     10. _____

4. On a scale of 1 to 10, list your current level of motivation to work toward a cure. For example: 1 = not motivated, 10 = highly motivated. _____

5. Collect pictures of situations and things that cause you anxiety. You will use them soon to help desensitize your fears. If you can't find pictures try to find a printed word of the feared object. If that is not possible, draw a picture or write the word that describes the object.

6. Name your Boo voice. A whimsical or derogatory slur is appropriate. You'll be talking to it a lot. _____

7. Reread this chapter several times. Eighty-five percent of anything read or heard once will be forgotten.

You are not crazy; you are not neurotic—you are phobic, and phobias and OCD are easy to cure. Change. Do it. Accept the fact that you
are a phoboc; human beings have fears. Normal human beings have psychological problems and that's okay.

# 2

# Tools and Strategies to Combat Anxiety

*Ingredients:*

1 rubber Boo monster
1 brain in bag
1 rubber brain
1 plastic brain with large knife-blade switch
1 bag large marshmallows
1 large squirt gun

*Directions:*

Display prominently in front of seventy mortified adults and children. (In the second class, participants are often more anxious because they have started the process of non-avoidance but they haven't gotten any tools yet to deal with their heightened anxiety.)

## Two Sides—Two Minds

Your brain has two sides—a right side and a left side. How's that for a profound revelation? And you thought I wasted twelve years of postgraduate work. The right side of the brain is the creative side. This side conjures up the anticipated horrors that accompany all phobias and obsessions. The right side created your Booland. The right brain is the survival side and the side that creates future fears. Most important, *it is the biochemical adrenaline-stimulating side. When you are in your right brain, you are in the adrenaline-secreting side.*

The left side of the brain is the critical, calculating, action-oriented side. *When you are using your left brain, you shut off adrenaline.* Everyone has experienced this phenomenon. You are about to play in a championship ball game. You're running to the bathroom every ten minutes—adrenaline is a great laxative. Your heart is pounding; you are tense and agitated. The game starts and you rapidly calm down. Or you're about to act in the school play. Just prior to the curtain raising, you're screaming, "Give me the first line—I can't remember anything." The play starts and you remember two hours of dialogue. In both examples, when the actual event begins, you switched to your left brain, focused on the present moment and what you were doing, and shut off the anxiety-producing adrenaline.

In class, I demonstrate this important process by using a prop made by my oldest successful graduate—ninety-six years young. I thought thirty-one years of being phobic was long; he was phobic for more than seventy years. He sawed a plastic pumpkin in half and painted one side black and left the other orange to represent both sides of the brain. On the top he placed a large knife-blade switch that could be moved from the right side to the left. This process is called *cortical switching*. If you are feeling anxious, you purposefully choose behaviors that will get you from the right adrenaline-stimulating side of the brain to the non-squirting left side. Start by choosing *three things you can do*: talking to or telephoning someone, dancing, singing, yodeling. Play a video game, do a crossword puzzle, interact with your pet, prepare a meal, do some mathematical problems in your head or spell words backward. Another cortical shifting strategy is to focus on *three things you can see*. You might count ceiling tiles, look for cloud designs, read labels in the supermarket. The more intensely you focus, the more likely you are to reduce anxiety. You might focus on *three things you can hear:* birds chirping, ocean sounds, construction noises, background music, or the speaker's voice. Finally, focus on *three things you can feel or smell*. Some find a powerful cortical switch by holding someone's hand. I bought a small rabbit pelt and kept it in my car. When I got anxious in heavy traffic or traversing bridges, I felt solace in petting that fur. Some find useful release by sniffing colognes or other aromas. Find out if one or all of these work for you.

Your first tool, cortical switching, gets you out of your right brain and allays your anxiety.

## Two Minds

The brain acts as if it has two minds. One is the logical, rational mind so characteristic of phobocs. We are always in our heads, ruminating, intellectualizing, and researching in an effort to resolve our anxiety disorder. The other mind is the experiential or survival mind. Its prime function is to keep you alive. It stores emotional memories in the primitive area of the brain called the amygdala. If any situation is perceived as a mortal threat, the amygdala hijacks the entire brain, provokes a massive outpouring of adrenaline, and mobilizes the body's defenses for survival.

The rational mind has virtually no influence over the experiential mind, while the experiential mind has tremendous influence on the rational processes. In essence, the brain is a *"show me"* organ. It does not believe what you tell it—only what you do. For thirty-one years, I tried to talk myself out of my fears—it didn't work. Only experiential victories can reprogram our amygdala's survival programs.

### Thoughts About Thoughts

Are thoughts powerful? You have probably heard, "to think it so create" and that all great inventions have been preceded by a thought. Statements like that give you the impression that thoughts are powerful. Well, I test that theory by asking my large classes to close their eyes and at the count of three, use their collective brainpower to turn off the lights in the room. "One, two, three. Think lights off. . . . Okay, open your eyes." Lo and behold, the lights are still on. "Well, you're beginners, let's try an easier task. Close your eyes again and at the count of three, I want everyone to visualize turning the page of my notes. One, two, three. See the page turning." They open their eyes again, and again, get some bad news. Seventy focused brains failed to turn one page.

Incredibly, I could do both of those tasks with the tip of my little finger. *Thoughts have no power unless you give power to them.* Thoughts are just thoughts. They are not necessarily truths. They are not commands to action and they are not forces. They never take over your will and they are not indications of your secret evil desires. Thinking is not acting. Thoughts are involuntary—we cannot control the content of our spontaneous thoughts. Morality is voluntary—we do not do things we choose not to do and your thoughts will never make you do them. It is best to think of thoughts as suggestions. I always suggest to my classes that they put all of their money in a paper bag and give it to me and I will spend it. In nineteen years, not one person has ever done that. You never have to act on your thoughts unless you choose to. Thoughts are not important unless you deem them to be. Thoughts are the spontaneous, neurobiological creations of your high-speed computer brain. Your brain is a thought machine, it thinks of everything. Never judge yourself on the content of your thoughts— just your behaviors. One hundred percent of people have intrusive thoughts but "normals" dismiss them while phobocs "buy" them as possible truths or indications of hidden evil desires, which creates our anxiety. Anxiety gives credence and power to any negative thought. Since anxiety connotes mortal threat, anxious thoughts will be repeated. The end point is to accept all thoughts non-emotionally and judge them as non-important.

## Faulty Thought Processes

Mismanaged thoughts are the basis for all phobias and obsessions. Here are the nine faulty thought processes that maintain and perpetuate our anxiety disorders: "The cat and camel can create responsible magic" is a useful mnemonic to help you recognize and challenge these destructive mistakes.

**The.** Thought Action Fusion (TAF) means if you think it, it will happen. So, don't think about cancer or your parents dying because it will happen. The problem is that you can't choose not to think about things. In fact, when you try not to think of something, you will increase the frequency of that thought. Some patients won't write about feared topics, lest they come to fruition. This becomes a problem when you try to desensitize to anxious thoughts, as you will learn to do in the next chapter.

If you think thoughts are so powerful that they can create a catastrophe, then create me a diamond. If your thoughts can kill your parents or cause cancer, perhaps a little more effort on your part can create that gem for me. Obviously, you can't because, as you have heard, thoughts are powerless.

**Cat.** Catastrophic misinterpretation is the basis for all phobias and obsessions—the exaggerated catastrophic thoughts, inaccurate perceptions, and interpretations created by your Boo. All dangers are greatly magnified.

We enhance catastrophic misinterpretations when we analyze why we had that thought or what it means. If it's an unacceptable or disturbing thought we might wrongly conclude that it means we are dangerous, evil, or crazy. Remind yourself that thoughts are like television programs. You can't control the subject matter, but you can change the station. You can't control the content of your thoughts but you can control your interpretation of them.

**Camel.** The illusion of thought control. A famous experiment asks participants to close their eyes and raise their right hand. They are then instructed to lower their hand if they think of a camel. Of course, you instruct them not to visualize that pack of camel cigarettes and not to remember that camel in the zoo chewing its cud. Tell them not to see a camel walking in front of an Egyptian pyramid. If any of those negative commands conjures up a camel image, you have to put your hand down.

When we do this exercise in class, most arms are down in the first fifteen seconds. When patients, particularly those with OCD, call and say they can't stop obsessing—the answer I give is, "camels." You can't not think of things. Indeed, you will soon learn, *if you want to think of something less, you have to think of it more!*

**C**AN.   Circular thinking. I thought it because it was important and it's important because I thought it. We attach importance to a thought simply because we think it. Nothing could be further from the truth. Thoughts, as you recall, have no importance until you bestow it on them. The great majority of thoughts are nothing more than neurobiological garbage created by an efficient thought machine—your brain.

Avoid circular thinking. Thoughts are just thoughts, not facts, forces, or truths and not important unless you deem them to be so.

C**A**N.   Avoidance. When you avoid, you are exaggerating and magnifying your fears. Avoidance constitutes fear rehearsal and negative reinforcement. Stay in the fear situation or cold pool and learn that you will habituate. Non-avoidance is the path to cure, it teaches you that anxiety is not dangerous and it will go away if you stay in the fear situation.

CA**N**.   Neutralization. Anything you do other than face your fear to relieve your anxiety is neutralization. It can be very subtle and must be recognized and eliminated as you proceed on your road to recovery. I had a fear of vomiting in social settings. If I couldn't avoid the situation, I would eat white turkey breast and mashed potatoes with white gravy—neutralization. I thought if I threw up it would be less offensive than brown gravy. I also chewed my food more thoroughly to aid digestion so I would be less likely to get nauseated—neutralization. When you neutralize, the Boo gets that famous point and you know how long you get to keep your phobia.

Rituals and compulsions are good examples of behavioral neutralizations designed to relieve anxiety. They must eventually be stopped and the resulting anxiety dealt with.

**Create**.   Creative coincidence. A psychiatrist observes a young man snapping his fingers. "Excuse me, I'm a student of human behavior, I was wondering why you are snapping your fingers?" The man responds, "It keeps the wild elephants away." "Why, there isn't a wild elephant within 2,000 miles of here," replies the psychiatrist. "Works like a charm, doesn't it?"

We do a behavior, the feared event doesn't happen, and we conclude our behavior must have prevented it. Obviously, there is no relationship between the snapping fingers and the absence of elephants. We don't step on a crack and our mother's back is not broken. Can you hear the fingers snapping? All compulsive rituals are good examples of creative coincidence. A woman in San Francisco combed her hair four times on the right and four times on the left to keep her daughter safe in Italy. Snap Snap. When people describe their rituals, class members are invited to snap their fingers—this identifies the practice of creative coincidence.

You must stop the compulsive behavior and see if the feared consequence happens. Stop the snapping and listen for the rampaging herd of elephants. If you are ritualizing, try snapping your fingers to remind you of your faulty thought processing.

**Responsible.** Phobics are awesomely responsible. We appoint ourselves caretakers of the entire world. The greater we perceive our responsibility in a role, the more anxious we become. Presumed responsibility is at the core of many checking rituals. I check doors and windows and stoves to keep my family safe. I pick up rocks and pebbles on a dirt walking trail so others won't trip and fall.

One young lady wouldn't invite her sister over to her house because if her sister was killed driving there, she would be responsible and would never be able to forgive herself. Her dilemma, she realized, as is common, was that if she didn't invite her sister and her sister was killed at home, she would also be responsible. Those concerns are "what if" products of a vicious, devious Boo and we don't answer "what if" questions.

Cure demands the recognition that everyone is 100 percent responsible only for their own life and their own choices.

**Magic.** Magical thinking is the process whereby we accept unsubstantiated, unsupported, unproven beliefs as truths. It is the basis for all compulsive behaviors. Do you recall the two requirements to get your birthday wishes? Of course, you can't tell anyone your secret wish and most important, you must blow out all your candles with one breath. For fifty-two years, I was blowing my brains out trying to fulfill that last requirement.

Did you ever investigate the research data concerning these stipulations? Did you read the Danish article that showed you had a better chance of getting your wish if you told three people? Did you read the English translation of a Russian researcher who found if you took three breaths to blow out your candles and left one burning, you had a 17 percent greater chance of having your wish granted? Of course not, there is no such research. You bought a ridiculous, unproven, unsubstantiated hypothesis and carried it out faithfully.

We do the same with all compulsions. We do these rituals without ever challenging their veracity. We don't step on a crack in order to spare our mother's back. Have you read the research data that proves such a claim? Of course not, it is non-existent. One patient wore his hat sideways before boarding a plane and knocked three times on the fuselage to keep the plane airborne. Thanks very much, but I'll put my faith in the pilot. All superstitions embrace the magical thinking doctrine. To cure you must recognize that these beliefs are merely unproven hypotheses and not facts. Then, when ready, you refrain from doing the compulsive ritual and deal with the ensuing anxiety.

## Booland

Booland is our own personal haunted house. It is our most feared "worst case scenario." It is where our greatest phoboc fears and consequences actually happen. It is where we throw up at the weekly conference with the boss watching. It is where we have a bowel accident on national TV. It is where we have a panic attack in the worst place possible—it is our land of abject terror. The Booland scenario is produced, directed, and scripted by our Boo. Our ticket to Booland is our inability to recognize and challenge the thoughts that buy our ticket to this frightening land.

Here, every fear is exaggerated, every catastrophe occurs, and there is no escape. The Boo becomes our dominant master and we are its pitiful slaves. If we fail to follow our Boo's commands in exquisite detail, bad things will happen to us or our loved ones.

If you are doing rituals, the following Boo rules apply:

1. "You keep doing them until I tell you to stop. Alas, I never do."
2. "You keep doing them until you get them right. Unfortunately, there is no right in Booland."
3. "You can never be clean enough, apologize enough, or check enough, but keep on trying anyway."

Booland is your personal horror movie. Like any movie, the characters and scenes are make-believe. You avoid buying your ticket by utilizing the tools and strategies presented in this chapter.

## The Emotional Cascade

A destructive habit of phobocs is the tendency to rapidly add one frightening thought upon another. The result is predictable. Each negative thought produces a squirt of adrenaline. Multiple negative thoughts produce a massive outpouring of adrenaline and extremely high levels of anxiety. This is called an emotional cascade. My bridge phobia led to the following adrenaline cascade:

"What if I have a panic attack on the bridge today?" (squirt).

"What if I lose control?" (squirt).

"What if I crash head on into another car?" (squirt).

"And kill all seven people?" (squirt).

"I am arrested and jailed" (squirt).

"The judge says, 'What were you doing on the bridge if you knew you could have a panic attack?'" (squirt).

"I'm suspending your license" (squirt).

As a result:

"I lose my home" (squirt).

"My wife leaves me" (squirt).

"I am homeless" (squirt, squirt, squirt).

In seconds, I've gone from total calm to abject terror, drowning in an ocean of thought-provoking adrenaline. Emotional cascades happen at warp speed. Anxiety is voiced in shorthand—bridge, panic, death. While the emotional cascade takes a second, the physiological consequence of massive stress hormone secretion can last for hours or days.

## Thought Stoppage

A powerful tool to prevent and circumvent emotional cascades is thought stoppage. At the first sign of anxiety or the identification of a scary Boo message say, "stop" and take a calmative breath. Thought stoppage is an anachronism. You can't stop initial thoughts, they come too fast, but you can cut short the deleterious effects of an unchallenged emotional cascade. Thought stoppage is a reminder to immediately utilize your phoboc tools to limit the scope of your frightening thoughts. It should be used instantaneously any time you experience your first symptoms of anxiety. This is important because, over time, our fear thoughts become automatic. We don't hear our Boo yelling "bridge, panic, death," rather we just start feeling anxious. You will always know the Boo has spoken because it always speaks in adrenaline. Some people snap a rubber band on their wrist or shake a small "brain in the bag" at the same time they say "stop" to strengthen the thought stoppage message. The goal is to challenge and shorten emotional cascades. The shorter your cascade, the faster your anxious recovery.

## Fear Levels—Subjective Units of Discomfort (SUDs)

It is important to be able to accurately assess the level of fear you are experiencing. You can use it to judge the effectiveness of your anti-anxiety tools. Such an approach changes you into a detached, non-involved, scientific observer. There are traditionally ten levels, number one—minimal anxiety, to number ten—the worst panic you ever experienced. I like to think that you ascend one level every time you squirt adrenaline. Ten scary thoughts and ten scary squirts gets you to level ten. You would then understand why the emotional cascade, the unchecked flow of multiple scary thoughts, can produce an extraordinary amount of intolerable symptoms in an incredibly short period of time.

Here is my fear level list and the symptoms I experienced at each level.

1. Mild fear, butterflies, mild concern
2. Warm feeling, palms are sweating, need to go to the bathroom
3. Heart rate rapid, knees may tremble, knees weak—scared, but functioning intellectually

Best to stay at this level; retreat if it goes higher, relax and *return*. As fear level increases, you may have difficulty thinking clearly.

4. May feel unsteady, more concerned
5. Mouth is dry. Feel I must leave the scene, concerned about what people think. (You know you're at level five because it is the first time you think of leaving the scene.)
6. Increasing discomfort, can't swallow, feel severe muscle tenseness

Finally, as level of fear increases·

7. Severe headache, a feeling of doom; can't function intellectually: hyperventilate, chest tightens, can't get a deep breath
8. Same as number seven above, but more intense
9. Feel dizzy, nausea, visual distortion, numb all over, a feeling of losing control
10. Panic attack. Feel I'm going to die, having difficulty functioning, delusional; chest tightness is severe, frantic

Not everyone experiences all of these symptoms. You may have some that were not mentioned or may note that your symptoms appear at different levels. What is important is to get an idea about what you experience at a level three or four because that will be a critical level for you. If using your tools doesn't lower your fear level or keep it at a four, you may have to leave.

Of course, phobocs always ask, "What if I can't leave? What if I'm on an airplane and I can't get out?" That's a good time to find out if all you learned in Phobease is true: "If I stay in the fear situation and use my tools, it will go away. Anxiety is not dangerous, it is marshmallows on my bare feet. Comfort is not my goal, living is. I will handle it."

Remember all these symptoms are normal and are caused by adrenaline secreted in your body. All of these emotions will fade—you won't die.

I love medicine and its pompous sophistication. Subjective units of discomfort scale indeed. In the children's class we call them scare units. How scared are you feeling on a level of one to ten? You don't have to remember all the listed symptoms; you can make your own personal decisions about what level you are experiencing.

Using your own fear levels, we are going to ask you from now on, anytime you feel anxious to assess your level of fear. Particularly when you start doing your exposure projects, it is imperative that you grade your levels every few minutes. When you do that, you become a *detached scientist*. You are acting as a non-involved neutral observer of an anxiety reaction. You know now there is no danger; it's just adrenaline. So now when you wake up at 3:00 A.M. with panic symptoms, you ask, "My God, what is happening?" Squirt. Think, "I'm having a heart attack." Squirt. "I can't get a deep breath." Squirt. "If it doesn't stop, I'm going to go crazy." Squirt. "Why is God punishing me like this?" Squirt. "There must be something terribly wrong." Squirt. "I've got to see another doctor." Squirt. "I hope I won't be like this forever." Squirt, squirt, squirt, squirt, and squirt. These are the ramblings of an untrained phoboc.

A Phobease-trained phoboc wakes up at 3:00 A.M. with panic symptoms and says, "Stop, one, two, three, four, I must have had a scary dream and squirted adrenaline. I'm at level six, pulse rate of eighty-six, I will do some more calmative breathing." One minute later, "I'm at level two." The most important reason for grading your fear level is to find out, when handled correctly, that you can go from high levels to near zero in seconds. For thirty-one years, I left situations with high levels of anxiety. Without tools I didn't know that if I stayed my fear levels would come down. Instead my high level "proved" that the situation must have been dangerous. The only tool I ever used was avoidance. Remember, adrenaline only works for minutes. If you don't add to the initial dose with fearful thoughts, your anxiety will rapidly wane. The first time you demonstrate that you can effectively lower your fears with your tools is when you realize you have power over your Boo. Once you realize that your fear is not going to spiral out of control and reach a level of 800, you realize there is hope for a cure. It's also a time when you might consider buying a little coffin for your Boo because its demise is imminent. *From now on and forever, every few minutes, ask yourself, "What is my SUDs level?"*

## Fatigue

High levels of anxiety exact a very expensive physical price. When we secrete large amounts of adrenaline, glycogen is mobilized from the muscles and converted to simple sugars that can then be readily utilized for combat. Glycogen is muscle fuel. If you take too much glycogen out of the muscle, it becomes temporarily weak. The result is a three-day feeling of fatigue and utter exhaustion. We feel like that famous wet noodle. Chronic fatigue is common in untrained phobocs. This frightening symptom often leads to multiple doctor visits to rule out significant disease. If you drink a gallon of whiskey at one sitting, you will be quite drunk and sobering up will be a long slow process. When we are in our anxiety producing Booland, the results are similar. Massive amounts of adrenaline secretion produce exaggerated physical symptoms, and recovery, likewise, is long and slow. As you perfect your coping tools, you secrete less adrenaline and experience less anxiety, and recovery is far more rapid. Finally, over time, you squirt so little scare juice that your body gets resistant to adrenaline effects, and fear symptoms are minimal and rapidly dissipate. That is the end point of Phobease training.

## Fear Tools and Strategies

Destroying your Boo requires going to war with your adversary. I am going to give you over thirty effective tools and strategies that you can use to minimize anxiety symptoms.

## Recognize

The most important of all the tools is to recognize your Boo. As I mentioned before, your ability to cure your phobias or obsessive disorders is 100 percent dependent on how well you recognize and deal with your Boo. If you recognize a Boo message, you now know it's a lie. It's an exaggeration and a catastrophizing threat. The Boo does not own a crystal ball and thus cannot predict the future. If the Boo says it will happen, it won't. It can't make anything happen. You always know if the Boo has spoken, even if you don't hear it, because the Boo speaks in adrenaline and you experience anxiety. *The Boo always squirts first and speaks later*. You don't have to know what it said to cure, just deal with the anxiety. Your tools will work whether or not you even know how your disorder began—it's not important.

## Accept

Accept anything the Boo says. The best way to deal with the Boo is to treat it the same way you would treat "Chicken Little." If you recall, Chicken bursts into your house yelling, "The sky is falling." Now, if you recognize Mr. Little, you are not going to run for your hard hat, dive under a table, stand under a door frame, or run screaming into the street. Rather, knowing the source, you will handle the warning non-emotionally. You would probably humor or cajole the misinformed poultry. "There, there, Chicken, I know it's falling but only small pieces and this is an extremely well built house. Would you like some fresh lemonade? You look a little pale." When you recognize and accept your Boo's ramblings and threats you will be well on your way to your cure.

## Thought Stoppage and Calmative Breathing

At the first sign of anxiety or the first recognition of a negative message say, "Stop," take a deep breath through your nose, hold for a count of four, and exhale slowly through pursed lips—immediately and every time.

Now you remember that thought stoppage doesn't stop the initial thought—it comes too fast. You will even read in some places that thought stoppage doesn't work. They are wrong. While it doesn't work to stop the initial thought, it is a reminder to put on your battle gear and mobilize your Phobease tools and strategies because you are about to go to war with your Boo. Thought stoppage reminds you to stop any subsequent thoughts that could create an emotional cascade. If I take only one shot of alcohol, I'm not going to get very drunk— the small amount of alcohol will metabolize quickly and I will sober up rapidly. Thought stoppage works the same way. If all the adrenaline I get is from the initial thought and I do not add to it, my anxiety will be mild and its effects will dissipate rapidly. While I will never be able to control the content of my initial thoughts or even their frequency, I will *always* be able to assess their importance. If I recognize the Boo origin, I will be able to dismiss it non-emotionally. If you don't water your weeds, they will wither and die. If you don't water your thoughts with attention, they will also wither and lose their emotional power.

Following thought stoppage with a calmative breath assures your brain that some senseless babble has been heard and summarily dismissed. You've got your Boo on the ropes.

## Dispute and Reframe

You recall that my nickname is Dr. Fear? The word "Fear" stands for "false exaggerations appearing real." Well, the "Dr." stands for dispute and reframe. Here's a chance to really shut your Boo up. It wouldn't make much sense to demand proof from Chicken Little that the sky really is falling. "Where is it falling? How much is falling? Do you have pieces to prove it?" The warning is better handled by simply ignoring it. Then you could read Mr. Little the riot act for barging into your house and disturbing your peace and warn him not to do it again.

We teach you how to *boss back* your Boo. Are you tired of this swine dictating what you can do? Are you tired of being confined and constricted by its vacuous threats? Are you tired of that idiot taking up large parts of your brain territory? Well then, stand up, spread your legs to shoulder width, hands on hips, lean slightly forward on your toes, jut your chin out a little, and let him have it. Out loud and angrily tell him, "I'm sick and tired of you telling me what to do. I'm sick and tired of you threatening and bullying me. I'm sick and tired of your constant lies. I'm tired of your incessant drivel. So shut up your face. Stick it where the sun don't shine. I'm not going to take it anymore. Squirt all the adrenaline you want but I'm staying. I know all you can do is go Boo. You are a powerless fake." You might further invoke what I call the "two-word" cure. You might choose, "Shut up," "Up yours," or even better, "Screw you," or the two best words, which, for social propriety, must be left unwritten. However, using the two-word ultimate boss back means you have read and understood all the material from page one. You know the precise limitations of your adversary and are daring it to carry out its empty threats. When you are trained and confident you will find strength in constantly disputing your Boo.

## Reframing

You want divine guidance? Listen carefully to your Boo and then do the opposite. Reframe every Boo "what if." I was flying back from Buenos Aires—isn't it nice to cure a travel phobia? I had done a phobia presentation on our cruise ship entitled, "How to Fly, Bus, and Camel with Half Your Fears." After the lecture, we drove to the airport with some friends we met on the ship. They were flying American and we were flying United. Everyone flying on American that day had to have their checked luggage searched because security was looking for a bomb. Halfway home my Boo casually asked, "What if someone on this plane had a bomb and it blew the plane to smithereens?" Before my cure I would have begun to carefully assess the people around me for terrorist potential, giving the Boo a few points and me a bucket of adrenaline. But trained, I recognized the Boo message, said "Stop," calmative breathed, and reframed. "What if nobody on this plane has a bomb and the plane lands safely?" *Boo:* "What if the wings fall off the plane?" *Me:* "What if the wings don't fall off and the plane lands safely?" *Boo:* "What if both your children are shot to death at school?" *Me:* "What if they aren't?" Isn't that delectable? Reframe everything and the Boo is rendered powerless.

From now on, challenge every "what if" question or worry with a reframed happy resolution. Take that, Boo.

## Dismiss

Have you noticed that every one of these tools and strategies represent subtle forms of neutralization? At the beginning we need them. They are like training wheels on our first two-wheel bike. As we gain confidence and skills we dispense with the wheels and ride off into the sunset dragging our bedraggled Boo behind us.

Eventually, we don't have to go through this long reframing approach. When you have recognized, disputed, and reframed a few hundred Boo threats, you can save a lot of time and energy by accepting its relentless babbling non-emotionally and simply dismiss it as irrelevant and non-important. Nothing shrinks a Boo faster.

## Interoceptive Exposure

As you recall, the major concern of patients experiencing panic attacks is that their physical symptoms are indications of impending medical disasters. We fear our racing hearts are going to burst out of our chest or result in heart attacks or strokes. Thus we stop doing anything that increases our heart rate. We might avoid carrying grocery bags in the house. We get so out of condition that brushing our teeth becomes a physical threat and produces the exact symptoms we're trying to avoid. The dizziness we feel is an impending stroke and dissociative symptoms are the first signs of insanity. We might avoid hot weather because it feels like an early panic attack.

Interoceptive exposures are exercises that create, on purpose, the very symptoms you fear and avoid. If you are concerned about rapid heart and breathing rates, I would have you start walking daily on level ground for short distances. Over time, I would have you increase distance; add inclines, stairs, and hills; and finally have you running up and down the stadium stairs with a piano on your back—a slight exaggeration—not in Phobease.

If you're afraid that getting warm might precipitate a panic attack, you begin to study local temperatures and avoid going into hot zones.

Interoceptive exposures would have you sit in a hot bathroom, then saunas for progressively longer periods of time. Finally, I would ask you to visit areas like Las Vegas in July and deal with searing temperatures of 114 degrees Fahrenheit.

Interoceptive exposures for patients who don't like a tight feeling in their chest begin by their wrapping on a tight ace bandage, then progressing to placing heavier and heavier weights on their chest—20, 30, 40, 50 pounds, your Saint Bernard, your 250-pound husband, and finally, a small elephant. Small elephants are considered overkill—a powerful tool to kill tight chest fears.

Afraid of not getting enough air to breathe? Start by breathing through one nostril, then a regular straw, a snorkel, and finally a small cocktail straw.

Don't like being dizzy? Have a friend spin you sitting down, then spin standing up with someone to spot you to keep you from falling. Finally, on a beach where falling won't hurt you, spin repeatedly until you do fall.

What symptoms do you fear? Devise an activity that will create and exaggerate that symptom. What is it you don't like? Do it and then do it again.

## Cortical Shifting

Cortical shifting, you remember, is a purposeful maneuver to switch you from the creative adrenaline-secreting right brain to the non-secreting left side. There are twelve things you can utilize to reduce anxiety:

> Three things you can do (talk, sing, call someone, play a video
>     game, do a crossword puzzle, or pet your dog)
> Three things you can see
> Three things you can hear
> Three things you can touch

Through experimentation, find the strategies that work best for you. Use those that provoke rapid resolution of your anxiety symptoms.

## Competitive Behaviors

Competitive behaviors are used in many of the impulsive disorders: hair pulling (trichotillomania), skin picking, nail biting, and self-mutilation. It is any maneuver that prevents you from carrying out your undesirable impulse. Thus if you clench your fists you would not be able to pull your hair, bite your fingernails, or cut yourself. You are using the same muscles needed to perform your impulse. Like thought stoppage, competitive behavior gives you time to mount coping strategies in order to stave off the performance of your undesirable behavior. We ask people to hold the competitive behavior for three minutes, by the clock, and take that time to calmative breathe, cortical shift, boss back the Boo, and voice protective affirmations. Much like anxiety, *all urges go away*. People invent their own competitive behaviors including showering, petting the dog, hand squeezers, push-ups. Just be sure to maintain it long enough for the urge intensity to diminish. You can use a modified form of SUDs to grade your urges from very strong, to moderate, to minimal.

## Conditioned Responses

We use conditioned responses to change our perspective of feared things or events. If you are phobic about rats, you have programmed your brain to react to the thought, word, picture, or the animal itself. In the next chapter, when you begin to desensitize to that feared rodent, we will ask you to suck a lollipop or listen to patriotic music or pet your dog at the same time you say the word "rat" or look at a picture of the animal. In a short time, the brain will be conditioned, and thus reprogrammed, to look at a pleasant relationship between you and the rat. (You'll get a chance to suck lots of lollipops before you finish this course.)

## Commit to Cure

This is the only commitment we will ever ask you to make. If you make the commitment, you will cure. Don't let personal crises or the expected setbacks deter you from your goals. Stay firm in your desire to free yourself from your phoboc constraints.

## SUDs (Scare Units)

Remember, from now on, any time you are experiencing anxiety, rate it from one to ten. If you are in a fear situation, try to stay until you have noticed a 50 percent reduction in your level of anxiety. This will be proof that your fear tools are working. Assigning fear levels makes you a detached observer, non-emotionally involved in assessing a non-threatening physiological event. What level am I? What level am I now?

Finally, if you leave situations at high levels of anxiety, something I did for thirty-one years, all you learn is that the particular situation was indeed scary and your high level of anxiety proved it. What you do when you leave at high levels is practice how to fail, and I failed often. Had I known about cold pools and anti-anxiety tools and strategies, I could have stayed, reduced my fear levels, and turned every one of my defeats into a glorious victory. What level are you now?

## Best Case Scenario

The Boo only talks in exaggerated catastrophes. One way of disputing and reframing is to create a "best case scenario." The Boo says, "What if the elevator gets stuck and you can't get to a bathroom and you have a bowel accident and offend all the passengers trapped with you?" That was my favorite elevator catastrophe. To avoid that, I walked a few million stairs. A best case scenario approach would ask, "What if the elevator gets stuck and you have a sexual escapade with the partner of your choice?" That image might not squirt adrenaline.

Instead of going down in flames and failing miserably as the Boo predicted, you make the best presentation of your life. Your boss, who is in attendance, gives you a standing ovation and doubles your salary on the spot. "Best case" raises the possibility of alternatives to high-anxiety Booland disasters.

## Success Rehearsal

Success rehearsal is a variation of "best case scenario." If you have an upcoming significant challenge, perhaps your first airplane flight in fifteen years, I would ask you to write a victory postcard in advance. Describe how well you handled driving to the airport and stood, relaxed, in a long security check line. Write how you boarded the plane in a crowded tramway, handled take-off anxiety, mid-flight turbulence, and landed with an anxiety level of two. Explain how you comfortably arranged hotel transportation through bumper-to-bumper commuter traffic, checked in, and fell victorious on your king-sized bed at your hotel room on the 104th floor. Then we invite you, when the time comes, to duplicate those successes in real life.

Got a phobic challenge coming up? Write a victory card in advance and you will have a script for your forthcoming successful venture. (P.S.: Make sure you write that you had some anxiety but you managed it effectively rather than handling all these challenging events at a zero SUDs level.)

## Expose and Block

If you have OCD, this will be an important technique for you. If you recall, obsessives avoid anxiety by creating a compulsive ritual. The ritual behavior allays the anxiety caused by the obsessive concern. The goal in Phobease is not to avoid anxiety, indeed, but to provoke it, on purpose, and then deal with it. So, if you fear contamination from dirt, chemicals, or germs and you touch a "dirty" doorknob, you would run and cleanse your hands by washing or wiping with an antiseptic towelette. Exposing and blocking requires you, on purpose, to touch that same doorknob (expose) but then refrain (block) from doing your cleansing compulsion. Of course, this creates anxiety and as you will learn in subsequent chapters, this is your pathway to cure. Thus, if you have OCD, you have double work. While a phobic only has to gradually expose to the feared object to cure, an OCD has to expose and block. In either case, cure demands purposeful exposure to the thing you fear and effective management of the provoked anxiety.

**Some other examples**.   You overhear or inadvertently read a dirty word written in graffiti. In the past, you would have reacted by reciting your Hail Marys, the Shema, or asking God for forgiveness. When trained and ready, on purpose, you write or speak dirty words (expose) but don't (block) recite the ritualistic prayers. You are concerned about burglars breaking into your house and killing your family, so you repeatedly check to see if the doors and windows are locked. When ready, you leave the "safest" window unlocked (expose) but don't (block) check it to see if an intruder has opened it further.

While these approaches may seem impossible to you right now, you will find, to the contrary, that all phobias and obsessions can be cured and exposure and blocking is the key to OCD cure.

## Extension to Absurdity

Another disputing and reframing technique is extension to absurdity. You take your worst feared event, your worst case scenario, your ultimate Booland disaster, and turn it into a ludicrous farce. One of my many phobias, you remember the average phoboc has twelve to fifteen separate issues, was getting nauseated and throwing up on an airplane. I reviewed and rehearsed my fear hundreds of times by visualizing how disgusting and vile that would be. I could feel the scorn of disapproving passengers and feel the devastating humiliation and embarrassment. Take the same fear and see yourself throwing up so much that the plane is four feet deep in vomit. Passengers are standing on their seats while you keep spewing. The stewardess is filling up a wheelbarrow with the mess and throwing the contents out of the plane door, coating the entire side of the plane. The plane lands, skidding on the slimy mess. Extension to absurdity provides delightful levity to a perceived disaster and can be a powerful tool if you share my perverse sense of humor.

## Embarrassment Immunization

Social phobics are people who have an intense fear of being embarrassed in a social situation. As you have already repeatedly read, conquering phobias and obsessions requires the purposeful exposure to the thing you fear. In the same way that you get vaccinated to prevent serious diseases, "embarrassment immunization" is a safe, gradual approach to inoculating you against "terminal" humiliation. When ready, we will ask you to do embarrassing things: count floors out loud in an elevator, stand up in a restaurant, and sing "Happy Birthday" to yourself. You might want to walk a banana on a leash; wear an outrageous outfit, a costume to work, or two different color shoes; or go to a market and buy one walnut. If you are a confirmed perfectionist who wouldn't be caught dead without makeup, wear half of it. Wear stockings with multiple runs, clothes with stains. We have our vomit phobics (emetophobics) make a vomit sound and "throw up" fake rubber or plastic vomit in class, then on the hospital volunteers, finally on friends, families, and strangers.

Much of our embarrassment fears stem from exaggerated concerns when we were young. At that time, embarrassment was viewed as devastating and intolerable. We carry that same fear into adulthood, not realizing that we could, indeed, handle those situations now. When I went to grammar school, it was fashionable and cruel for bullies to run up behind some unsuspecting victim and pull his pants down. I didn't know then that I was phoboc, but I did know if that happened, I would die of embarrassment. So I wore two pairs of underwear and cinched my belt up so tight my legs would swell. My tactics worked and I was never "pantsed." Each year in July, in a small town called Laguna Niguel, virtually the entire town's population along with a few thousand happy revelers line up on the railroad tracks and moon the 12 o'clock Amtrak train. What would have been a terror in grammar school becomes a delightful afternoon.

If it's embarrassment you fear, do embarrassing things and then do them again. When you practice embarrassment immunization, you, too, may find that you can moon the whole world and tolerate it.

## Study, Study, Study

While knowledge alone can never cure phobias and obsessions, lack of knowledge will maintain and perpetuate anxiety disorders. So study, reread chapters, do your homework assignments, and become an expert on the subject. Knowledge alone can't cure because it appeals solely to the logical, rational mind. To cure we need to reprogram the experiential mind with numerous purposeful victories.

If you read materials outside of Phobease that contradict its doctrines, please check with us. Much is written that is inaccurate and untested and may lead you astray. There are no magic bullets, no vitamin replacements, and virtually no single treatment that can affect a cure. You need the whole ball of wax, that famous psycho-educational, cognitive behavioral therapy, and experiential desensitization, but it all begins with knowledge.

## Model and Mirror

"Modeling and mirroring" means copying the behavior of someone in the situation who is handling it well. Let's say that you are an inexperienced flier. During the flight you encounter some rough turbulence. Your lying Boo tells you, "The plane will crash and you're about to die." You say, "Stop," take your calmative breath, and look over at the person next to you, busily working on her laptop. (There is always someone with a laptop these days!) She is totally unperturbed and unmoved by the turbulence and continues to complete her task. Without being able to assess the threat of the events (airplanes never crash from turbulence) you copy (mirror) her calm demeanor.

As you approach the landing you hear a "horrible" noise and the plane shudders a little. Actually, the pilot has lowered the plane's landing gear but the Boo says, "It sounds like the engine is tearing off and you're about to die." You say, "Stop," take your calmative breath, and look for someone to model and mirror. You observe the stewardess calmly collecting papers and empty soft drink cans and you realize your Boo has lied again, for the millionth time. Obviously, if the plane were in jeopardy, a seasoned stewardess wouldn't be calmly collecting garbage. You confidently mirror her calm demeanor. I once told my class, jokingly, if you look over and the stewardess is pulling on a parachute, you are in deep trouble. One of my class members asked her stewardess if they had parachutes and she said, "Of course not." She later accused me of lying to the class. I always wondered how that scene might play out. The plane gets in trouble, the crew parachutes out and waves good-bye to the passengers as the pilotless plane plunges to its demise. I don't think that would be a great headline: "Two Hundred Passengers Dead, but All of the Crew Survived." However, back to modeling and mirroring. If the stewardess is not pulling on a parachute, you can trust that nothing untoward is happening.

My grandson, age five and the product of a very phoboc mother, was at Disneyland. He desperately wanted to go on the Matterhorn ride but was frightened by the screams he heard emanating from the mountain. The first thing we did was go to the attractions exit and count the number of dead people there—none. Amusement parks like to keep that figure low in order to maintain high ridership numbers. We counted the number of people exiting that knelt down and kissed the ground—none. What we did recognize is that the vast majority, many as young as age two or three, ran smiling to get back in line to repeat the ride. Buoyed by that evidence, we modeled and mirrored their behavior and enjoyed his first Matterhorn excursion, secure in the fact that probability for survival was high. We tested that probability four times that afternoon. When in doubt: model and mirror.

## Master the Topic

You master phobias and obsessions with repeated victories. A victory is the purposeful, voluntary exposure to the thing you fear. People say, "It can't be that simple," but it is. There are no shortcuts. The only way out is through. You need to find out experientially that anxiety is not dangerous, it will go away—even if I stay in the fearful situation. I stay in that cold pool and use my tools, my body habituates, and in time, I master my fear and get to live that expansive life I so desire.

## Anticipate Anxiety

If you always get anxious driving over a bridge you might predict it will happen next time, too. Well, now you have tools. Review your coping strategies in advance. Write out a script of what you will say if you feel rising anxiety and take it with you. Remind yourself of the tools you will use: thought stoppage, calmative breathing, disputing and reframing, your SUDs score. Bring along whatever you will need to cortical shift. You are a Boo killer now, so go into battle with all of your weapons.

My stepdaughter is famous for turning a fully laden airliner around and having it deposit her back at the terminal. Untrained, she told them "If you don't let me off, I will have a panic attack, go crazy, and die." They believed her. Subsequently, she took Phobease, cured her flying phobia, and then flew all over the United States leading software seminars. She now teaches multiple Phobease classes. When she began her flying desensitization program, she boarded the plane prepared. She took a number of cortical shifters, an audiotape of *Les Misérables*, her class relaxation tape, a puzzle book, and her "lucky" one-eyed stuffed toy rabbit. (Do you hear those fingers snapping?) Whatever you need to get on and stay on that plane is okay. She took water and snacks because they don't feed you for an hour and hunger can feel like an impending anxiety attack. She arrived early—because coming late is stressful. She did some calmative breathing and took a fifteen-minute walk through the airport. Finally, she read the victory list she had accumulated since the start of her class. She was prepared.

Soldiers don't go into battle without their weapons and a plan and neither should you. You know your adversary well. This is war with your Boo so flank it, outwit it, and subdue it. You don't even have to fight fair.

## Neutralize the Boo

How can you tell when something scary is about to happen in a horror movie? It's the music. It builds to a crescendo, the theater shakes, your pulse quickens as you approach your encounter with the monster. You know disaster lies ahead. Well the Boo speaks with the same intensity. What would happen if you sang the Boo threat, in a gentle lilting melody, "Ladies and gentlemen, hear this lovely tale, Howie is about to throw up in the garbage pail"? You could diffuse the Boo by pretending to hold a microphone and playing the role of a news reporter. You announce to the world, "Ladies and gentlemen,

Howie is about to throw up on two or three people. Tune in to the 11 o'clock news for close-ups of the event." You could voice the threat in slow motion or in a Donald Duck voice or with a thick French accent. All of these techniques are ways to weaken, discount, and diminish the power of your Boo. You know the Boo is a paper tiger. Mocking the Boo is effective "bossing back."

## Bending the Ritual

Most compulsive rituals are done with a specific precision in order to appease your Boo god and ward off any implied disasters. Doing it "right" adds to the magical power. You must touch your left ear four times and your right ear four times while standing on one leg or your children will die. You must scrub the left hand for ten minutes and the right for ten minutes or contaminate the world. You must chant your prayers at a specific tone and speed or you will burn in eternal damnation.

When you are ready, alter your rituals slightly and see if the threatening Boo catastrophes actually occur. You, of course, must deal with the increased anxiety by purposely doing it wrong. That's precisely why you are doing it—the "wronger" the better. So, you do the ear-touch five times. It still adds up to eight but you have bent the ritual and you may have put your children in dire jeopardy. You scrub your left hand for ten minutes and wash your right for five minutes and see if the world survives. You chant your prayers at the wrong pace and in the wrong key and wait for the thunderbolt from heaven. Remember to listen for the snapping fingers when you are doing your compulsions and look both ways for rampaging elephants when crossing the street. When you learn about hierarchies you will learn how to gradually decrease the time you spend doing your rituals until you can abandon them completely.

## The Three D's

Three more strategies to deal with anxiety are delay, distract, and detach. One of the ways you can gradually weaken the power of your obsessions is by delaying the performance of your compulsion. After

you contaminate, instead of running to wash, you delay for five minutes and see if you can manage the resultant anxiety. If your SUDs
level is low after five minutes, you are invited to delay again and again.
The longer you delay, the more likely the anxiety will dissipate and
subsequent compulsive behavior will be easier to resist.

In general anxiety disorder, we invite patients to set up distant
worry periods. Then if you have a worry during the day, you capture
it on paper, but delay worrying about it until your designated evening
worry session. At that time, you review your list and worry about each
one for a total of fifteen minutes.

Distracting and detaching are cortical shifting strategies and are
always done secondarily. You must first recognize, accept, thought
stop, calmative breathe, cortical shift, and delay. If anxiety persists
unchanged at a high SUDs level, then detach—leave the scene and
distract with your cortical shifting procedures. There are times when
your tools are less effective—often when external stressors are piling
up. On days like that, you concede a point to the Boo, but warn it
you'll be back tomorrow with guns blazing. You can lose battles and
still win the war. If today's battle is going poorly it's okay to distract
and detach.

## Eye Movement Desensitization and Reprogramming (EMDR)

EMDR is a powerful technique of imaginal desensitization with
accompanying eye movements—the three courses I took had slightly
different approaches. One had the participant follow a moving finger
at the same time he focused on past emotional events. Another asked
him to move his eyes in rhythm with a metronome, while a third had
him focus on an optikinetic spinning cylinder. The common denominator was the very insightful therapists who coached progressive
relaxation while focusing on past traumatic experiences. It has been
recognized as one of the useful tools for dealing with PTSD.

Dr. Callahan *(The Five Minute Phobia Cure)* offered his own ver-
sion, utilizing acupressure combined with various eye maneuvers. He

had patients tapping classical acupressure points with their eyes open, closed, looking down to the right, left, and circling the eyes again while thinking of anxiety-producing topics.

While there is some controversy about the contribution of eye movements, there is none regarding the efficacy of imaginal desensitization. This will soon become an important tool in your phobic arsenal.

## Humor

Phobias and obsessions are not too funny when they are devastating your life. As you get better, you may find humor a powerful tool to employ against your Boo. Some therapists treat these disorders with humor as a primary therapeutic tool. One can try assigning responsibilities to your Boo. If it tells you to check to see if the stove is on, you can tell your Boo, "You check it if you're so worried." When your Boo tells you, "If you don't wash you'll die," remind it, "If I die, you're going with me and I'm going to bury you underneath me." Humor doesn't squirt adrenaline. Even death, a constant concern, can be dealt with lightly. We always remind our class participants if you die any time during a Phobease class, you don't have to do that week's homework. You might remind yourself of that fact if you are concerned about your plane crashing or not waking up after an anesthetic—yippee! No homework! You remember the stuck elevator and the sexual escapade? Make up your own hilarious scripts for your most feared situations. Some therapists make up funny songs about phoboc topics. Humor diffuses anxiety, so find ways to incorporate it into your phoboc strategies.

## Here and Now

All worries are "what if" questions in disguise and we never answer "what ifs." All fears and fear rehearsals are future concerns. One of the most powerful tools to use against worries and fear rehearsals is Here and Now. The danger of answering future "what if" questions is that you pay the emotional price as if the event were happening now.

What if both your children are shot to death tomorrow? If you are caught up in the emotional pain of such an event, you are reacting physiologically and biochemically as if it has actually happened. To counteract unnecessary remorse, simply ask, "Is it happening now?" This immediately identifies the future characteristics of the question. In that context, you have identified your catastrophizing Boo and can end the debacle by stating, "If it happens, I will handle it." "What if my stress causes me to develop cancer twenty years from now?" Ask, "Is it happening now?" "No," then "I will handle it." These events would be terrible but they are products of your thoughts and not truths or accurate predictions. Constantly come back to the here and now and save yourself a lot of emotional pain.

## Overkill

When you are working on your hierarchies, we ask that people overkill their phobias or obsessions. If you can't even say the word "snake" and you progress to being comfortable holding a three-foot boa constrictor, overkill would be doing a snake routine in North Beach with five ten-foot boas and three yellow pythons.

My son had a contamination obsession—did I mention this runs in families? He completed his cure when he stuck his hand in a public toilet and didn't wash it for three days! When he ate, he put on a glove, but he recontaminated after meals with a toilet-soaked rag he kept in a ziplock bag. We call that "stepping on the neck of your Boo." If you stop halfway in your hierarchy, your Boo will know and come back to bite you. Practice overkill and you will have a toothless Boo.

So, after you cure your flying phobia, become a pilot and fly around the world upside down and blindfolded. If you hate driving, I would suggest buying your own taxi and driving fourteen hours a day in downtown Manhattan. You shut your Boo up with pretentious victories. If you don't like crowds, wait for million-man rallies and join the throng, "swim" your way into the center of the mob, and stay there. Once you get your foot on the neck of the Boo, keep it there. Find every opportunity to challenge and overkill your phoboc fears.

## Worst Case Scenario

This is the only time you get to answer "what if" questions. This powerful exercise asks that you write or record a four-page script of your worst fears. You capture your Booland scenario on paper or tape. No calming tools allowed. You write how you suffer a panic attack in the worst place imaginable, recorded by CNN for the world to see. You are ridiculed and shunned, you are fired and committed to an insane asylum for life! Then you read or listen to it repeatedly for forty-five minutes every day until you can do so with little or no anxiety. Most patients find this a truly difficult exercise. Many fear if they even write it, it will happen (thought action fusion). Others find their fear level so high they can't complete the project. The first time you read it, anxiety levels are often in the seven or eight SUDs range. By the third day, it becomes a total bore. You desensitize to thoughts and obsessions the same way you desensitize to your snake or cat phobia— simply by repeated exposure.

Worst case is capturing the vague horror script that floats around in our brain whenever we face our phoboc challenge. It's a useful tool in all phobias and obsessions, but particularly with PTSD. In worst case, it is not a life-threatening event but a terminal one. You and your family are horribly beaten and killed. The earthquake flattens your home and you are hopelessly trapped for days until you die of thirst and starvation. For me, worst case was where I have the feared bowel accident at the hospital with peer witnesses. You must write about the shame and demeaning glances and the abject humiliation. You relate how you hear degrading comments for days afterward, the whole world knows because the events are captured in newspaper headlines and featured on the nightly news.

A psychotherapist gave up her private practice for fear she would make a mistake and as a result, a patient would commit suicide. In her worst case scenario, she wrote about the dreaded phone call from the parents of the deceased. They were screaming, "You killed our daughter. You told her to write her worst case and she was so traumatized she hung herself. She left a suicide note saying it was all your fault. You are an incompetent therapist and we are reporting you to the Review Board." At the meeting, her license is revoked. The panel is in agreement that she never should have been doing therapy. "You are a disgusting, pathetic, incompetent murderer." She read it repeatedly and then read it aloud in the Phobease class. Eventually, she cured her obsessive fear and returned to a productive practice.

When read repeatedly you desensitize to your scary thoughts and realize your Boo was the producer, writer, and director of that script. You get in the here and now and realize if it happened, you would be able to handle it. You realize that your worst case is fear rehearsing at its best and just thoughts—not facts. When you are ready, I will ask you to do this challenging exercise for one or two of your phobic or obsessive fears.

## Intentional Paradox

Intentional paradox is another way to mock your Boo. The Boo holds us hostage with its catastrophic threats. Here you challenge the Boo to carry out its implied disasters. Do you remember from grammar school what has to happen if you double-dare someone? They absolutely, positively have to do it. If you dare someone they have a choice but double-dare them and they have no choice—they must carry out your request or die or something worse. The Boo says, "If you don't get out of here, you will die." You tell the Boo, "Okay, I'm waiting. I double-dare you to kill me in ten seconds or I'll clean out the cat box." You bare your watch and count down: ten, nine, eight . . . and impatiently repeat, "I'm waiting, I double-dare you. What's the matter big boy? Lost your magic?" Intentional paradox is standing up to your Boo bully. Intentional paradox means you have recognized that the Boo is powerless and all it can do is go "boo" and squirt adrenaline. You know a lot about adrenaline now. It's a normal bodily secretion that prepares you for mortal combat—a drug that lasts only ten minutes and is no more dangerous than dropping marshmallows on your bare feet. From now on, any time the Boo utters a threat, spread your legs, get those hands on your hips, thrust that chin out, and double-dare the Boo to "put up or shut up." Intentional paradox shuts up the Boo—employ it frequently.

## Pronounced Efficaciousness

When I wrote my children's class manual, I asked them if I should retain those big words. The vote was a unanimous "yes." Children love words like "supercalifragilisticexpealidocious." Translated, efficaciousness simply means, "I will handle it." Bullies hate that kind of language. The Boo is always implying that you won't be able to handle it. The Boo is wrong. Thirty-eight years of working in rehabilitation taught me that patients can handle any crisis. People can handle being paralyzed from the neck down for life. They can handle being diagnosed with multiple sclerosis or terminal cancer. You know why? Because they have no choice. The Boo always says, "You won't handle it well." Well, you don't have to handle it well, you just have to handle it, and you will. We can handle phoboc fears, family crises, societal disasters, and devastating injuries. There is no scientific limit to what people can tolerate. People have experienced inhuman tortures and prolonged confinement in concentration camps and survived.

At first, when I employed the "I will handle it" tool, neither the Boo nor I believed it. After all, I hadn't handled it in thirty-one years, why now? If the Boo brings up your past record, repeat, "I will handle it." After the third challenge, detach and do something else. In time, when you have accumulated untold victories, you will have convinced the Boo that you, indeed, will handle it.

I never believed in all my phoboc years that I would ever awaken knowing that whatever comes along that day, *I will handle it*. If you persist and do the work, you will cure too. It's a wonderful feeling.

You now have all the tools and strategies you need to begin your journey on your path to cure. As you begin to face your fears, you will recognize those that work best for you in reducing anxiety levels. Everyone is different, so initially there is a trial-and-error approach. Forty tools may be too many to remember, but there are a basic core that we call "The phobease golden dozen":

Recognize and accept the Boo
Thought stoppage and calmative breathing
Dispute and reframe
Cortical shift

SUDs evaluation
Model and mirror
Get in the here and now
Anticipate and prepare
Write it down
Study the subject
"I will handle it"

## Chapter 2 Highlights

1. Recognize your Boo as the most important primary tool—remember all it can do is go "Boo."

2. Accept the Boo's ramblings and treat it like Chicken Little. Listen to it carefully and then do the opposite.

3. Thought stop and calmative breathe immediately and every time you feel anxious.

4. Dispute and reframe constantly. Tell your Boo, "I will handle it."

5. Invent situations that create the symptoms you are trying to avoid—interoceptive exposure.

6. Look for three things you can do, feel, smell, or touch to get you into your left brain—cortical shifting.

7. Study the topic—knowledge is power but knowledge alone can't cure anxiety disorders.

8. Repeatedly assess your SUDs level any time you are anxious—remember, "Comfort is not your goal—living is."

9. Remember that only victories, purposeful exposures to the thing you fear, cure phobias. And when you get them, write them down.

10. Use the following tools: cortical shifting, calmative breathing, humor, mirroring, modeling, best and worst case scenarios, intentional paradox, exposure and response prevention, knowledge of subject, neutralizing Boo by singing, repeating in slow motion, or announcing its threats, and overkilling your phobias and obsessions—all are effective.

11. Spread your legs to shoulder width, put your hands on your hips, lean forward, and loudly boss back your Boo.

12. Remember that all phobias and obsessions are curable. (Did I mention that?)

## Chapter 2 Assignment

Remember that this is a workbook. You cure phobias with action so *please* do all your assignments.

Do relaxation exercise daily.

Continue daily diary. Are you doing thought stoppage immediately and every time?

Exercise daily. It burns adrenaline. Try for twenty-five to thirty minutes continuous activity. It desensitizes you to the rapid breathing and heart rate felt during panic

1. Rearrange your fear list from worst to least. What's limiting your life the most should be at the top of your list:

| | |
|---|---|
| 1. _____ | 9. _____ |
| 2. _____ | 10. _____ |
| 3. _____ | 11. _____ |
| 4. _____ | 12. _____ |
| 5. _____ | 13. _____ |
| 6. _____ | 14. _____ |
| 7. _____ | 15. _____ |
| 8. _____ | 16. _____ |

2. Make a victory card. List *any* discernible change in your phoboc behavior no matter how small. If you can sit just one seat in from an aisle when you couldn't before, list it. Write it down. You're going to use these phoboc victories often. Carry the victory card with you so you can read it to your brain.

3.  Memorize a level "4" anxiety level. What symptoms do you experience just before you have to leave a situation? Review the fear level chart and get an idea of how your fear symptoms escalate. Begin to grade any fear level you experience. This makes you a scientist rather than a scared observer. "Oh, I'm a level 2, but I can handle that."

4.  Practice looking at your pictures of fear situations using Thought Stoppage, Recognition, Calmative Breathing, and Positive Self-Talk. This is a form of familiarization and desensitization. Carry the pictures with you and look at them many times. Some patients say, "Don't even mention the word airplane." This is an extreme form of avoidance. Looking at pictures and relaxing are safe ways to practice non-avoidance. By doing this in a calm environment, you are reprogramming your brain.

5.  Think of "escape routes" for your phobias. Escape routes are ways of getting control at this stage—anything you need is okay. One patient took a stick for her elevator practice so she could put it in the door at the last second and not risk losing her hand if the door didn't open. Phobocs like to hold things. If you need water or a cell phone, then get it. Some patients make sure they have a quarter for a phone call or a twenty-dollar bill for a taxi. Use your creative skills to think up ways to get out of situations in advance. Be prepared!

    Are you afraid of getting stuck on the road? Buy a cell phone or CB radio. Are you afraid of not finding a bathroom on the road? Carry a bedpan and sheet in your car trunk and you'll have your own portable potty.

Change! Risk!

Do it slowly, but do it!

Retreat is okay!

Write down your victories!

Reward yourself for victories!

# 3

# Desensitizing to Phobias and Obsessions

**Ingredients:**

1 brain in bag
1 loaded squirt gun
1 Boo monster
1 bag large marshmallows
1 Right/Left brain prop
1 working pen for each participant
An assortment of fake vomit, hypodermic syringes, rubber
mice, rats, and snakes; toy toilet, devil doll, bats, bees, dogs,
and so on.

**Directions:**

Display prominently before seventy frightened adults and
children.

---

FOR YEARS, fear and anxiety have stalked you. Now it's your turn to
make fear the hunted. Seek it out, embrace it, and destroy it. For
years, you have studiously avoided scary things. I am now going to

ask you to invite them, *on purpose*, into your life. For years, you have
been doing the exact opposite of what you needed to do to cure. The
only way to cure phobias and obsessions is with experiential victories.
A victory is the purposeful exposure to the thing that you fear. There
are no shortcuts—the only way out is through. "Darn." You will learn
how to safely creep up on any fear or obsession. You do this by creating a hierarchy. A hierarchy is a gradual, safe, planned, safe, incremental, safe, controlled, safe way of approaching any fear situation.
(Did I mention safe?) As a claustrophobic, I thought the treatment
would be to lock me in a "small" (adrenaline-secreting trigger word)
closet, throw away the key, and leave me in there for three months.
That belief kept me from seeking treatment for years. I didn't know
there was a less odious approach that would expose me to gradual,
tolerable levels of anxiety: hierarchies.

The trouble with phobias and obsessions is they severely restrict
and constrict our lives. It's the iceberg phenomenon—only 10 percent
of an iceberg floats above the water, while the remaining 90 percent
is hidden from view. Simple phobias have this hidden devastating
effect on our lives. My simple claustrophobia compromised and limited every aspect of my existence. At the height of my phobia, I was
anxious about everything: anything confining including restaurants,
elevators, airplanes, buses, rapid transit, theaters, courts, attending or
giving lectures or conferences, social events, dances, fear of bowel
accidents, doctors, dentists, being far from home, cruise ships, and
life. I was limited to a twelve-mile space between my home and the
hospital where I worked.

The reason you want to cure your disorder is so you can live an
expansive life, unrestricted by fear. Is it possible? Absolutely, if you
do the work, you will cure. The key is to desensitize to your particular twelve to fifteen fears. Desensitization is a process whereby you
become familiar with and tolerant of your anxiety symptoms. Familiar is derived from the word "family." Most of us are more comfortable with family members than with strangers. We have been taught
since childhood that strangers are dangerous; they kidnap, rape, and
kill you. Nice messages for a phoboc child. Years later, when you
are invited to a social event where you don't know anybody (i.e.,

"strangers"), you may experience high levels of anxiety. Simply, we become familiar by repeated exposures to the things we fear.

One of our class members loved flowers and was phobic about frogs. As she pored through one month's flower magazine, she turned to page thirty and was startled to find a beautiful Anthyrium harboring a tiny green tree frog with huge bulging red eyes staring back at her. She threw down the magazine, assessed her SUDs level as a fourteen, and vowed to cancel her subscription. An alternative would be to ask her to do some calmative breathing, suck a lollipop, listen to patriotic music, and, when comfortable, turn from page twenty-nine to thirty about 250,000 times. I can assure you, if she carried out the assignment, on the last page-turning her anxiety level would be zero and her Boo would be bored silent. Like the cold swimming pool example, we habituate to repeated and continuous exposure to fear stimuli.

On the 250,000th exposure, we are not going to be surprised or startled to see that cute, darling little frog. After a quarter of a million glimpses, the prominent red eyes are not going to provoke an adrenaline response. This exaggerated example defines the approach to diminishing fear of anything. The essence of desensitization is total and dedicated repetitive non-avoidance. If you fear rats when ready, I will ask you to challenge your rodent-free world by writing "rats," saying "rats," wearing a rat T-shirt and earrings. I will ask you to buy toy rats, rubber rats, pet rats, and for overkill, sleep with 200 or 300 (just kidding—a little) of your favorite hairy little rodents.

## Write It Down

Whoever said, "The pen is mightier than the sword" probably knew a lot about treating anxiety disorders. Getting things on paper is a crucial initial step to your phoboc cure. We phobocs tend to be in our rational, logical minds a good deal of the time. The average person can think 300 to 400 words per minute, speak 140 to 180 words per minute, but can only write 20 words per minute. So writing slows things down and allows us to capture concrete examples of our vague fear thoughts. It further limits our creative scare scenarios.

Dealing with anxious topics in a safe, calm environment helps to reprogram our fear centers (amygdalae). I'll ask you to add that lollipop and patriotic music while writing your fear to tell your brain that the topic is being declassified from threatening to non-threatening.

When you start your exposure hierarchies, I will ask you to identify, on paper, everything you do now to avoid your fear. You will use that information to construct your personal non-avoidant hierarchies. Finally, and most important, I will ask you to keep a daily diary with emphasis on recording, in exquisite detail, every phoboc victory you accomplish. If you report any victory in a Phobease class or workshop you will repeatedly hear the words: "Did you write it down?" You need to write it down immediately to fend off another weapon the Boo has: a large brain eraser. If you don't write it down immediately, the Boo will erase the important nuances and minimize your victory. All victories are major and must be underlined in red with a liberal sprinkling of exclamation points. There are no minor victories in Phobease.

## Decreasing Adrenaline Effects

There are two major ways to decrease the exaggerated symptom responses produced by adrenaline—reduce your scary thoughts and embrace a daily exercise program. If you are experiencing chronic anxiety or intermittent high SUDs levels of anxiety, you have probably become sensitized to the drug. Over time, receptor neurons become exquisitely sensitive to even minimal increases in the concentration of circulating stress hormones. I was always impressed, as a medical scientist, how I could go from calm to abject terror in a thousandth of a second. I was always at a moderate level of anxiety, going through life with moist, warm palms, waiting for the next crisis—which was often. The slightest challenge, with my sensitized neurons, would result in intolerable panic symptoms.

The first way to diminish those symptoms is to increase your resistance to adrenaline. You do that only through exercise. I am going to ask you to embrace a daily program. Start slowly if you are out of condition and progress to twenty-five to thirty minutes of continuous exercise. If there are health concerns, get a physical checkup, but most people can simply and safely begin with a walking program. One can gradually increase time and pace and progress to slopes, hills, and mountains. You may vary the activity: bike, jog, run, swim, mow your lawn by hand, or take dance classes, tai chi, chi gong, or tae bo, but make sure you do it on a daily basis. Exercise burns the adrenaline you secrete. As you become better conditioned, your heart becomes more resistant to adrenaline stimulation. Your resting pulse rate slows, which gives you more tolerance to cardiac stressors. Being out of condition makes every disease worse. If you avoid exercise, lesser physical activities will exaggerate cardiac symptoms. One patient was so out of condition that just showering caused a significant physical challenge and resulted in an elevated pulse rate. Do you know the average pulse rate of world-class marathoners? The average for most individuals is seventy to eighty beats per minute. Elite marathoners have resting pulse rates of twenty-eight to thirty beats per minute. Conditioning equates to cardiac resistance to adrenaline secretion. That resting pulse rate allows some people to run full out and average under five minutes per mile for 26.2 miles! Start your exercise program today, burn circulating adrenaline, and get more resistant to your stimulating hormone.

The second way to reduce adrenaline effects is to stop secreting the drug. Using the knowledge and tools you've learned in the first two chapters is a good start. As you create victories from successful approaches to your hierarchies, you will further diminish secretions. In subsequent chapters you will learn effective tools to change the way we talk to ourselves—cognitive restructuring. The life skills you will learn will build your social confidence. All of these result in an overall reduction of adrenaline secretion and a diminishing of anxious symptoms.

## Stress Is Additive

The body is a stress-adding machine. You may find that as you ascend your hierarchy, you are able to accomplish goals at a low level of anxiety. But unexpected external stresses may make it harder for you to accomplish those same levels. If you are going to be investigated by the IRS, getting married or divorced, or moving, getting fired or hired, facing impending surgery, or dealing with deaths or births, your phoboc accomplishments may be set back. Any external stressor may lower your set point for anxiety symptoms and will be manifested by a sudden increase in your phoboc fears. Your Boo will become a screaming monster. Any illness or hormonal surges at menses or pregnancy may also increase phoboc symptoms. Be forewarned, when you are vulnerable, you will hear from your Boo; so tell it, "I was expecting to hear from you" and then go back to page one, review the Phobease doctrines and strategies, and put them into practice.

## Familiarity Breeds Contentment

Repetition is another cornerstone of the Phobease doctrine. When you begin desensitization hierarchies, I am going to ask you to repeat your exposures hundreds of times—no, thousands of times. (Have I resorted to exaggeration again?) You expose again and again until you can recognize that your initial SUDs level is lower. Repeat until you habituate. Repeat until you are comfortable. One exposure every six months doesn't work. The only time I ever drove on a bridge was when out-of-town company requested the mandatory crossing of the Golden Gate Bridge. As always, I would get through the challenge, but at high levels of anxiety. Then, I would not go back until the next time I was forced to. That meant for the next 180 days, I would remind myself that I didn't *have* to cross the bridge that day. For 180 days I was avoiding and thereby rehearsing and negatively reinforcing my fear. That's a powerful lot of fear exaggeration, which, of course, guaranteed the persistence of my phobia. When I was ready, I purposely drove every one of the seven Bay Area bridges every weekend and at least two to four trips daily. I arranged on one bridge to pay only once because the toll collectors offered a pass that allowed me to cross six or seven times per day. Repeating is what shuts up a loquacious Boo. The more times and the more frequently you can expose yourself to your fears, the more likely and quickly you will habituate, master, and conquer them. Repeating exposures is so critical that I am going to repeatedly repeat it and then I'm going to repeat it again. (My English teacher just turned over in her grave.)

## Every Phobia and Obsession Is Curable

Did you read that or would you like me to repeat it? *Every phobia and obsession is curable—including yours!* About 15,000 successful Phobease graduates can't be wrong. You recall that all phobias and obsessions have the same creation formula and more important, the same cure formula:

1. *Face your specific fear*. I will help you identify the "specifics" of your disorder.
2. *Experience the fear*. That's the part we would prefer to avoid.
3. *Habituate to and master the fear*.

Remember, while the disease is intellectual—we create it by how we talk to ourselves—the cure is automatic and devoid of intellectual processing. Stay in the cold pool—your fear situation—and the body will habituate and your anxiety will decrease.

Over 93 percent of participants in the Phobease classes and workshops show significant improvement. Many phobocs immediately decide that they'll be one of the 7 percent that don't improve. *If you do the work, you will cure!* The major reason people don't do the work is they have fully embraced myth number 3: "I am incurable." Without tools, they are probably right, but once "trained," many then go on to prove that, indeed, *all phobias and obsessions are curable*.

## Never Forced

You will never be asked or forced to do anything you are not ready to do. When they are not ready, people generally experience high levels of anxiety and the exposure is exceedingly uncomfortable. There is an approach called "flooding" in which that is done on purpose. The patient, usually because of deadline emergencies ("I have to fly next week and I can't even look at the word *airplane*"), is placed in their feared situation and left there until they habituate. Without tools, that might take several hours, but they will find out that all anxiety eventually goes away. A hospital nutritionist in the ninth month of her first pregnancy informed me, on a Friday, that she was claustrophobic and terrified of being on the delivery room stirrup table. On the following Sunday I arranged to have her placed on an unused stirrup table, armed with a few basic tools and the assurance that the experience wouldn't hurt her or the baby. She spent over three hours on the table. She estimated her initial SUDs level at twenty-three on a scale of one to ten! I played the role of both obstetrician and Boo and informed her that the baby was breech and would have to be delivered by forceps or caesarian. These were her greatest concerns. We reviewed "here and now" and "I will handle it" repeatedly. By the third hour, her back and legs ached and her SUDs level was between zero and one. She delivered a healthy baby boy the following Tuesday. She subsequently took the ten-week Phobease class to hone her skills at a more casual pace.

While you will never be forced to face your fear, you must realize that there will never be a perfect time to do so. I'm often told that exposure exercises are too hard. My answer is always the same, "Is a few minutes of 'hard' worth a lifetime of peace of mind and an exciting expansive life?" Let me tell you, "It is!" Remember that the more fear you are willing to tolerate, the closer you are to a cure. It is only adrenaline. Anxiety is what you are seeking. There is an old saying that, "Life by the yard is hard, but life by the inch is a cinch." If you construct and practice your hierarchies correctly, you will inch toward your chosen goals and won't be experiencing extreme levels of anxiety.

## Imagined and In Vivo (Real Life)

There are two ways to practice your hierarchies. In imagination, you visualize being in your feared situation. You can see yourself handling your anxiety, utilizing your tools, arriving at your greatest fear with crowds cheering your accomplishment. Traditionally, there are eight to ten levels to an exposure hierarchy. That allows that gradual exposure you are seeking. If there were only two levels, a severe snake phobic would go from writing the word "snake" to holding a ten-foot boa and you and your Boo would know it's too big a jump. If there were thirty levels you would be working at your hierarchy for years. Eight to ten levels give a consistent meaningful anxiety exposure at each level. It's important that each step creates some anxiety so you can experience it and learn that it is not dangerous. There is an extremely important difference between imaginary and in vivo exposures. In imagination you will be asked to do your *entire* hierarchy— all ten steps—repeatedly throughout the day. In vivo, you go only one step at a time, *never* going to the next step until you are comfortable with the one below. Comfortable doesn't mean anxiety-free, but an acceptable managed level for you. Thus, you rarely experience dramatic jumps in anxiety with your in vivo exposures.

Obviously, imaginary exposures are "safer" than real-life exposures but they still provide a very useful, non-avoidant approach to a number of unique situations. If you are not a multimillionaire and can't afford ten airplane flights per day to Australia, you can do them daily in imagination for free. If you are concerned about being burned to death in a home fire, we are not going to recommend burning your house down with you in it. However, you can create a ten-step hierarchy in imagination. You might progress from first smelling smoke to number ten when you realize you are trapped in a room with non-removeable window bars and will be burned to death in that room. Fear of being struck by lightning and going to hell are other examples that can be faced in imagination. It offers a unique and effective way of desensitizing to fear-provoking thoughts and worries. Fear of diseases such as cancer, AIDS, leukemia, flesh-eating, and *E. coli*, are best practiced in imagination or worst-case scenario.

Sometimes you can combine both techniques. If you are afraid of AIDS, you might do in vivo exposures, for example, write the word "AIDS" for fifteen minutes, read brochures on the subject, watch movies on the topic, visit AIDS wards, hug or massage an AIDS patient, and finish with several imaginary hierarchy steps—the doctor informs you that you are HIV positive, then diagnoses you with AIDS, and the last step you die of your disease.

A good way to practice imaginary desensitization is after you have created your ten-step hierarchy, you number ten pieces of paper 1 through 10. On the back write the proposed exposure for that corresponding level. Throughout the day take out your papers, turn them over, and visualize being in that challenge and handling it successfully. Remember in imagination, you do the whole hierarchy but in vivo—one step at a time—never going to the next step until you have accomplished your current level.

## Incremental and Decremental

Hierarchies can be incremental, progressively increasing your exposure to things that exaggerate your anxiety. Increasing distances from your home would be a good example. If you are uncomfortable leaving your house you might start going to the curb, then one quarter of a block, the supermarket one mile away, and eventually, gradually increasing your comfort zone until you accomplish your ultimate travel destination, a mere 9,000 miles away.

Claustrophobics can use incremental hierarchies to increase time in confined environments. For patients with CT-scan or MRI fears, I ask them to purchase a large square garbage pail and gradually build up a tolerance for lying inside for forty-five to sixty minutes. You can also practice lying under your bed for progressively longer periods of time. Patients with eating disorders—anorexia nervosa or voluntary starvation—can gradually increase the amounts of food and calories they are ingesting as they recover from their disorder. "Dark and alone" phobias respond well to incremental phoboc approaches—gradually increasing time in their feared environment.

Decremental or decreasing hierarchies are commonly employed with compulsive rituals. Begin by counting and recording the number of times you do the behavior you want to change. If you are washing or showering thirteen hours per day, you could gradually decrease by hours from thirteen to one until you can refrain from washing in a twenty-four hour period. Overkill might mean not washing for a week. You can similarly reduce checking, hair pulling, apologizing, or reassurance-seeking behaviors by the same decremental approach. Cognitive rituals such as repetitive prayers, chants, or magical phrases lend themselves readily to decremental hierarchies.

## The Six R's

React

Retreat

Relax

Recover

Repeat

Reward

This will be the format you will use every time you do your hierarchies.


### React

React means to place yourself in situations that will create anxiety. That wonderful state I assiduously avoided for thirty-one years and thereby insured that I would keep my constricted phobic lifestyle for those same thirty-one years. The construction of a hierarchy allows for the gradual but persistent exposure to your fears. Some have suggested the ten steps represent 10 percent increments of anxiety. The tenth level would be your 100 percent most feared event. Your beginning first level would be a tolerable 10 percent of your perceived fear. Thus, even at the higher levels you are just going 10 percent above the last accomplished level. All of us can tolerate small increments like that. The steps must create anxiety, otherwise they have to be strengthened. We must, on purpose, constantly invite fear and anxiety into our life. Only then can we experientially find out everything we need to cure: *anxiety is not dangerous, all anxiety fades, and if you stay in the fear situation, your body will habituate to the fear stimulus.* Make sure when you conquer a level that you write it down—immediately and every time. Don't neglect that step because you think the victory is inconsequential—there are no small Phobease victories.

## Retreat

Retreat is not cowardly. Initially, when you are sensitive to adrenaline, it is best to leave a situation if you are at an extremely high SUDs
level and your tools are not effective. Now, here's where every phoboc
asks the same question, "What if you can't leave? What if you're on an
airplane and you can't get off?" Well, you will have another wonderful opportunity to find out experientially what you need to know.
High levels of anxiety are a personal invitation to do battle with your
Boo. So, start with thought stoppage, calmative breathe, recite your
dispute and reframing coping statements, use the materials you
brought to cortical shift, model and mirror, humor your Boo, and
then boss it back and end with "I will handle it." Now, aren't you
sorry you asked that question? Anyway, at this stage of the game, you
are not permitted to answer "what if" questions. You may schedule
specific retreats into your hierarchy. For years, I always felt trapped in
meetings, theaters, restaurants, and courts. I was afraid if I left, everyone would know I was phobic; there could be no other explanation, if
anyone leaves, they have to be phobic. Later, we'll find that this is a
mistaken belief that we will have to test and challenge. For my cure,
I began to retreat and leave every situation on purpose, and then most
important, return. Not once, but twice! Why? Because if you leave
once, people will assume you could be going to make a call, or going
to the bathroom, but if you leave twice, then they will know,
absolutely, you are phobic. Do you see the core of my concern was
actually the WPTs? What trapped me was not physical barriers but
my distorted belief. I knew intellectually that I could leave but rational
logic doesn't work. As I progressed, I left in specific ways to provoke
being noticed. If there were slides being shown I would walk in front
of the projector when I left and even when I returned. No more sitting by an exit and stealthily sneaking out. If it's being noticed that
you fear, then leave with a flourish. Slide under or climb over a table,
drop a book but don't go quietly. When I found out experientially
that I could leave, I no longer had to leave. As I became comfortable
with retreating, I no longer felt trapped. The important difference is
that inherent in this retreating strategy is that after you relax and

recover, you must reenter. Retreating then is a temporary strategy to regroup and then reenter the fray.

## Relax and Recover

Once you're out of the fear situation, do your calmative breathing, cortical shift, and get your SUDs level down as close to zero as you can because you are going back in the fray. When you enter anxious challenges, even at moderate SUDs levels, you will rapidly ascend to intolerable symptoms. Most times, if you retreat and recover, you'll be able to stay on this second attempt. Again, use your tools and bring your SUDs level down. If not, retreat, relax, recover, and repeat again and again and again. That's how you shut up a Boo.

## Repeat, Repeat, Repeat, and Repeat, and Then Repeat Again

(Do you get a feeling of déjà vu?) This is the most important section in this chapter and possibly the most important key to phoboc cure. Exposure once every six months does not qualify for effective phoboc challenge. *You stop being phoboc when you stop thinking phoboc, and you stop thinking phoboc when you accumulate multiple victories that allow you to gain the needed confidence to master your fear.*

For example, you have an escalator or elevator phobia. Your first exposure results in a SUDs level of six. You exit, relax, recover, and repeat. On the tenth exposure, your SUDs is two. On the thirtieth transit, your SUDs is zero. Why? Because what cures phobias are victories and you have just had thirty of them. You now confidently expect that the next trial will show similar results. You return the next day and your first attempt shows a barely perceptible SUDs level of less than one and falls to zero on the second attempt. You repeat twenty-eight more trials at SUDs zero. You have mastered your fear and quieted a "bored to death" Boo. You step on the neck of your Boo by multiple low-anxiety victories. For overkill you get a job as a full-time elevator operator.

When I conduct "Bashful Bladder" workshops, I ask people to overhydrate so they can urinate in various social settings, thirty to fifty times per day, and then repeat that same exposure the next day. One hundred successful exposure victories does a lot for building urinary confidence. Confidence, borne from multiple experiential victories, is what cures phobias and obsessions. So cross the bridge ten times in one day, do thirty freeway on-ramps, contaminate repeatedly in one day, or ask 180 people for a bathroom—I did. Repeat, repeat, repeat, repeat, and then do it again. Only victories, repeated experiential victories, cure, so get 'em and then write them down.

## Repeat, Repeat, Repeat, and Repeat, and Then Repeat Again

This is definitely the most important section in this chapter and I am taking my own advice—I'm repeating it. I know I already wrote this, but I'm trying to drive home the most important strategy for phoboc cures. Immerse yourself in your fear challenges and you will cure. Repeat, repeat, and you know, repeat it again.

## Rewards

Phobocs are usually filled with so much self-contempt because of our disorders that we have difficulty regaling ourselves. That is about to stop. I am going to ask you to reward yourself for every accomplished level of your hierarchies. More important, I will ask you to pick a significant reward when you achieve your number ten level. Five-carat diamonds, Rolls Royces, Humvees, and private jets are considered reasonable choices for that incredible accomplishment. Post a picture of it where you can see it each day. This is a powerful form of goal-oriented behavior.

When I was working on my travel phobias, I began by taking our Bay Area Rapid Transit (BART). I started with one station. At the conclusion, I rewarded myself with a grape Popsicle. My greatest fear was going through the tube under the San Francisco Bay. "What if the tube ruptures and I am trapped hundreds of feet below the Bay?" You wouldn't answer that question now. But after a few single stations with decreasing anxiety, I decided to do the tube. I approached the station just as the train pulled in. I fumbled for the ticket, ran up two flights of stairs, and swore as the train pulled out. I was shaken, my SUDs level was an eight. I had to wait twenty minutes for the next train. Twenty minutes to create a host of "what if" questions. By the time it arrived, I was still at a level four. Not a good level to start your first tube trial. Unfortunately, I was unaware that there was a long dark tunnel to traverse before even reaching the tube. I shot to an eight or nine and got off the train and went home without my Popsicle.

I did everything wrong. I didn't have a plan or script. I hadn't prepared for a long wait or an unexpected tunnel. I was still creating "what if" questions and not using my tools. That night I reviewed the first three chapters and outlined a specific plan for subsequent exposures. The next day, I returned, intent on walking casually no matter when the train came. I brought the sports page to help cortical shift while waiting for the train. I "thought stopped" every "what if" disaster and calmative breathed. I answered every Boo threat with "I will handle it." I reminded myself if the tube ruptured and I drowned, I wouldn't have to do that week's homework. I boarded at a level one and never got above a level three even as I traversed the long, dark (trigger words) tunnel and the sub-Bay tube for the first time. On the way home, my level was zero. That was common for me when I was heading back to my "safe" home. I truly enjoyed that Popsicle that day. My ultimate reward for traversing the tube three times in one day was an expensive French micro-spinning fishing reel. Twenty years later, when I use it, I still remember its significance.

I realized weekend BART was bereft of people. Crowds and crowded trains would be a much stronger claustrophobic challenge for me. So, on my vacation, I rode the trains at morning and evening commute times with 250,000 other daily riders and earned another well-deserved Popsicle. If it's crowds you are avoiding, then it's crowds you must face.

An addendum to this story is that I went to the Opening Ceremony for the 1984 Olympic Games in Los Angeles. Two million visitors couldn't raise my SUDs level above a one. While there, my Boo arranged to have my car stolen. I flew back to Northern California and realized the only way to get home from the airport was to take BART. I smiled all the way home—even a stolen car couldn't dampen the fact that I could now take a train through tunnels and tubes without anxiety. Let's try a raspberry Popsicle today.

## Set a Time, but Not a Time Table

I'm going to ask you to think of a time when you could devote at least thirty to forty minutes each day to work on your phobias and obsessions. Perhaps after you've gotten the children off to school or after dinner or even in place of another daily obligation. If you have trouble finding the time, you might consider selling your children, divorcing your wife or husband, or winning the lottery so you can quit work. *Write that time down now*. Try, on a daily basis, to meet that commitment. Whether you read, do the homework, or work on your hierarchy, that will be Phobease time. If you really can't find that big a slice of time, then do mini-Phobease exposures throughout the day. Figure out creative ways to constantly face your fears.

While I ask you to set a specific time to do your Phobease work, refrain from imposing deadlines for accomplishing your hierarchy goals. It just adds unnecessary stress and pressure. "I should do two chapters a week and thus will be 100 percent cured in six weeks." Stringent time lines may be hard to attain. We tend to work at different speeds. It's not uncommon to progress quite unevenly due to other external stressors. Be gentle in your self-imposed demands. By the same token, do get started—there is no perfect time. See if you can fulfill your daily commitment.

You might want to adopt the strategy of successful writers. They write 1,000 words per day. If they are unmotivated, they write 1,000 words. If they are sick or tired, they write 1,000 words. If busy, out of town, or frustrated, they still write 1,000 words. Make a commitment to cure and you'll be able to write your Phobease 1,000 words per day.

## Choose Two or Three

I am going to ask you to pick two or three phobias or obsessions to work on. Then create a ten-step hierarchy for each one. Choose those that are limiting your life the most. You need to get a feeling for the various incremental approaches to different phobias and obsessions. When you are creating your personal hierarchy (fear ladder), begin by writing the number 10 in ink, your greatest fear. Then, in ink, write number 1—something you could do today, to begin your non-avoidant path to cure. Then, in pencil, guess at a number 5 level and fill the rest of the levels in. Why pencil? Hierarchies are really guesses: *There are no right or wrong hierarchies*. Keep an eraser handy to change levels in case they are too easy or too big a jump. You use ink on level 1 and 10 to remind you of your commitment. Don't stop until you have conquered your highest level of fear on every fear ladder.

Now, while you will have two or three formal ten-step fear ladders, you can continue to challenge other fears not listed on your hierarchies. Remember, the average phoboc has twelve to fifteen issues. I chose my claustrophobia and fear of bowel accident as my two formal fear ladders. However, I had so many other issues that when I understood the path, I could find phoboc challenges at every turn. Elevators, restaurants, business meetings, buses, BART, courts, airplanes, cruise ships, bridges, control issues (driver versus passenger), parties, and dances—all gave me ample opportunities to place myself in daily fear situations, utilize my tools, and savor low-anxiety victories.

For years I utilized the stairs. Why? It is good exercise and cardiac protective, burns calories, increases energy levels, and is more convenient than wasting time waiting for elevators. Nonsense. It was pure avoidance. The real reason I used the stairs was because I didn't want to become trapped in an elevator and not have access to a bathroom if I needed one. So to cure, I had to ride elevators. I rode the hospital elevators, on purpose, twenty to thirty times per day. Before work, at lunch, after work, and when I was on weekend call I logged a couple of million elevator miles. I joined singles clubs, accepted every social invitation, and purchased a dance studio membership because I was claustrophobic in the dance position. I practiced weekly excursions on BART, took bus trips, allowed others to drive, and sat in inside seats, farthest from the door. The beauty of having twelve to fifteen phoboc issues was that I could find phoboc challenges everywhere and I met them. Every trigger pointed to areas I needed to confront. I chose to be uncomfortable all the time and delighted myself with victory after victory. My confidence, self-worth, and self-esteem soared and in four weeks, eight hours of instruction and hundreds of hours of exposure, I was 95 percent better. I was comfortably doing things I hadn't done in thirty-one years.

## Avoidance and Neutralizations

You begin your quest for freedom from your restrictive phobias and obsessions by identifying, on paper, everything you do to avoid or minimize anxiety. Be tireless in this pursuit. Neutralizations, things you do other than avoid to reduce anxiety, can be very subtle. Avoidance is easy, if you don't like flying, you don't fly, but neutralizations can be tricky. Someone with a choking phobia who won't eat unless they have a person schooled in the Heimlich maneuver in attendance or a glass of water to prevent choking is neutralizing. I chewed food thoroughly and avoided spicy foods and red sauces and ate more easily digestible foods prior to social events to prevent stomach upset and vomiting—that's neutralizing. Neutralization is a form of fear rehearsal and negative reinforcement. Further, you need to identify, on paper, "trigger" words and trigger situations. Trigger words are adrenaline secreters. In the class, if someone utters a trigger word, we shake the brain in a bag. Bag shakers are words that exaggerate your fear in certain situations. Remember that long, dark tunnel. That is two bag shakes. Two shots of adrenaline. "Big, many, small, tight, close, narrow, windy, high" would be other examples. These will become guidelines for incorporation into the design of your personal hierarchies.

After your identification, incorporate all avoidant, neutralizing behaviors and trigger words (bag shakers, adrenaline squirters) into your exposure hierarchies. If phoboc situations arise that are not part of your two or three chosen fear ladders, challenge them separately. All victories count, all victories diminish your Boo, and all victories bring you closer to your expansive life. Incredibly, you can cure airplane phobias by riding elevators, asking attractive people out for dates, or petting a feared tarantula. You have only one enemy—the Boo. It is the common denominator in dealing with any phobia or obsession. You use the same Phobease tools and strategies for vanquishing your tormenting Boo and surmounting any fear. Thus, those little mini-victories are important stepping stones leading to your eventual cure.

## Personalize Your Hierarchy

All hierarchies must be personalized. Each of us has issues or triggers that make exposure situations easier or harder. I was concerned about people seeing me, a physician, having a panic attack. Thus, I was only comfortable doing things like driving and riding elevators alone and unobserved. Many would prefer people with them in case they have a panic attack and need assistance. For me, then, I needed to desensitize by adding people to fear situations, while others have to work toward being alone.

Other factors to consider might be:

day or night
size—big or small
gender—male or female
relationship—family, friend, or stranger
attractive versus unattractive
young or old
weather—clear, rain, fog, or snow
distance—close or far
crowded or uncrowded
windows or no windows
alone or with others
narrow and windy
high and higher
light or heavy traffic
fast or slow
near or far from an exit

You ask yourself which of these factors make you more uncomfortable. Which of these shake your bag and squirt adrenaline? They would be important factors to include when you create your hierarchies.

I was uncomfortable with crowds, older people, and strangers. I was much more uncomfortable with attractive young women, peers, authority figures, and especially being far away from home. My levels in my hierarchies reflected those specific factors. Remember the cure formula demands that you face your specific fear. For me, my number ten level on my driving fear ladder was to be in a two-door car, sitting in the backseat between two attractive women with three more in the front seat. It took some time to find that particular situation, but an outing to a San Francisco musical with members of my wife's tap dance class provided the opportunity to accomplish that challenge. Chalk up another victory and yes, I wrote it down. As you work on your respective hierarchies, you may have to change your intermediate hierarchy levels to accommodate your variable factors. That's why we write them in pencil—so keep your eraser handy.

## Phobease Swim School

I am thinking of starting my own swim training school. You show up, terrified of water, pay your money, and I push you into twelve feet of water. As you go down for the third time, I drag you out and tell you "same time tomorrow." Not too many people would return. This is what many of us do with our phoboc exposures—constantly drowning in our fears because we lack the tools and have inadequate training. Successful swim schools offer a more conventional approach. You stand in two feet of water, splash some water in your face, then gradually put your face in the water and blow bubbles. You do a dead man's float, holding on to the wall in shallow water until you gain enough confidence to do a dead man's float in deeper and deeper water. Then you add arm strokes and eventually swim across the pool in three, four, five, and nine feet of water and eventually swim the English Channel. You can do the same with any phobia or obsession. You can safely creep up on any fear.

## All Mountains Have Been Climbed

Surmounting your phobias is similar to climbing a mountain. You must train for it and learn specific skills. You know in advance that all mountains have been climbed. You start on a path but may slip back and have to change your route. Some segments are hard and may impede progress. Others are easy and you may make giant strides. It may take longer than anticipated because of unforeseen circumstances. But, if you persist, you know that all mountains—phobias and obsessions—can be conquered.

Another mountain metaphor is in the admonition to never look down when you're climbing. It's not a good idea to see nothing but 3,000 feet of air between you and the ground. In Phobease, you are advised to look up to see your goal but also to look down to see from whence you came. The view gets more impressive as your victories pile up. When you suffer a setback, it helps to realize you have not slid all the way back to ground zero.

## Worst Case Scenario

Worst case is a powerful tool to deal with worries and anxiety-producing phobic and obsessive thoughts. You will be asked to write a three- or four-page story about your worst fears without using any anti-anxiety tools. Worst case is your unspoken Booland. Your most feared "what ifs" come to life on paper. You read it daily for forty-five minutes in order to experience the severe discomfort it produces. If reading does not produce high anxiety, you may wish to record and listen to it for the same duration. In worst case you die, go to hell, your children die, you contract your most feared diseases. Initially, it provokes high SUDs levels, but in a short time you desensitize to the script and realize the Boo was the producer, writer, and director, and indeed, if it happened—you would handle it.

## Learned Helplessness

I don't condone the following experiment so please don't write to me about it. Purportedly, you take a dog and throw it in a pool of water and force it to keep on swimming. When it becomes so fatigued that it is in danger of drowning, you fish it out, let it recover, and throw it back in the pool. Irrelevant of what the dog does—moan, whine, look dolefully—it still gets thrown back in the pool. Eventually, it gives up, no longer struggles to stay afloat, and would drown if not rescued.

This is combined with a second experiment. A small cage is equipped with an electronically charged floor. When a light comes on, half of the floor delivers an uncomfortable shock. Animals of all species—mice, rats, guinea pigs, cats, and dogs—learn quickly to move to the non-electrified side when that light comes on.

Now, you place the dog that was in the drowning experiment in the same cage. When the light comes on, *the dog stays*. It tolerates the painful shock and does not move. The dog has learned that no matter what it does, it cannot escape the discomfort, so it does nothing. This experiment demonstrates "learned helplessness."

Many phobocs, especially those of us who have had extensive unsuccessful treatments, arrive at the same conclusion. For thirty-one years, I had psychotherapy, analysis, and drug trials and my phobias were unchanged. Like the drowning dog, I had given up. I embraced the third myth: that I was incurable. I would be like that for the rest of my life. No wonder 30 to 60 percent of phobocs get depressed. Depression is defined as an utter lack of hope and an overwhelming feeling of helplessness. The good news is that when you accomplish the first level of your hierarchy, you dispel both destructive beliefs. If you can do one level, you are not helpless and there is definitely hope. Both phobocs and that drowning dog can be retrained so that when that light comes on, we move. You are not hopeless and helpless. *You are curable*.

## Hierarchy Hints

Here are some suggestions for approaching treatment for the various components of the anxiety spectrum:

### Generalized Anxiety Disorder (GAD)

You recall the target symptom in GAD is worry. Begin by constructing a twenty-four hour diary. Record all worries during that period and then arrange them by SUDs level in order of your greatest fears. Assign twice daily fifteen minute worry periods. During the day, if any worries pop up, write them down, but delay dealing with them until the designated worry time. That frees up hours of your day that were previously interrupted by intrusive concerns. You desensitize to worries and obsessions the same way you would overcome a fear of spiders or snakes—by purposeful, repeated exposures. When your worry period arrives, you get out your favorite lollipop, put on your favorite music and worry about the thoughts you wrote down that day. You can record and listen to them, you can write them repeatedly, or you can have a friend read them to you. When you are in your worry time, do not use any tools. The goal is to get you to experience the anxiety created by harmless thoughts until you habituate and accept them non-emotionally.

During the day you can use thought stoppage, calmative breathing, and then get in the here & now. Ask yourself, "Is it happening now?" and remind yourself that if it were, "I would handle it." One annoying characteristic of worries and obsessions is that they can't be proven. If you worry about developing cancer in twenty years, no amount of testing or reassurance will allay your fears. You have to deal with the intolerable nature of uncertainty. Get in the here and now and let your Boo know you would handle it.

Another exercise is to divide your worries into those that can be solved and those that cannot be solved. If you're concerned that your father is ignoring his yearly physicals, you can call him and encourage him not to do so. If you're worried about getting old, you might accept that eventuality as unsolvable. Finding ways to actively assail your worries gives you a sense of empowerment. Finally, the all-important worst case scenario; take your worst worry—highest SUDs level—and write a four-page story of your worst fears and your imagined catastrophes coming true in excruciating detail. Record it if it is more frightening and then read or listen to it daily for forty-five minutes until you can do so with minimal anxiety.

## Panic

The target symptom is fear of physical symptoms and fear of the panic attack itself. Begin, as always, by identifying avoidant and neutralizing behaviors. Where would you least like to have a panic attack? Are there specific situations you fear that will create a panic attack? Getting hot, tired, or physically challenged are common concerns. Can you recognize any trigger words that increase your apprehension? Create specific interoceptive exposures to precipitate the symptoms of your fear. Do these daily. Create a hierarchy incorporating your avoidant behaviors and bag shakers. Practice the entire hierarchy daily in imagination and one level in vivo. Write a worst case scenario about your number ten level fear.

## Obsessive Compulsive Disorder (OCD)

The target symptom is anxiety-producing thoughts. Write them down and arrange them by SUDs level. You know by now to get a lollipop and some nice music and write your obsessive thoughts for fifteen minutes or tape-record them and listen for that same period of time. You are desensitizing to thoughts. They are neurobiological brain garbage—Boo products that are neither truths nor facts. They are not important unless you deem them so. They are not commands to action and will never take over your will. Identify your avoidant and neutralizing behaviors, especially your compulsive rituals, and incorporate them into exposure and blocking hierarchies. Do what makes you anxious but don't do any compulsions that you use to allay your anxiety. A simple rule is to accept your obsessive thoughts—they are all Boo garbage—but resist doing your compulsions.

Finally, construct a worst case scenario of your number ten level. Create your own horror movie. Include in exquisite detail your most frightening consequences. Carry it out to the infinite disaster and then read or record it and listen for forty-five minutes daily until you can do so non-emotionally.

## Post Traumatic Stress Disorder (PTSD)

The target symptom in PTSD is memories. You know by now we begin by identifying on paper avoidant and neutralizing behaviors and add trigger words. Use these to construct an exposure hierarchy. Do the entire hierarchy several times daily in imagination and one level in vivo—never going to the next level until you are comfortable at your present level.

Worst case scenario is a particularly powerful tool for PTSD. Since this condition often results after multiple traumas, you might choose one event you wish to write about. If the events were too emotionally painful to review, you can write a narrative worst case first. You describe the events as if you were a news reporter. After you desensitize to that scenario you can rewrite it with all your painful responses and feelings. Read that sequel for the required forty-five minutes daily.

## Impulsive Disorders
## (Hair Pulling, Nail Biting, Self-Mutilation)

The target symptom is urges. Begin by constructing a twenty-four-hour behavior diary. Record where, why, what, when, how many or how much time is spent doing the behavior. Identify your antecedent behaviors—what are the circumstances that precede you carrying out your unwanted behavior? Fatigue, external stresses, despair, rejection, menses, deadlines, and frustration are common precipitators. Certain environments, alone in your bedroom with no date on a Friday night may provoke expression of your habit. It's important to know your provoking stimuli so you can prepare a strategy in advance. If being alone, tired, in your bedroom on a Friday night is when you pull hair, then go to a movie or invite a friend to your house. Recognizing antecedent situations is important to combat impulsive behaviors.

Remember that all urges are temporary and go away. You need to find that out experientially. You can use many of the Phobease tools to counteract impulsive behaviors. Thought stoppage, calmative breathing, bossing back the Boo, cortical shifting, anticipating, distracting and delaying—all may be useful.

Competitive behaviors are very important in resisting impulsive behaviors. You substitute a physical behavior that uses the same muscles needed to carry out your unwelcome behavior. If you make a fist and hold it, you can't pick skin, pull hair, or cut yourself. You hold that for three minutes. Use that time to employ your Phobease tools. If the urge is still strong, hold the fist for an additional three minutes. If necessary, detach, or leave the scene.

Identify avoidant and neutralizing behaviors and triggers and incorporate them into desensitizing hierarchies. Create goal-oriented rewards for abstaining. Finally, realize that will power and motivation are less important than an effective plan. Substitute a different behavior for the one you are trying to replace. Strong urge—jog for an hour, play the piano, pet the dog—choose things that are pleasant and enticing. You can also utilize punitive measures if you yield to your unwanted urges. Pull a hair and you have to do fifty push-ups, clean out the cat box, or wash your neighbor's car.

## Addiction and Negative Habits

Again, we are dealing with a target symptom of urges. Begin with a twenty-four-hour diary containing what, where, when, and how much time is devoted to the habit. Identify antecedent behaviors and triggers and create anti-habit strategies. Identify environmental triggers, social settings, and people that contribute to your undesirable behaviors. Identify what it is in your lifestyle that contributes to your habit. If you have difficulty controlling your weight, and your car, pantry, and drawers at home and work are filled with treats, you want to eliminate those calorie sources. You may decide to shop only after you have eaten and only purchase items on a written list. If you love candy and bargains as I do, you must avoid shopping the day after Valentine's Day or Easter when candy is dispensed at half price.

Again, anticipate your urges and use your Phobease tools and strategies to surmount them. Post short-, medium-, and long-term goals. Share your specific plans with others to add pressure to conform to your chosen objective. If you need a buddy, get one prior to withdrawing from any addiction. Don't count on willpower or high motivation, but rather create effective alternative behaviors when urges are strong. Choose rewards for achieving your short-, medium-, and long-term goals. Make the final reward significant—you earned it and you deserve it.

You might want to consider other unique motivators:

1. *Blackmail contracts.* Choose your most hated organization and write them a sizable donation. If you violate your self-imposed goals, mail them your check.

2. *Public revelations.* Write a letter to your peers or your local paper about your negative behaviors. Again, if you fail to meet your objectives, mail the letter.

3. *Punitive measures.* Find a behavior you dislike and assign yourself to perform it if you don't meet your self-assigned goals. Whether it's cleaning out the cat box, doing fifty push-ups, or washing your neighbor's car, you have to perform it when you slip.

Finally, though relapses are extremely common, in fact a normal expectation in addiction withdrawal, all addictions have been overcome by someone.

## Composing Your Fear Ladder

Review the following fear ladder hierarchiess. Then turn to a blank fear ladder and write your worst fear at number ten and then something you could do tomorrow at number one. Fill in the remaining eight steps in pencil. Do this for the two or three phobias or obsessions you have chosen to work on.

Good luck on your journey. Remember, *All Phobias and obsessions are curable*.

# Hierarchy Fear Ladder

Phobia or obsession to work on: _____.

Reward: _____.

| Level | Fear | Date Accomplished |
|---|---|---|
| 10 (your worst fear; in ink) | | |
| 9 (in pencil) | | |
| 8 (in pencil) | | |
| 7 (in pencil) | | |
| 6 (in pencil) | | |
| 5 (in pencil) | | |
| 4 (in pencil) | | |
| 3 (in pencil) | | |
| 2 (in pencil) | | |
| 1 (something you could do now; in ink) | | |

Remember, hierarchies are guesses. It's okay to erase and change levels any time.

## Hierarchy Fear Ladder

Phobia or obsession to work on: ___cat phobia_____.

Reward: _____.

| Level | Fear | Date Accomplished |
|---|---|---|
| 10 (your worst fear; in ink) | Hold an adult cat | Write the date you |
| 9 (in pencil) | | desensitized yourself and |
| 8 (in pencil) | | could perform the event |
| 7 (in pencil) | | with minimal or no fear. |
| 6 (in pencil) | | Thus, every rung will |
| 5 (in pencil) | | eventually have a success |
| 4 (in pencil) | | date. You should reward |
| 3 (in pencil) | | yourself every time you |
| 2 (in pencil) | | accomplish a rung. |
| | | Remember to write it on |
| | | your victory card. |
| 1 (something you could do now; in ink) | Look at word "c_t" | |

Begin to formulate a gradual program that will result in you reaching your highest rung.

## Example: Cat Phobia

*Note:* This is an example for a simple or specific phobia. You could substitute spider, snake, dog, bat, and so forth with a similar format.

## Hierarchy Fear Ladder

Reward: <u>Buy myself a pair of cultured pearl earrings.</u>

| Level | Fear | Date Accomplished |
|---|---|---|
| 10 (your worst fear; in ink) | Hold an adult cat | |
| 9 (in pencil) | Hold a larger cat | |
| 8 (in pencil) | Hold de-clawed small cat | |
| 7 (in pencil) | Hold kitten yourself | |
| 6 (in pencil) | Touch kitten held by someone else | |
| 5 (in pencil) | Hold stuffed toy cat | |
| 4 (in pencil) | Look at picture of cat | |
| 3 (in pencil) | Look at picture of kitten and say "cat" for 15 minutes | 2/4 |
| 2 (in pencil) | Look at word "cat" for 15 minutes. | 1/17 |
| 1 (something you could do now; in ink) | Look at word "c_t" for 15 minutes | 1/1 |

Make a set of ten hierarchy cards to practice imagined desensitization. Consider wearing cat jewelry: pins or earrings. Hold a stuffed toy cat while watching TV. Buy a cat pillow or cat T-shirt.

*Overkill:* After you have reached level 10, baby-sit a neighbor's cat. Buy a cat for a house pet; join the circus and do a lion and tiger act.

## Example: Airplane Phobia
## Hierarchy Fear Ladder

Reward: <u>View New York's Thanksgiving Day Parade.</u>

| Level | Fear | Date Accomplished |
|---|---|---|
| 10 (your worst fear; in ink) | Fly to New York alone | 6/4 |
| 9 (in pencil) | Fly to New York with support person | 5/3 |
| 8 (in pencil) | Fly to Las Vegas alone | 4/1 |
| 7 (in pencil) | Fly San Francisco to Las Vegas (1 hour 30 minutes) with support person | 3/17 |
| 6 (in pencil) | Fly San Francisco to Los Angeles (50 minutes) with support person | 3/3 |
| 5 (in pencil) | Fly San Francisco to Sacramento (28 minutes) with support person | 2/17 |
| 4 (in pencil) | Fly San Francisco to San Jose (14 minutes) with support person | 2/4 |
| 3 (in pencil) | Sit in parked aircraft | 1/20 |
| 2 (in pencil) | With support person, drive to airport and observe planes | 1/14 |
| 1 (something you could do now; in ink) | Look at picture of airplane for 15 minutes, say "airplane" aloud for 15 minutes | 1/9 |

*Overkill:* After you have reached level 10, fly to Europe, Asia, or Australia. Take flying lessons and become a pilot or flight attendant.

## Example:
## Mixed Hierarchy Fear Ladder

| Level | Fear | Date Accomplished |
|---|---|---|
| 10 (your worst fear; in ink) | Fly to New York | |
| 9 (in pencil) | Fly to Las Vegas | |
| 8 (in pencil) | Fly to Sacramento | |
| 7 (in pencil) | Drive to Tahoe | |
| 6 (in pencil) | Drive to Sacramento | |
| 5 (in pencil) | Drive to Fairfield | |
| 4 (in pencil) | Speak at church meeting | |
| 3 (in pencil) | Speak at PTA meeting | |
| 2 (in pencil) | Speak at Phobease meeting | |
| 1 (something you could do now; in ink) | Stand up and say hello | |

Some prefer to mix phobias but still follow a hierarchical approach arranged according to perceived SUD levels of their various fears. By now you understand that irrelevant of your phobia or obsession, the goal is the same—the effective management of your anxiety. For that reason, victory over any fear enhances your ability to deal with non-related fears. Curing a public speaking phobia will help you fly comfortably to New York.

## My Car Phobia

This is how I constructed my control hierarchy as it pertained to my car phobia. (Triggers representing avoidant or neutralizing behaviors are in italics.) I was totally comfortable driving alone or driving with family. I was less comfortable driving with *friends*. My discomfort escalated if someone else drove and I was in the *backseat* and my discomfort was intolerable if I was in the *middle space* of the *backseat* in a *two-door car*. (Note: all underlined words are bag shaking, adrenaline secreting, triggers.) Remember, your Boo knows every variation that increases or diminishes your fears. *Friends, strangers, family, male, female, young, old, attractive, unattractive, front seat, backseat, two door or four door*; these can all be used to help you create your hierarchies.

My level ten was *being driven while sitting in the middle space* of the *backseat* of a two-door car with the other five occupants being *single, attractive women*. My first rung of the hierarchy ladder was to be driven by my daughter with me seated next to her in the front seat. Filling in the other eight levels was easy by moving slowly toward the backseat first with family, then strangers, eventually in a four-door car, and finally, the eventual goal of the tenth level. I killed that phobia by riding over 160 miles with strangers in the *backseat* of a *two-door car*. What a great victory! Now I love to have someone chauffeur me while I lounge in the backseat—having an anxiety level of zero.

### Example: My Car Phobia
### Hierarchy Fear Ladder

Reward: <u>Leather jacket.</u> (I got it!)

| Level | Fear | Date Accomplished |
|---|---|---|
| 10 (your worst fear; in ink) | Driving with 5 female strangers in the middle of backseat of 2-door car | |
| 9 (in pencil) | Driving with friends in middle of backseat of 2-door car | |
| 8 (in pencil) | Driving with strangers in the middle of backseat of 4-door car | |
| 7 (in pencil) | Driving with friends in the middle of backseat of 4-door car | |
| 6 (in pencil) | Driving with strangers sitting in backseat of a 2-door car | |

| Level | Fear | Date Accomplished |
|---|---|---|
| 5 (in pencil | Driving with friends while I sat in the backseat of a 2-door car | |
| 4 (in pencil) | Driving with friends while I sat in the backseat near the door of a 4-door car | |
| 3 (in pencil) | Driving with stranger while I sit in front passenger seat | |
| 2 (in pencil) | Driving with friends sitting in passenger seat | |
| 1 (something you could do now; in ink) | Driving with daughter in front seat | |

## Imagined Hierarchy

Some phobias and obsessions can be dealt with only in Imagined Hierarchies. Fear of cancer or going to hell can be practiced in imagination. Worst case scenario is an exceedingly powerful tool for these kinds of situations.

## Imagined Hierarchy Fear Ladder

Obsession: <u>Fear of dying of cancer.</u>

| Level | Fear | Date Accomplished |
|-------|------|-------------------|
| 10 (your worst fear; in ink) | You die of cancer | |
| 9 (in pencil) | You are told the tumor is growing and spreading | |
| 8 (in pencil) | Repeat studies reveal poor response and change therapy | |
| 7 (in pencil) | Chemotherapy begins with severe side effects: fatigue, hair loss | |
| 6 (in pencil) | Studies show extensive spread | |
| 5 (in pencil) | Biopsy is positive for malignancy | |
| 4 (in pencil) | Doctor visit results in biopsy | |
| 3 (in pencil) | You find a large lump | |
| 2 (in pencil) | Say "I have cancer" for 15 minutes | |
| 1 (something you could do now; in ink) | Write word "cancer" for 15 minutes | |

Combine all these levels into a worst case scenario. Read or listen to recording for forty-five minutes daily until you desensitize.

## Interoceptive Exposure

Phobocs are often excessively concerned about physical symptoms (for example, tight chest, dizziness, rapid heart rate or breathing rate, or visual distortions) because they exaggerate the consequences (heart attacks, death, or insanity), when in reality, all symptoms created by anxiety and panic attacks are harmless.

You may be uncomfortable, but you are never in danger. They are symptoms produced by the body in preparation for mortal combat. In actuality, they strengthen both the heart and the lungs.

To desensitize, you must, as with any phobia, face your fears by creating the symptoms on purpose. This is called interoceptive exposure or in plain English—symptom exposure.

Concerned about breathing? Breathe through a snorkel tube, then a straw, and finally a small cocktail straw. Concerned about feeling dizzy? Rotate your head rapidly from side to side, sit up rapidly and repeatedly from lying down position. Have a friend spin you in an office chair. Spin rapidly standing with a friend spotting you. Face your specific fear and it will disappear.

### Example: Interoceptive Exposure
### Hierarchy Fear Ladder

Phobia: <u>Rapid heart rate and breathing.</u>

(*Note:* before embarking on any severe exercise program, you should check with your doctor.)

| Level | Fear | Date Accomplished |
|---|---|---|
| 10 (your worst fear; in ink) | Run up flight of stairs, two at a time | |
| 9 (in pencil) | Run up flight of stairs | |
| 8 (in pencil) | Walk up stairs, two at a time | |
| 7 (in pencil) | Walk up flight of stairs | |

| Level | Fear | Date Accomplished |
|---|---|---|
| 6 (in pencil) | Jog up incline | |
| 5 (in pencil) | Jog on level ground | |
| 4 (in pencil) | Walk briskly up incline | |
| 3 (in pencil) | Walk briskly on level ground | |
| 2 (in pencil) | Step up and down step stool 5–15 times | |
| 1 (something you could do now; in ink) | Go from sitting to standing 5–15 times | |

*Overkill:* Join a gym and learn to lift weights or join an aerobic step class. Train for, and run a road race; run a 26.2-mile marathon.

## Example Hierarchy Fear Ladder

Obsession: <u>Germ phobia</u>

Compulsion: <u>Washing</u>

Exposure and ritual prevention (blocking) is a highly successful technique used to treat obsessive compulsive patients. You expose the person to the event that precipitates their obsessive concerns and then progressively prevent (block) the ritual (compulsion) that they use to diminish their anxiety.

| Level | Fear | Date Accomplished |
|---|---|---|
| 10 (your worst fear; in ink) | Roll on dirty floor | |
| 9 (in pencil) | *Touch public toilet seat | |
| 8 (in pencil) | Touch own toilet seat | |
| 7 (in pencil) | *Shake hands with "dirty" person | |

| Level | Fear | Date Accomplished |
|---|---|---|
| 6 (in pencil) | Shake hands with "clean" person | |
| 5 (in pencil) | Put hand in mud | |
| 4 (in pencil) | Touch ground with one hand | |
| 3 (in pencil) | Touch ground with one finger | |
| 2 (in pencil) | *Touch doorknob with whole hand | |
| I (something you could do now; in ink) | Touch doorknob with one finger | |

Blocking, postponing or delaying washing after above contaminations is an effective tool for destroying compulsions. You simply acknowledge that you will wash at a specific future time. When that time arrives, try to delay it again. Doing this allows you to deal with the anxieties that delays produce and eventually will allow you to dispense with the performance of the ritual. Avoid any neutralization or avoidance strategies.

*Overkill:* After you reach level 10, sleep with contaminated tissues; sleep with toilet seat; contaminate and don't wash for three days; get a job as a garbage collector.

*Rag trick: Wipe rag on feared object, label, and place in a ziplock bag. You can then recontaminate repeatedly without having to revisit sites.

## Chapter 3 Highlights

1. Remember: all fears restrict us. Desensitize by making the scary familiar with imagined and in vivo hierarchies.
2. Be aware that all phobias and obsessions can be gradually and safely approached with exposure hierarchies.
3. Try the cure formula: "Face your specific fear, experience the fear, habituate to and master your fear—it is automatic."

4. Stay in the cold pool and your fear will diminish. Comfort is not your goal—living is.

5. Accept your obsessions and resist your compulsions—the only way out is through.

6. Step on the neck of your Boo with repeated victories.

7. Reprogram your amygdala—your storehouse of survival memories—with victories: get 'em and then write them down.

8. The best way to approach fearful worries and thoughts is worst case.

9. Remember that the only thing the Boo can do is go "Boo," squirt adrenaline, and make you feel uncomfortable.

10. Be aware if you want to think of something less, you have to think of it more.

11. Desensitize to obsessive thoughts and worries the same way you desensitize to dogs, cats or spiders, by repeatedly exposing yourself to them.

12. Remind yourself that you are not hopeless and helpless: *All phobias and obsessions can be cured.*

## Chapter 3 Assignment

Do daily relaxation process.

Exercise fifteen to thirty minutes daily.

Do daily diary entries.

1. List two or three fears or obsessions that you wish to work on.

1. _____

2. _____

3. _____

2. Make a Hierarchy Success Ladder sheet. Complete one ladder for each fear.

3. For number 10, write in ink the thing that would be the most fear provoking for you. Then, at the number 1 level, list something—no matter how trivial—you could do now.

4. Identify everything you do to avoid or neutralize your fear and incorporate that into your hierarchy.

5. Now, in pencil, see if you can fill in the other eight levels for each of the phobias or obsessions you have selected.

6. For each hierarchy, number the pieces of paper from 1 to 10. On the reverse side, write down the corresponding hierarchy step. Carry them with you.

7. Daily—many times per day—go through your hierarchy in fantasy. Turn over each paper one at a time, read the step described and then see yourself accomplishing that task successfully. In fantasy, do every level of your hierarchy.

8. Start doing In Vivo Desensitization with your hierarchies. Get to fear level 4, stay there, use your tools, breathing, cortical shifting into "here and now" and Positive Self-Talk. Retreat if fear goes above four. *Recover, relax*, and *repeat*. Try to do your in vivo hierarchy daily. When you desensitize (i.e., can do a level with minimal or no fear), write the date accomplished in the column so designated on your Hierarchy Fear Ladder. Reward yourself for every level; then and only then, proceed to the next level.

9. Tell someone about your phobia or OCD. Self-revelation is very important.

10. Practice Thought Stoppage, Boo Recognition, Success Rehearsal, and Positive Self Talk, both in fantasy and in vivo.

11. Worst case scenario: Write four or five pages or record in detail a fifteen- to twenty-minute tape of the most feared event on your hierarchy. Listen to it daily for forty-five minutes until you habituate to it. Use no neutralizing strategies. Experience the anxiety. This is the only time you get to answer "what if" questions.

Face the fear correctly! Do it! Change!

If it makes you anxious, do it—and then do it again!

## Phobease Word Puzzle

Fill in the blanks with the correct letters:

1. The Boo voice always L _ _ S.

2. Panic attacks always G_ A_ _Y.

3. C_ _ _ _ RT is not your goal.

4. S _ _ P. 1, 2, 3, 4.

5. _ A _ _ _ LL breathing.

6. Face the fear C_RR_ _ _LY.

7. I will _ AN_ _ E it!

8. Eliminate _ AFF_ _ _ _.

9. Fear juice is called A_R_N_ _ _ N_.

10. Eat a balanced _IE_.

11. Exercise produces _ND_ _ _ HI_ _.

12. _ _ IT_ it down!

13. _ _ MMI_ to a cure!

14. The brain doesn't want to die or be _MBA_ _ _ _ _ _ _.

15. Face your fear RE_ _ _ _ EDLY.

16. You can ask for _NY_ _ _ _G.

17. The only way _U_ is T_R_ _G_.

18. Practice, practice, _RA_T_ _E.

19. _R_I_in the bag.

20. Follow the six _'s.

21. All phobocs are C_R_ _ _E.

22. BE P_ _P_R_D when you travel.

23. Write your _ _ RS_ case scenario.

24. Adrenaline lasts only _ _ _ minutes.

25. Climb your H_ _R_ _ _ _Y ladder.

26. The disease of phobias is _V_ _D_ _ _ E.

27. Listen daily to your _E_A_AT_ _N tape.

28. _H_ _ _CS = phobias/obsession.

29. Write down your _I_T_ _ _E_.

30. Knowledge is _OW_ _!

# 4

# Phoboc Potpourri

*Ingredients:*
1 rubber Boo
1 squirt gun
1 squeak hammer
1 bag large marshmallows
1 brain in bag

*Directions:*
Display prominently in front of seventy uncomfortable adults
and children.

———

THERE ARE A NUMBER of common conditions that require unique
hierarchies. The examples presented are composites of actual cases
treated in my Phobease classes and not intended to represent any one
individual. (Triggers representing avoidant or neutralizing behaviors
are in italics.)

## Anorexia Nervosa (Voluntary Starvation)

The OCD Boo at its deadliest: A fourteen-year-old high school junior had exhibited symptoms of anorexia nervosa for three years. Her weight of ninety-seven pounds represented a twenty-eight-pound weight loss. She had been hospitalized three times, discharged at target weight, but relapsed after each discharge. She ate only half a bowl of breakfast cereal with *nonfat milk* at breakfast and nothing else for the rest of the day. She performed 200 abdominal crunches several times throughout the day and jogged four to eight miles per day. Despite her obvious emaciation, she viewed herself as obese and having a *bulging abdomen*—both visual distortions characteristic of body dysmorphic disorder (imagined ugliness). It is the Boo that is responsible for such inaccurate mirror interpretations.

Anorexia nervosa is the deadliest eating disorder because along with the characteristic severe food restriction, one often sees other weight reduction strategies—purging through induced vomiting, laxatives, enemas, weight reduction pills, or excessive exercising. Subsequent starvation induces organ atrophy and electrolyte imbalances that can lead to fatal arrhythmias, organ failure, and death. Loss of menstruation is a common finding. It is characterized as a disorder of the three W's—white, wealthy, women. In all societies, the rare and unique are recognized and regaled. Thus, in our abundant society, plump is common while thin, very thin, is unique. As societies are Westernized or economically enhanced, one sees a concomitant increase in eating disorders. Our society's preoccupation with thinness and dieting are prime factors in the precipitation of anorexia. It is common to find six- and seven-year-olds who are already dieting or concerned about their weight.

## Treatment

I view anorexia as a severe form of OCD. Patients show the classic features of the anxiety spectrum: highly intelligent, sensitive, empathetic human beings born with the neurobiochemical potential to develop OCD. They show frequent associated phobic, anxious, panic, and depressive symptoms. They invariably embrace the three phoboc myths: I am the only one; I am crazy or will go crazy; and finally and most devastating—*I am incurable*. Perfectionism, decreased self-worth and esteem, self-contempt, and excessive amounts of guilt and shame are common contributing components. Finally, they all show a distorted body image that is best viewed and treated as a severe form of body dysmorphic disorder (BDD). Their Boo (scare) voice reigns supreme and rules their mirror. It takes salacious delight in taunting its starving victim—telling them they could still lose a few pounds and people would truly love them more if they were thinner. The Boo introduces frightening obsessions regarding food intake—"If you eat, you may not be able to stop," "There's too much fat in meat—become a vegetarian," or "You eat one marshmallow, you will gain fifty pounds." Obsessions regarding digestion, foodstuffs, and elimination are common and many patients show other common obsessive compulsive behaviors not related to weight issues.

Once created, it has an expanding life of its own. Compulsions to avoid weight gain are invented to allay or dispel anxiety. Purging, enemas, laxatives, diuretics and excessive exercise become the anorexic's ritual behaviors. Anorexia nervosa is not the result of poor parenting, but a neurobiochemical manifestation of OCD.

## Result

This student attended the Phobease class and accepted that her problem was not weight but a manifestation of her genetic predisposition to develop an anxiety disorder: OCD. Her mother had suffered from anorexia; her father had a history of panic disorders. She embraced the Boo concept, named it a definite unmentionable and created the following hierarchies to combat her disorders by exposing to her obsessive concern about weight gain and calories. Her incremental eating hierarchy:

1. One teaspoon nonfat yogurt four times per day
2. Two teaspoons nonfat yogurt four times per day
3. Three teaspoons nonfat yogurt four times per day
4. Four teaspoons nonfat yogurt four times per day
5. Two teaspoons lowfat yogurt four times per day
6. Four teaspoons lowfat yogurt four times per day

7. Four teaspoons regular yogurt four times per day

8. Four tablespoons regular yogurt four times per day

9. Four ounces flavored yogurt twice daily

10. Eight ounces flavored yogurt at one sitting

She used similar incremental hierarchies for eggs, cheese, and eventually pizza. She combined this with a decremental blocking exercise hierarchy. She began by counting her abdominal crunches: 1,600/day $(200 \times 8)$

1. Start with $150 \times 8 = 1,200$/day

2. Reduce to $125 \times 8 = 1,000$/day

3. Reduce to $100 \times 6 = 600$/day

4. Reduce to $100 \times 4 = 400$/day

5. Reduce to 200 daily

*6. Reduce to 200 three times per week.

She felt this would maintain her tone and abdominal strength and agreed she would only exercise if she maintained ideal body weight within 10 percent of normal.

For a decremental running hierarchy, this student used time as her criteria rather than distance.

1. Begin at four hours per day

2. Reduce to three and a half hours per day

3. Reduce to three hours per day

4. Reduce to two and a half hours per day

5. Reduce to two hours per day

6. Reduce to one and a half hours per day

7. Reduce to one hour per day

*8. Reduce to one hour three times per week

---

*It would be preferable to eliminate all crunches and running sessions but she refused. Over one year, she attained normal body weight and has maintained it for two years.

She agreed to that final level only if she maintained ideal body weight within 10 percent of predicted normal.

Avoidant behaviors included wearing loose blouses to hide her abdomen and never wearing tight-fitting T-shirts. She neutralized by not eating for six hours prior to venturing out. Her Boo bulging abdomen hierarchy:

10. Attend school football game with folded bath towel under her tight fitting T-shirt

9. Wear T-shirt to school with folded bath towel underneath

8. Wear T-shirt to movie with folded towel underneath

7. Wear T-shirt to school with hand towel underneath

6. Wear T-shirt to school with folded pillow case underneath

5. Wear T-shirt to school with washcloth underneath

4. Wear T-shirt to next class after lunch

3. Wear T-shirt to school cafeteria

2. Wear T-shirt until noon

1. Wear T-shirt to first period at school

She began by counting the number of girls with dates at a high school football game that had plump or bulging abdomens. She concluded it was more than half and that perhaps that was not a significant deterrent to attracting a partner.

## Fear of Blushing

A thirty-five-year-old male had been fearful of blushing for more than twenty years. He chose not to go to college because of his phobic fear. He rarely dated and when he did, he went to a particular restaurant that was *dimly lit* (neutralization). He always wore red shirts or sweaters to give his face a reddish hue that hid an impending blush. He had investigated the possibility of undergoing a $14,500 surgical procedure to cut the nerves to his face.

Blushing, or fear of blushing, is another social phobia that produces devastating consequences. Like many phobias, the extent of its compromise is underestimated (the iceberg phenomenon). I have had patients who quit their jobs lest their boss find out or see them blush. Avoidance of social and intimate relationships is the norm.

Anxiety and the fear of blushing predisposes the individual to having their attacks. The disorder is a vascular sensitivity, genetic and familial in origin. The individual sufferer sees a blush as a window to self-deficiencies. It tells the world that the individual is immature, weak, fragile, incompetent, and unable to control his or her domain. Blushers have a diminished self-worth and self-esteem. Social isolation is common. Shame and guilt are prominent features. Depression and suicidal ideation are not uncommon. In severe cases, patients become housebound. They are so adept at avoiding that even best friends and family are unaware of their condition. Blushing is just one component of the social phobic. Invariably, they avoid public speaking, are often non-assertive, and lack communicative and social skills.

## Treatment

Treatment, as always, must be a universal approach to challenge the phobias and all their components. Psychoeducation, cognitive behavioral therapy and cognitive restructuring, life skill training, allaying of guilt and shame, and restoration of self-worth and self-esteem are essential.

His desensitization approach began with the self-revelation required of all class participants and identification of all avoidant behaviors and triggers.

### Levels

1. Announce to class he had a fear of blushing
2. Write the words "I blush" for fifteen minutes
3. Wear a T-shirt with the initials "WGB"—"world's greatest blusher" in class, outside of class, home, and eventually to work
4. Recite in class and outside that whenever Rudolph can't lead Santa's sled, Santa calls on him to illuminate the way

5. Wear only white shirts to class and work

6. Wear Halloween red face makeup to class, home, and work

7. Tell off-color jokes to class participants, family, friends, and peers

8. Sing happy birthday out loud in a crowded hospital cafeteria, buy one walnut at the supermarket, return an item to the wrong store without a receipt. Embarrassment Immunization exercises are required of all shy, social phobocs.

9. Ask every woman in the class for a date

10. Sign up for two night college classes

He became comfortable with his blushing.

## Result

He decided not to have the radical surgery and used a portion of the money he saved to purchase several new suits with white dress shirts as his reward.

## Body Dysmorphic Disorder— Imagined Ugliness

A thirty-two-year-old single attractive woman was told in grammar school that she had thin lips. From that time on, when in close proximity to others she *covered* her lips when she spoke. She rarely *dated* and *never wore lipstick* because it brought attention to her lips. She rarely attended any *social events* for fear they would lead to kissing and intimate relationships. Examination revealed normal lip size and configuration. Reassurance of this had proved nonproductive throughout the years. Reassurance is practically useless because it appeals to the rational, logical mind and is invariably discounted. Exposure hierarchies are needed to attain experiential victories. The goal is not to prove that her lips weren't thin. The nature of obsessive concerns is that they can't be proven or disproven. Rather, the goal is to convince you that even if you had the thinnest lips in the world, they would be tolerated by a very resilient, accepting world.

BDD is one of the most painful, devastating, and debilitating obsessive-compulsive spectrum disorders. Defined as an intense pre-occupation with an imagined or slight defect, it virtually destroys people's lives. It carries the highest depression rate—85 percent—of any of the anxiety disorders. Eighty-five percent admit to suicidal thoughts and over 25 percent attempt suicide.

It is estimated that 2 percent of the general population and 8 to 10 percent of patients suffering from social phobias have BDD. It impairs individuals at every level of their existence. Patients may spend hours obsessing on their imagined defect. They are often "trapped" in their mirrors, checking and compulsively examining their supposed defect. It most commonly involves the skin and facial components—nose, hair, mouth, ears, and eyes—but can involve any part of the body. Obsessive thoughts can focus on texture, size, symmetry, color, and even odors. Concerns regarding breasts and genitalia are common. Patients with BDD are continually comparing unfavorably with other people or models portrayed in glamour magazines. Questioning reassurance is constantly sought from family, friends, and spouses but does little to mollify their overwhelming concerns. The condition is virtually never discussed and is rarely diagnosed, because patients seek non-psychiatric medical advice and treatment. It is estimated that 10 percent of patients seeking cosmetic surgery or dermatologic skin consultation have BDD. Many patients have multiple cosmetic surgeries, averaging two to six, which are frequently viewed as failures and thus compound their distress. They are often refused treatment because their condition does not warrant it.

The emotional distress caused by BDD is enormous. Sufferers are frequently unemployed and unmarried because social situations and intimacy compound and magnify their difficulties. Many have been housebound for long periods. Patients often live with parents, who are frustrated by their inability to understand or help their offspring. Camouflage with hats, makeup, wigs, clothes, and hairpieces may take up enormous amounts of time and do little to aid the process. Sufferers are filled with shame and guilt over their seemingly vain focus on their appearance, not realizing that it has nothing to do with vanity, but rather an underlying psychiatric disorder.

## Treatment

BDD appears to be a genetically determined neurobiological vulnerability that predisposes the individual to develop an anxiety disorder. It runs in families, affects the sexes equally, and generally appears in the late teens. It is not due to poor parenting, weakness of character, or moral fortitude. It is simply a manifestation of an obsessive-compulsive spectrum disorder. In reality, these individuals are born to have BDD.

## Result

The woman embraced the concept that a lying Boo was making the mirror interpretation and she was willing to adopt a progressive lip exposure hierarchy.

*Levels*

1. Announced to the class that she had small lips (self revelation)
2. Allowed every class member to come and stare at her lips; none fainted
3. Smiled at everyone in the class
4. At dress-up day, wore bright red lipstick for the first time in her adult life
5. On purpose, smeared red lipstick all over her lips and went into the hospital cafeteria and drank a cup of coffee
6. Wore red lipstick to work
7. Participated in two shy group date class projects; she enrolled in a dance class
8. Joined a singles group
9. Went to her first singles dance with red lipstick
10. Accepted her first real date in two years and wore red lipstick

# Fear of Bowel Accident
# (Irritable Bowel Syndrome)

An unusually handsome fifty-two-year-old claustrophobic physician suffered for thirty-one years from the fear (guess who?). My target organs, where I experienced my anxious symptoms, were my stomach and bowel. When I got anxious, I experienced increased bowel motility and urgency. I lived in constant fear of the unanswered "what if" question. What if you needed a bathroom and couldn't get to it? My Booland was that scenario of losing bowel control, offending people with the odor, and the utter shame and embarrassment that would surely follow such an event.

## Irritable Bowel Syndrome (IBS)

I was diagnosed with IBS. IBS is the most common functional gastrointestinal problem in the world. It is nicknamed "brain gut" disease—you scare the brain, it scares your gut. It is recognized as a "psycho-bio-social disorder." In English, that means that the production of symptoms—bloating, pain, gas, and alternating diarrhea and constipation—are caused by a combination of factors. Any strong negative thought or emotion—anger, guilt, worry, fear, shame, or depression—results in increased bowel motility and a resultant increase in bowel symptoms.

"Psycho" doesn't mean you are crazy or that your symptoms are imagined, but that they are caused by scary thoughts and destructive beliefs, which result in intense anxiety, which aggravates all bowel symptoms. Concern that symptoms represent serious disease and fear of bowel accidents, of offending people with stomach noises, of gas passing, or of frequent visits to the bathroom are common worries. They lead to an excess focus on the bowel and result in the heightened anxiety that perpetuates and intensifies the bowel symptoms.

"Bio" refers to the fact that people with IBS were born with extrasensitive bowels. They demonstrate an increase in the number of pain fibers and a lowered threshold to pain when the bowel is artificially stretched. Bowel motility is less fluid and the bowel shows an excessive reaction to anxiety-produced stress chemicals. There is increased sensitivity to certain foods, spices, and food allergies, which further compound the problem.

"Social" refers to the difficulty of dealing with a disorder that is so unacceptable in society. Bowel movements, sounds, gas, and smells are offensive topics, especially to women. The inability to have perfect control over a bodily function, combined with a fear of losing control and experiencing a bowel accident, creates further stress and a resultant exaggeration of bowel symptoms. Concerns that people will negatively evaluate you and your condition are common.

The combination of all these factors and the inability of medical treatment to cure or even accurately define the problem leads to a destructive vicious cycle. Anxious thoughts result in increased pain, bloating, bowel motility, and diarrhea. The explosiveness of the bowel movement reinforces the fear of bowel accident and creates more anxiety, more preoccupation and magnification of bowel symptoms, resulting in ever-increasing anxiety and the cycle is repeated anew.

## Treatment

Treatment begins with the recognition of this "brain-gut connection." The focus is to reduce and manage anxiety. Education, training in anti-anxiety tools and strategies, symptom diaries, relaxation, cognitive therapy, training in assertiveness, conversation and arguing skills, recognition of co-enabling tendencies, and experiential desensitization are the basis for most effective programs.

It is imperative that patients learn that their symptoms are "real" and not imagined. That recognizing and changing scary thoughts and destructive beliefs will diminish the intensity of bowel symptoms and lead to the desired control and predictability of bowel function. Finally, desensitization hierarchies are employed to master all of the activities one has avoided in the constant quest to be "safe."

In a short time, anxiety is markedly reduced, confidence is enhanced, and one can enjoy a rapid expansion of social and geographical enterprises. I soon realized I didn't have IBS; I had an anxious bowel. When I used my newfound tools, I could control my anxiety. I was able to reduce bowel stimulation and increase bowel holding time.

As with any phobia or obsessive fear, I had to identify the avoidant and neutralizing strategies I used. There were many. If I was going out, I would visit the bathroom and strain to have one or more bowel movements prior to leaving the house. I would take an imodium (constipating drug) for "important" social functions. I would be very selective in my diet to avoid stomach upset—no spicy or exotic foods. I strongly considered buying a small RV to have a bathroom nearby at all times. I settled for a "runner's bathroom"—a bedpan and sheet hidden in my trunk for bowel emergencies. I avoided sick people who might give me the stomach flu and always sought aisle seats or seats close to the exit. I challenged all of those perpetuators when I constructed my exposure hierarchy. I wrote a detailed "worst case" scenario and dutifully read it those painful forty-five minutes per day. It rapidly reduced my anxiety about the event, realizing if it did happen, it would be embarrassing, but I would survive. The next realization was anxious bowel urgency was not the same as diarrhea urgency. There is no prolonged holding time with the latter, but there is with anxious stimulation. I began by resisting the bowel urge for progressively longer times. I found that if I controlled my anxiety, bowel movements could be delayed for hours! Hours meant I had plenty of time to find a bathroom.

I constructed the following hierarchy: I was afraid to ask for bathrooms because people might guess I was phoboc. I thus began by asking over 100 people—salespersons, police officers, etc.—where the nearest bathroom was located and they all told me.

*Levels*

1. Ask for nearest public restroom; hug a sick person
2. Increase holding time with bowel urgency with available bathroom
3. Go to close "safe" location without prophylactic home bowel movement ("safe" means available toilet)
4. Increase distance and sites, without prior home bowel movement
5. Go to safe place after eating "wrong" foods without prior bowel movement

6. Go to friend's house without prior bowel movement with constipating drug

7. Go to social event without prior bowel movement without constipating drug

8. Go to theater without prior bowel movement; go to bathroom at theater

9. Go to major event without prior bowel movement; sit in inside seat

10. Travel to foreign country and use the same strategies

## Result

As you know, since my cure, I have taken thirty-five comfortable cruises and visited over fifty foreign countries. I have eaten and digested cuisine from every one of those nations. I found that every country has ample available bathrooms, loos, and water closets. They will still be there for you when you cure your bowel accident phobia.

## Fear of Choking and Gagging

A young woman was extremely concerned about choking to death. She never ate *alone* and only with persons who could perform the Heimlich maneuver. At restaurants she would not begin eating until she had a large glass of water. She opted for predominately liquid or creamy diets and avoided *food with high choking potential*—popcorn, French bread, peanut butter, and peanuts. She *counted* and *chewed* foods eighty times to facilitate swallowing. Her chewing ritual was so time consuming that her husband often left the table before she was half way through her meal. She could not swallow *pills* whole because their texture provoked an exaggerated gagging response. Similarly, dental procedures involving her back teeth required anesthetic sprays to suppress her gagging reflex.

If you recall, two things your brain doesn't want to do are die and be embarrassed. Thus, the fear of choking to death is a common phobia. All body survival mechanisms are set on hair-triggers—

designed to be exquisitely sensitive. Thus you can choke on saliva or
water but you can't choke to death on saliva or water. Indeed, unless
you suppress your cough reflex with an inordinate amount of alcohol
and then ingest an unchewed piece of meat 2 × 3 inches you cannot
choke to death. You can choke on chicken or fish bones, popcorn, or
bread fragments, but you can't choke to death on them because they
are not big enough to obstruct your breathing apparatus. The trachea
is a solid non-collapsible rigid tube 1 inch in diameter. It is protected
by a dense array of sensory nerves that identify any foreign object
approaching its opening. Intruding particles are dispersed with coughs
so powerful they approach sonic speeds.

## Treatment

Identify all avoidant and neutralizing behaviors (any activity you do to
relieve your concern about choking). This might include swallowing
studies—bite size, eating slowly, and carefully monitoring your swallowing—available liquids, over-chewing foods, counting chews, types
and consistencies of foods you avoid: chewy, dry, crunchy. Avoiding
distractions—talking to someone, reading with others, not eating
alone for fear of choking and not having help, avoiding media examples or pictures of choking and tight things around your neck. Use
these and any others to construct a progressive hierarchy that ends in
eating your most feared foods in your most feared situations. Remember, only victories cure obsessions.

Write a four- to five-page "worst case scenario" of choking to
death. Record it and read or listen to it for forty-five minutes daily
until you can do so without significant anxiety.

### Tongue Exercises

Patients with swallowing, gagging, and choking concerns are so
protective that they often have weak, deconditioned tongues. To
strengthen and retrain do the following exercises *hourly*. Using your
thumb and first two fingers resist protrusion of your tongue for six
seconds. Then press your tongue firmly against the roof of your
mouth and the floor of your mouth for six seconds each. Protrude
your tongue as far as you can and then wiggle it from side to side as

fast as you can. Protrude and retract it as fast as you can. Finally, swallow repeatedly as fast as you can.

## Gagging Treatment

In front of a mirror, touch the middle and sides of your tongue with a cotton swab for one second. Progress toward the back of your tongue in one-half-inch increments. Any gagging should be treated with calmative breathing and repeat stimulation at that site. Progress to longer and firmer stimulations (i.e., five seconds with the swab and then with a tongue depressor and finally a teaspoon). Practice daily for forty-five minutes until resistance to gagging is attained. Finally, have someone else do the stimulations with the same format.

## Pill Swallowing Regimen

Purchase varied size candies—small round cake decorations, Tic Tacs, M&M's, Good & Plenty. Start with swallowing water, progress to single small candies, then to the larger ones. Finally, start over with multiples—three to four of the little ones and two to three of the bigger ones. Practice daily with various vitamins to maintain your skills. Keep a daily record of all efforts.

### Her hierarchy
1. Eat dinner reducing chews from eighty to twenty
2. Eat dinner with fluids—husband in next room
3. Eat dinner while reading newspaper or watching TV
4. Eat dinner while watching TV alone—husband gone
5. Eat French bread with liquids while watching TV—husband gone
6. Eat peanut butter and jelly sandwich while watching TV—husband present
7. Eat peanut butter and jelly sandwich with liquids—husband gone
8. Eat popcorn without fluids—husband present
9. Eat popcorn with fluids—totally alone
10. Eat popcorn without fluids and totally alone

She adopted two affirmations:
"I swallow all foods and pills with ease."
"My cough reflex protects me at all times."

## Result

The young woman rapidly progressed along her hierarchy and was able to swallow three pills at one time in front of her last Phobease class. She could stimulate the back of her tongue without gagging and allowed me to examine her throat with a tongue depressor in front of the same audience. She was able to accomplish her number ten level, eating a small bag of popcorn, without counting chews, without liquids, and totally alone.

## Compulsive Hoarding

A middle-aged woman joined the class because of generalized anxiety, frequent panic attacks, and driving, freeway, and bridge phobias. She showed rapid reduction of anxiety symptoms and by the sixth week she was free of panic attacks. At the tenth-week graduation class, she bragged that she had driven across the Golden Gate Bridge alone for the first time in thirteen years. She returned to repeat the class even though she had remained panic-free and was driving comfortably. She had even driven to Lake Tahoe, over windy mountain roads and more than 300 miles to Santa Barbara.

The woman's reason for the second stint was that she was a compulsive hoarder. She saved everything because throwing anything away created severe anxiety. She slept in a recliner because her bed had disappeared long ago under a mountain of clutter. She ate from a TV tray because her kitchen table likewise had long since vanished. She resorted to birdbaths at the kitchen sink because her shower/tub was filled with storage items. Her one-bedroom condominium was filled to the ceiling with accumulated items. She literally had to walk sideways through narrow pathways connecting the rooms. No one, including her family, had ever been invited into the house.

Compulsive hoarding is a common condition (estimated 8 to 12 percent) of patients with OCD. It is a combination of excessive acquisition of objects of limited or no value and an extreme difficulty with organizing and discarding items. It invokes many of the problem areas that are commonly seen in patients with OCD—indecisiveness and avoidance. There are exaggerated concerns about needing things in the future, and exaggerated emotional attachments with an inability to organize, categorize, or assign realistic values. This leads to clutter that can virtually fill an entire living space from floor to ceiling.

Symptoms include compulsive, excessive buying or acquisition of free things or items without intrinsic value—rocks, bottle caps, rubber bands, junk mail, and store samples. Since discarding items often causes severe emotional distress, hoarders often invent plausible excuses for keeping things. "I like them, you never know when you might need these"; "My mother used to save these"; "These possessions have a strong sentimental value to me." Often an exaggerated conscience is involved. "I don't want to waste these things—people are starving." In reality, this is not an intellectual process, but a manifestation of a disorder that compels sufferers to save and they create any excuse to account for their collecting. Some patients collect animals. One individual with twenty-five cats received three more kittens. She found them a nuisance and gave them away. However, she was so consumed with remorse and grief that she subsequently bought them back and vowed that she would never, ever give another cat away. She maintained that doctrine despite an ever-growing population and a horrendous cost in time and money in managing her flock.

Excessive acquisition and the inability to discard leads to unbelievable clutter. Furniture, sinks, and toilets literally disappear under a mountain of debris. Socialization is compromised because people cannot be invited into such disarray. Inability to organize, sort, and categorize leads to ever-growing piles. Since discarding creates so much psychic distress, the untreated hoarder, as do most phobocs, avoids and the process continues. In time, a serious fire or health hazard has been created. Some patients cannot discard garbage, so rodent infestation becomes an issue. Family members, exasperated by the mess, often have a purging—throw everything out, much to the consternation of the hoarder, who rapidly replaces the litter. Sometimes, valuables are thrown out with the worthless materials because the hoarder often mixes expensive jewelry and important deeds and stock certificates with worthless acquisitions. The problem is not sloppiness or laziness—it is OCD and that is the core of the treatment.

Since many patients have concerns about finding things, "important" materials are often duplicated and placed in different locations so they can be found more easily. It is not uncommon for phobocs to make fifteen to eighteen copies of documents such as football and baseball schedules and announcements of upcoming social events as well as wills, deeds, or trusts. All possessions are viewed as equal in value. The patient has difficulties assigning relative values to anything—so everything is deemed unique and important. One excuse is that they leave things out where they can be seen so they can be located more easily. This faulty reasoning has to be challenged when treatment begins. Commonly, patients are so embarrassed about their habit that they may go months or years without even telling their therapists.

## Treatment

Treatment begins by photographing or videotaping the "before" mess. I start with the standard psychoeducation given to any patient suffering from an anxiety disorder. They learn the genetic basis and cognitive distortions that perpetuate the condition. They learn to recognize their patterns of avoidance and learn techniques to deal with indecisiveness. Desensitization, exposure, and blocking techniques are used to deal with acquisition and discarding anxieties.

Discarding hierarchies are created. Patients are asked to list those items they would burn for fuel if they were freezing to death. They often feel less anxious if items are donated rather than thrown out. Goodwill Industries loves our class. Patients discard lesser articles and progress to more "valued and esteemed" items. If indecisive, the patient is asked to make rules, that is, all magazines or all newspapers. Organization strategies are used to store materials. Some empty entire rooms to provide rapid evidence of progress; others empty rooms of selected items. A specific goal of absence of clutter is the chosen outcome. Cognitive restructuring deals with future concerns about how to find things in the future. Libraries, the Internet, and available encyclopedias are offered as solutions.

Non-acquisition exposure and blocking techniques include viewing TV shopping channels *without* purchase, window-shopping with a support person, window-shopping alone, browsing with a support person, and then browsing alone *without* purchase. The final step might be to go to a home or business show where free items are given out and acquire nothing. With successful treatment, hours, days, and eventually weeks pass without unnecessary acquisitions. Anti-anxiety tools, insight into obsession management, and cognitive restructuring of destructive core beliefs are imperative.

Organizing strategies are used to aid in storage of residual items— bookcases, file cabinets, and closet organizers are useful. Again, if difficulties in making decisions arise, the patient is encouraged to appoint a trusted conservator. Questions regarding what to save are posed to the conservator, whose decision is final. As the anxiety lessens, disposal becomes easier and often snowballs into massive satisfying contributions. The "touch one time" technique used in business is applied in discarding—you must store or discard, no piles for future categorization.

Finally, the patient must be instructed in future non-acquisition strategies. Recognition of increased vulnerability with stress, fatigue, illness, hormonal surges of menstruation and pregnancy, and strong negative moods and emotions often exacerbate hoarding tendencies. Those times require strict adherence to Phobease anti-anxiety principles as well as contact with class facilitators if necessary for added support. All phobias, obsessions, and clutter can be cured.

*Her hierarchy.* Some people choose to work on emptying rooms, others, including my patient, opt for function. Her three major goals were to empty her bed, kitchen table, and bathtub. She used the "three box" approach. One box was marked *discard*, the second *save* but move elsewhere, and the third was marked *donate*. Initially, the discard and donation boxes were ignored but with time and the ability to effectively deal with discard anxiety, those boxes were filled with a zealous fervor. She composed a key list of five things that couldn't be thrown out: credit cards, jewelry, stocks and bonds, antiques, and sporting equipment. She decided that all magazines, non-reference books, newspapers, and mail, which comprised the bulk of the accumulation, could be discarded without review. She had learned how the Internet and library resources could be used for future information access. She agreed, per written contract, to dispose of a minimum of one black garbage bag per day.

1. Empty half of kitchen table into the three boxes
2. Empty other half
3. Empty half of bathtub
4. Empty other half of tub (*Reward:* take her first bath in years)
5. Empty one side of bed
6. Empty other side of bed (*Reward:* sleep in bed for first time in years)
7. Donate every other blouse to Goodwill
8. Donate every other jacket and coat
9. Donate every other dress
10. Invite family and friends for Easter dinner—first party at her house in thirteen years

## Result

The patient realized that dealing with discard anxiety was no different from dealing with her freeway and bridge challenges. She used the same repeated exposure technique and rapidly became comfortable emptying out her house. Goodwill benefited and she felt better donating than discarding. She canceled five of her seven magazine subscriptions, discarded all newspapers, catalogs, and mail the same day. Any future clothing purchases had to be matched with donations of similar amounts. One future event forced continued non-hoarding compliance: she invited everyone back for Thanksgiving dinner five months later. (See appendix A for other hoarding hierarchies and strategies.)

## Hypochondriasis (Illness Phobia)

A divorced sixty-one-year-old woman presented with a combination of symptoms for over twenty years' duration. She had frequent panic attacks, was geographically limited by severe agoraphobia, displayed marked separation anxiety, and had an intense fear of being alone. She used her dog, friends, a roommate, even her four-year-old grandson, to avoid being alone at night. On rare occasions where she was alone at night, she slept sitting up with a loaded shotgun in her lap. However, her major anxiety disorder centered on an intense preoccupation with disease—especially cancer. On various occasions, she developed brain, lung, stomach, and bowel problems, which required sophisticated investigative procedures, some invasive, which she feared. She constantly ruminated about the meaning of her symptoms, convinced they were indications of terminal cancer. She repeatedly postponed the bronchoscopy for her lung "cancer," her gastroscopy for her stomach "cancer," and the sigmoidoscopy for her bowel "cancer." She constantly searched the Internet for medical information, purchased her own *Physicians' Desk Reference* to research available drug treatments, and made multiple emergency room and physician visits as well as innumerable phone calls seeking medical reassurance. All medical tests including the invasive ones were normal.

Hypochondriasis is an obsessive focus on bodily symptoms with the distorted belief that they are all indications of serious diseases. Ninety percent can trace onset to anxiety-produced somatic symptoms. Over 60 percent of hypochondriacs experience comorbid panic attacks, depression, and agoraphobia. Patients are rarely treated in a psychotherapeutic setting because they regard their symptoms as organic. In fact, referral for psychotherapy is often used as an excuse to dismiss physicians and change to one who believes the symptoms are real. Though most patients with panic symptoms are concerned about acute disorders—heart attacks or strokes—hypochondriacs are more often concerned about distant medical concerns—cancer, multiple sclerosis, AIDS, and even mad cow disease. Sufferers have a basic mistrust of physicians and a paranoid conviction that their physician has missed the diagnosis. They are knowledgeable patients and often insist on unwarranted new procedures they have discovered in their quest for medical information. Their constant microscopic focus on bodily symptoms identifies subtle changes in their chronic symptoms that they feel warrant re-investigation, repeat reassurance calls, and medical examinations. Anxiety itself mimics and magnifies all somatic symptoms.

Reassurance is virtually useless or at best temporary, as new symptoms will appear. It is a subtle form of neutralization and negative reinforcement. Hypochondriacs often display obsessive concerns about body functions and secretions. They frequently check blood pressure, heart and respiratory rates, urine color, and bowel movement volume, consistency, and color. Any normal variation can be misinterpreted as heralding disease onset. This again leads to the cycles of anxiety and worry that must be resolved medically. Frequent checking of bodily lumps or nodes produces mechanical irritation and pain, which again feeds into the endless ruminative cycle. Their symptoms are not maintained for secondary gain but are perpetuated by fear and untreated obsessive concerns.

## Treatment

Treatment begins on page one. Patients have to know the genetic and physiological contributions to their obsessive concern. They are highly resistant to any implication that their symptoms have a psychological basis. Despite the psychological contribution, they must be assured that their symptoms are real. It is their faulty interpretation that creates their anxiety. It is important that they have one primary medical manager who is knowledgeable about the cognitive behavioral treatment of anxiety disorders, and particularly hypochondriasis and illness phobias.

Nowhere is the Boo voice more evident than in the interpretation of physical symptoms in patients suffering from excessive physical concerns. The symptoms are real but the Boo decides that a headache, feelings of faintness, or scalp tingling is multiple sclerosis or a brain tumor; chest discomfort is an impending heart attack or stroke and any stomach discomfort is, of course, terminal cancer. These are *catastrophic misinterpretations* that fuel anxiety. All these symptoms must be immediately checked out by an ambulance ride to the nearest emergency room or at least a visit to a physician or the Web to check on their latest symptoms.

Since you can't trust your interpretations of physical symptoms, the Boo will always do it for you. As always, the Boo lies, exaggerates, and catastrophizes.

Begin by identifying, on paper, all avoidant and neutralizing behaviors that are perpetuating your anxiety disorders. Since hypochondriasis is an anxiety disorder, diminishing anxiety at any level improves the chances for cure. Construct exposure hierarchies for the systematic desensitization to all fear situations.

The patient began by recognizing the complexity of her many anxieties. She decided to attack them all simultaneously. She constructed a progressive "alone at night" hierarchy, culminating in her being able to stay alone for seven nights, in bed, without her shotgun. She attacked her agoraphobia with an incremental distance hierarchy. Eventually, she increased her comfort zone from eight miles to being able to drive alone almost 1,000 miles to Texas. She flew to Washington State for the first family reunion she had ever attended.

Finally, to deal with her illness phobia, she agreed to write a worst case scenario about her terminal cancer and dispose of her *PDR* and to abstain from visiting the Internet for medical information. She understood the importance of refraining from making reassurance calls or emergency room visits. Her primary physician was consulted and agreed to not answer any of her calls for reassurance. She agreed to flush her toilet without observing its contents. Since her physical symptoms were routinely misinterpreted, she agreed to the following guidelines:

*Seek medical advice only when you have:*

1. A temperature above 103 degrees Fahrenheit
2. A pint of blood pouring from any orifice (*Note:* bleeding gums from brushing or flossing trauma or a spot of blood on toilet paper does not qualify; it must be a puddle.)

3. A significant wound—a knife protruding from a body part or a through and through bullet wound—corroborated by an independent observer.

4. A visible tumor larger than a softball

All other symptoms are to be considered anxious in origin and treated with Phobease tools. Any medical advice call, visit, or seeking of information will give one point to your Boo and will perpetuate and maintain your somatic obsessions. Resist that advice call or medical visit and you receive a point. *Resisting your boo is the pathway to cure.*

## Result

The patient is now comfortable alone, drives freeways with comfort, flies with minimal distress, and has not developed new "cancer" symptoms since her class graduation in 2000. She has not visited the emergency room and now sees her doctor only once every six months for a "routine" medical checkup.

## Paruresis (Shy or Bashful Bladder)

A forty-one-year-old administrative assistant found he was unable to void while on vacation in Mexico. He purchased airplane tickets to return home but because of delays the trip took eleven hours. His bladder distension was so severe he required emergency catheterization on arrival in the United States. Prior to his trip, he exhibited classic symptoms of paruresis. He simply could not urinate if *others* were in the restroom or in *close proximity* to the door. He could not urinate at *work* but had located *private bathrooms* in the neighborhood he could use in emergencies. He frequently *restricted fluids* prior to social events because of the impossibility of finding private facilities. He gave up all plans for future *travel*.

Paruresis (literally, paralysis of urination) is an inability to comfortably use a public restroom in the proximity of others. It is a manifestation of a social phobia. An estimated seventeen million Americans have some paruretic symptoms. Ten million are virtually unable to use public restrooms; some can urinate in a closed stall while others cannot. Concerns about bathroom noises further complicate the issue. Forty percent of Americans flush prior to urinating or aim for the side of the urinal to mask the toilet's sound. Some can urinate comfortably only at home with no one in proximity. Often the subject has to leave work or school to return home to urinate. One strategy is to severely restrict fluid intake to reduce bathroom frequency. Another is to hold urine for inordinate periods of time. Ninety percent of paruretics are men, due to the absence of privacy when using urinals.

There are many gradations of the disorder. Some men can use a urinal if adequate partitions are present, but they cannot use the "troughs" where several participants stand shoulder to shoulder without privacy. Sports centers with large crowds often feature such accommodations and virtually eliminate paruretic attendance. Many can use a public restroom if it is empty but may have to leave if someone enters.

The most common associated condition is shyness. Again, there seems to be a genetic predisposition and commonly it is familial. Over 80 percent of sufferers can attribute onset to an embarrassing event early in life. Teasing remarks or the inability to urinate on demand for urine tests often escalate into a life constricting paruresis that persists for years. It is America's greatest kept secret. You recall that us phobocs are highly intelligent, creative, accomplishing rascals who would have a hard time telling someone that they can't urinate in a public restroom—and they don't. They rarely tell anyone. When they report their problems to a urologist, they are often blithely dismissed as "Everyone has an occasional problem urinating with someone close by" or worse, may unnecessarily undergo an extensive urodynamic workup. Years of prolonged holding of urine leads to stretching and dilation. Urologists who may not be knowledgeable about paruresis may wrongly conclude that a dilated bladder is the result of neurological damage to the bladder. Subsequent workups might include cystogram, cystoscopy, urodynamic voiding studies, and possibly even a sphincter electromyogram. Besides scaring the patient, such procedures could cost thousands of dollars. In truth, if you can urinate with a good stream in the privacy of your own home, your bladder is probably normal.

All paruretics share these famous three myths:

1. *I am the only one who has this.* Most are surprised when they find out there are millions of paruretics in the United States and millions more elsewhere. They usually have never heard of anyone else having their disorder. They are even more incredulous when I tell them there is an International Paruresis Association and I am a board member.

2. *I am crazy or I will go crazy. How did I get this way?* They don't know they were born with an anxious perception—born to develop an anxiety disorder. What they know is it is crazy to have something like this and not be able to resolve it. "Even four-year-olds can use a public restroom and I can't. How demoralizing."

3. *My case is so rare and unique that I am incurable.* I always tell them, "What you have is common, ordinary, and curable." We get over 90 percent, often 100 percent, significant improvement in our *one-weekend* paruretics workshops. Patients who have been paruretic for decades and received years of psychotherapy cured in sixteen hours of treatment!

The iceberg phenomenon is very much in evidence when dealing with paruretics. It impinges on every aspect of their lives. They may have to work *close to home*, they may not be able to *fly*—bathrooms are often placed in *near proximity to others* with *flimsy thin doors*. They may have difficulty with *intimate relationships*, trying to explain why they can't attend *social events* or void with their significant other in close proximity. Finally, many occupations require unannounced *on-site urine drug tests*. Paruretics have been fired because they couldn't urinate on demand. Some jobs even require someone to personally observe your voiding to eliminate normal urine substitutions. Similarly, inmates have been punished with solitary confinement for failure to produce a urine sample and are assumed to be drug-positive. Anti-anxiety medications are occasionally helpful, but medications that work primarily on the bladder are doomed to fail since this is a phobia. Patients can be taught how to self-catheterize—place a small tube into the bladder and mechanically drain their urine. Knowing that they can thus always empty their bladder can be very emancipating, but curing their phoboc disorder with CBT is preferred.

## Treatment

Treatment begins with education. Paruresis is an anxiety disorder. Cure the anxiety and you cure the disorder. Neuro-ethologists—those who study the science of the contribution of evolution—have suggested that the urinary sphincters are designed to shut off under mortal threat. Since anxiety is preparation for mortal combat, the sphincters of the bladder become target organs for stress hormone secretion and shut off during severe stress. Annoyingly, you can't voluntarily push out urine with abdominal straining. The initial act of urination requires relaxation. Thus, as always, you begin on page one; learn about the genetic contribution to anxiety disorders and the physiology of adrenaline secretion. Learn the various tools and strategies and the cognitive restructuring of negative beliefs and the hierarchy approaches to desensitize to shy bladder fears. As always, first identify, on paper, your avoidant and neutralizing behaviors. What keeps you from voiding? The proximity of people, absence of partitions, open troughs or stalls too close to urinals or sinks, avoiding noise by aiming at the side of the toilet or urinal, and flushing or running water to mask bathroom sounds are all common. We begin with non-voiding hierarchies.

The goal is to become comfortable in bathrooms without the added initial stress of having to void. It's a way of challenging a belief that you can't stand in front of a urinal without urinating because people would notice, care, or think bad things about you.

*Non-voiding hierarchy (to be done hourly or several times daily)*

1. Wash hands in public restroom
2. Wash hands in public restroom with friend present

3. Wash hands and face, comb hair, with people present

4. Sit in closed stall and read the newspaper—no attempt to void

5. Read newspaper and stand in closed stall without attempting to void

6. Stand at urinal, with partition, read newspaper—no attempt to void

7. Stand at urinal, with partition, for prolonged period of time without attempting to void

8. Stand at urinal without partitions for prolonged period of time without attempting to void (record was eighteen minutes)

When you are comfortable in bathrooms, you may proceed to voiding hierarchy. *Note:* it is very important to be well hydrated—drink up to a quart of water, tea, or coffee one hour prior to exposure. Carry a bottle of water with you for easy rehydration. Start at level one by identifying a situation in which you will be minimally challenged but probably successful—void for three seconds and stop the stream.

1. With door closed, friend thirty feet from the door—void for three seconds

2. Door closed, friend now fifteen feet from door—void for three seconds

3. Door closed—friend at door—void for three seconds

4. Door slightly open—friend at door—void for three seconds

5. Door open—friend standing behind you—void for three seconds

6. Public restroom—in closed stall—void for three seconds

7. In public restroom—partitioned urinal—void for three seconds

8. In public restroom without partitions, with one or more strangers—void for three seconds

9. In crowded public restroom—non-partitioned urinal—void for three seconds

10. Attend sports event and void in trough with seventy people standing next to and behind you

*Note:* The three-second rule applies to paruretic practice so you can get multiple exposures per hour. In real life, empty your entire bladder. Always aim for the middle of the toilet bowl or urinal. If you are shy about noises, go in a closed stall and make repeated farting sounds with the back of your hand and spill one quart of water directly into the toilet bowl. If you can leave without smiling, receive two extra points.

All victories are met with enthusiastic cheers, whistles, and foot stomping, and must be written down and rewarded.

## Results

The administrative assistant attended a Phobease workshop and was so offended by the rubber brain, the Boo, and the squirt guns that he left prematurely. He reluctantly returned the next day, realizing that leaving was the ultimate form of avoidance. He began his hierarchies that last morning. He purchased the self-help home course and now understood the path to cure. In a short time, he ascended his voiding hierarchy. He achieved his number ten level by not only voiding consistently at work, with his boss present, but telling his peers of his condition. He attended the next year's workshop as a staunch advocate of the Phobease approach and coached participants at various stages of their hierarchies. At that workshop, 100 percent of the twenty participants demonstrated significant progress in that one weekend. He eventually returned to his beloved Mexico and shared urinary experiences with over 200,000 Mardi Gras revelers. He considers himself a cured paruretic, able to void in any bathroom setting. The International Paruresis Association (IPA) web site is www.shybladder.org.

## Scrupulosity

A thirty-one-year-old Catholic married woman with an eight-year-old son attended the Phobease adult class. Her major fears revolved around religious concerns that she *would burn* in eternal damnation, the devil would *possess her* and her son, and if she attended church the *statue eyes* would come alive and turn red. Her concerns were so great that she *stopped going* to church, avoided anything pertaining to blasphemy or the *devil—words, pictures, movies*—and recited *Hail Marys* for hours on end to keep her and her son "safe." Her Boo often insisted she wasn't *reciting with conviction* and she had to do them repeatedly.

Scrupulosity is an obsessive compulsive disorder with an excessive concern about committing sin and blasphemy. There is an exaggerated fear of going to hell, which leads to an obsessive adherence to religious doctrine. Its incidence in the United States is estimated at 6 to 10 percent. In other countries with higher percentages of devout religionists, the incidence has been reported as high as 50 percent of all OCDs.

The condition causes extreme anxiety, despair, shame, and guilt. Blasphemous and sinful obsessive thoughts are viewed as intolerable acts of the devil or products of a deranged evil mind, and lead to endless compulsive praying. Religions with expiative prayers are fertile grounds for rampant obsessive compulsions. Themes of unpardonable sin, burning in eternal damnation, failing to confess everything, or going to hell are common obsessions.

Endless reciting of Hail Marys, mantras, or the Shema are common compulsions and can be done rapidly, slowly, or in varying magical cadences and rhythms. Exorcisms have been inadvertently carried out on patients who were not possessed by the devil, but experiencing untreated OCD.


## Treatment

Treatment begins by teaching the genetic basis for obsessive thoughts. They are neurobiological creations, spontaneously generated by our famous Boo voice. They never reflect on the character or secret desires of the individual. OCD thoughts are ego-dystonic—that means against the will of the patient. We have no control over our thoughts, only our behaviors. Thus, "it is not me, it's my OCD," "It's not me; it's Mr. Boo." Obsessive scrupulous thoughts are not products of the devil or God; they are OCD—a genetic biochemical brain aberration.

An important enlightenment is that since God is omniscient (i.e., knows every thing), He knows that your blasphemous thoughts are products of your OCD and not products of disdainful beliefs. Never judge yourself on the basis of the content of your thoughts; they are neurobiological garbage.

The cardinal rule of treatment is to recognize and accept your obsessions but to resist your compulsions. Learn to recognize that when you are endlessly picking something apart or dissecting every nuance of a religious subject, that is your OCD. Use thought stoppage to recognize the origin of that pattern and use tools of exposure, delay, distraction, relaxation, blocking, and delegation to handle your anxiety. There are more than forty Phobease tools that allay anxiety and neutralize obsessions—use them for your scrupulous thoughts.

A good analogy is to recognize that your Boo voice is playing the game of "gotcha." Remember in grammar school, the bully points to an imaginary spot on your shirt and when you look down, he drags his finger up your face—"gotcha!" Scrupulous thoughts are the religious equivalent of that game.

If you react with anguish and anxiety and launch into a soothing prayerful compulsion, your Boo bursts out laughing and yells, "gotcha." If you answer repeated questions about religious meaning or intent, your Boo voice yells, "gotcha." Answer one Boo voice question and you can be sure there will be an endless stream of follow-up questions. Recognize the Boo voice origin and never answer a Boo voice question again.

In time, as you master the skills of recognizing and non-emotionally accepting religious or blasphemous obsessions, resisting performing compulsive thoughts, prayers, or behaviors, your scrupulous thoughts will gradually fade and you will enjoy a normal relationship with your God and religion.

The patient came to realize that her obsessive concerns were just that—not truths or facts—just anxiety-producing thoughts. She recognized that God probably sent her to the Phobease class and understood that her hierarchy practice was not sinful but the path to her freedom.

She identified her avoidant and neutralizing behaviors, which included *saying or writing* the word *devil*; overhearing *swear words; not going to church* and when there, avoiding looking at the statues. Her hours of praying were viewed correctly as neutralizations.

*Response prevention hierarchy*

1. Write the word *devil* and three unacceptable swear words for fifteen minutes and not follow (block) with Hail Marys

2. Say the word *devil* and those three swear words out loud facing a mirror and block saying Hail Marys

3. Say, "I love the devil" for fifteen minutes and block saying Hail Marys

4. Purchase a devil doll at a novelty shop and place it on lap while eating and watching TV

5. Wear a set of devil horns and red face makeup to a Phobease class on costume night (a fourth-week homework assignment)

6. Have son wear the devil horns

7. Attend church and look at the statues and demand the eyes turn red (intentional paradox)

8. Reduce Hail Mary recitations from three to two hours nightly

9. Reduce further to one hour and say them "incorrectly" and insincerely

10. Refrain one night from reciting nightly prayers and Hail Marys

## Result

The patient became quite comfortable with her religion, returned to church, and believed that God approved of her hierarchy work and would not condemn her to eternal damnation because of her scrupulosity. She did a Parents' Night presentation on scrupulosity to an adult church congregation.

## Obsessional Suicide Concerns

A third-year college junior majoring in psychology attended the Phobease class with complaints of chronic worrying (GAD) and occasional panic attacks, but her main concern was that she would get so depressed she would lose control and kill herself. She had never had a major depressive episode nor was there a family history of depression. She had no concrete plan and was receiving follow-up care by her psychiatrist who felt she was not a suicide risk. Despite reassurance, she removed *sharp knives* from her kitchen, disposed of all *medicines*, never stayed *alone* at night, and avoided any *articles about suicide, death, coffins, mortuaries, or cemeteries*. One of her concerns was that she would *go crazy*, lose her mind, and kill herself in that state. Thus, frequently throughout the day she would do an *"orientation check."* She would repeat her name, address, and telephone number. As if to refute her Boo, she would repeat phrases such as "I would never do that" or "I will never lose control." These refutations are cognitive retreats that give power to the suicide obsessions.

Fear of suicide is a common phoboc obsessive concern. Remember the phoboc creation formula requires an anxiety-producing thought, image, or urge that is bought as a possible truth. Then it is, as this patient demonstrated, avoided, repressed, or suppressed. What better topic for a brain that doesn't want to die or be embarrassed. Thoughts that are opposite to the basic desires of a patient (ego-dystonic) are the ones that create the most anxiety. The patient was happy with her life and her career path, and therefore couldn't understand why she had that repetitive, intrusive thought.

In the first three sessions, she learned what she needed to know about thought dynamics. She realized her suicide thoughts were perpetuated because she deemed them as significant, important, and possible. Any thought that creates anxiety and alerts the brain to a possible mortal threat will be focused on and repeated. By identifying her avoidant patterns, the student recognized the subtle contributions they made to the credence of her disturbing thought. She learned that

100 percent of people have intrusive thoughts but dismiss them, while us phobocs ask why. Asking "why" suggests that you don't know that thoughts are the spontaneous neurobiological creations of an incredible thought-producing machine—your brain. They have no meaning until you give meaning to them. She realized her suicide thought was not a command or a future prognosis and that it would never take over her will. It was merely a suggestion she could choose to ignore.

She began by conquering her fear of being alone at night using a classic incremental hierarchy. She constructed the following exposure and response-prevention harming hierarchy. She introduced the anxiety-producing exposures but refrained from saying her anxiety neutralizing phrases (i.e., "I will never do that" and "I will never lose control"). She also stopped (blocked) her incessant self-orientation ritual, which was reinforcing her fear of going crazy and then killing herself.

### Her hierarchy

1. Write anxiety-producing synonyms for suicide or death for fifteen minutes daily; say those words out loud in front of a mirror

2. Look at pictures and stories depicting death and suicide

3. Visit a funeral parlor

4. Visit a cemetery

5. Eat with a plastic gun or rubber knife at the table with the family present

6. Eat with a real knife or gun at the table with the family

7. Read, watch TV, and sleep with a knife, rope, razor, gun, or pills on bedside nightstand (whichever of those you avoided for fear you would use it to end your life—the gun was unloaded)

8. Visit a gun or knife store and handle the merchandise

9. Imagine being in the emergency room for a failed suicide attempt

10. Imagine losing control and killing yourself—do a four-page worst case scenario on this event. Include the emotional pain

you feel just prior to the act, the anger you feel because the Boo is about to win, and the consequences of your act on your children, family, and friends. Read daily for forty-five minutes until you desensitize. Tape-record and listen daily for greater impact until you desensitize to the event.

She progressed well and found two techniques very beneficial. She set aside a fifteen-minute evening worry period for her decreasing suicide ruminations and dismissed such thoughts with the famous "two word" cure—"screw you." Apparently, it worked well because her new husband, with her consent, has started an exotic knife collection.

## Self-Mutilation

A single twenty-six-year-old mother of a two-year-old presented with an obsessive concern that everything she experienced was not real. The world she saw, the people she met, and the entire universe were suspect. "How can you be sure that this is not a parallel universe—that we are not players in a TV drama?" She complained that she often felt numb and detached and part of this unreal scenario. She had been in therapy for over a year and was on a moderate dose of anti-anxiety medication. She also admitted that she had routinely cut herself with a razor blade, that she had taped so she couldn't cut too deeply, since she was fifteen years old. She displayed both forearms, revealing multiple parallel cuts in various stages of healing. She said she felt little pain during the cutting but found a great sense of release when she saw the blood flow. She looked forward to the cutting with great anticipation and felt that it contradicted the feelings of unreality.

Self-mutilation behavior (SMB) is the intentional infliction of pain and injury by cutting, scratching, picking, or burning oneself. Sufferers usually injure the arms, legs, and face but can involve virtually any part of the body. Superficial wounding is rarely an indication of severe psychiatric disease and is not a suicidal gesture. It is simply another one of the impulsive disorders like hair pulling (trichotillomania) or nail biting. The incidence in the general population has been estimated at 4 to 8 percent but as high as 21 percent in patients presenting to anxiety clinics. Onset is generally in the pre-teens.

SMB is most commonly seen with dissociative symptoms, which are strange and often frightening feelings of depersonalization, unrealization, and detachment that frequently result from extreme stress situations. Depersonalization is the feeling that you are outside of yourself—viewing yourself from a distance. Derealization is a feeling that everything is muted and unreal. Patients describe it as feeling as though you are in a made-for-TV movie. Detachment is an emotional and physical numbness—the patient states, "I don't feel anything." All of these symptoms are extremely scary because they invoke concerns of being or going crazy—the famous phoboc second myth. Dissociative symptoms commonly follow extremely stressful life-threatening events. Sexual, physical, and psychological abuse, particularly if repetitive, severe anxiety states, post traumatic stress disorder, and depression are frequent precipitators.

Self-mutilation is an attempt to penetrate the veil of numbness in order to feel something—anything. Since mild stimulae don't seem to register, more intense, painful injuries are inflicted. It can be an attempt to ease tension or reduce anxiety and stress, or an attempt to counter painful memories, flashbacks, or loneliness. It can be an expression of self-contempt and self-hatred. Most patients feel self-mutilation temporarily disrupts the disturbing symptoms of the dissociative state and results in a diminution of negative feelings. Paradoxically, it gives a feeling of control even though many patients complain of an inability to control their destructive behavior. It frequently produces overwhelming feelings of shame and guilt. The majority of patients would like to be able to stop the habit but don't know how to do so.

Treatment is primarily directed at the underlying anxiety disorder and its impulsive/compulsive origins. It begins with the usual behavior diary to assist in recognizing triggers, antecedent behaviors, avoidant behaviors and neutralizations, concomitant emotional and psychological states, frequency, intensity, and duration. Treatment continues with psycho-education, allaying of guilt and shame, cognitive restructuring, experiential desensitization to anxiety-producing situations and memories, competitive behaviors, removal of physical tools and devices, restoration of self-worth, self-esteem, and finally self-acceptance and self-love. Medications may be considered as part of some treatment regimens. Prognosis is good with over 80 percent of patients showing marked reduction or elimination of self-mutilating episodes.

The patient came to realize that her obsessive concern about reality was a famous Boo strategy. You can never prove or disprove obsessive concerns—that is their very nature. As long as you keep trying, the Boo will hold you hostage in your personal Booland. The goal is to accept simply that it is an obsessive thought. Thus, it must be accepted non-emotionally without attaching any significance or importance. Although we can't control initial thought content we are fully in charge of how we choose to interpret those thoughts. Only then can we blithely dismiss them and move on with our life.

Cognitive challenges are fruitless. "If this universe is not real, why do we have to pay taxes?" This question is met with the usual query in response, "How do you know your money is really paying taxes?" Logic and rationality cannot subdue obsessive thoughts. Acceptance of their characteristic nature is the only solution. I like to categorize all obsessive thoughts as Boo messages and thus always *lies*, exaggerations, and catastrophies.

## Treatment

With an impulsive disorder—self-mutilation, trichotillomania, skin picking, or nail biting—the sufferer should begin with a twenty-four-hour diary, listing when, what, and how many associated emotions and those behaviors or situations (antecedent behaviors) that precede unwanted behaviors. The patient learned about the nature of urges. They are temporary, short-lived, and always go away. She found there were more constructive ways to diminish stress and tension. Virtually all Phobease anxiety-reducing tools and strategies can be used to reduce urge tension. She then constructed a decremental cutting hierarchy by decreasing her thrice-weekly cutting to:

1. Cut twice a week; eight cuts on each forearm
2. Cut twice a week; six cuts on each forearm
3. Cut once a week; eight times on one forearm
4. Cut once a week; four times on one forearm

## Result

*Note:* Writing out a cutting schedule invoked a rebellious response. By the fourth week, the patient had dispensed with her self-mutilation. Her apparent antecedent triggers were her menses and Friday nights with no weekend dates. She substituted dance classes and proudly displayed bilateral healed forearms to the entire class at the tenth-week Phobease graduation ceremony.

## Target Organs

An exceedingly handsome twenty-six-year-old second-year medical student (guess who again?) self-referred to the Student Health Service. He complained of chronic abdominal symptoms—bloating, pain, frequent daily bowel movements, and intermittent diarrhea. A subsequent workup that included a colonoscopy, upper GI series, and barium enema proved normal. Stools for giardia and ova and parasites were similarly negative. A diagnosis of irritable bowel syndrome (IBS) was made. Symptomatic treatment including low-residue, high-fiber bland diet and para-sympathomimetic drugs proved ineffective. Symptoms persisted and subsequent similar workups were nonrevealing. Further studies to rule out sprue, ulcerative colitis, and chronic amoebic dysentery were normal. I was diagnosed with IBS and again offered symptomatic treatment, which again proved to be of little benefit. I brilliantly concluded that I was going to be like that for the rest of my life (myth number 3).

Patients with anxiety disorders tend to display their symptoms in specific organs. Some get primarily cerebral symptoms—headaches, feelings of faintness or dizziness, or feelings of detachment or depersonalization. Those with cardiorespiratory symptoms are acutely aware of rapid-pounding heart rates, skipped beats, chest tightness, and shortness of breath. Others have primary peripheral symptoms— warm sweaty palms and armpits, cold, numb hands or feet, itching or burning skin, and finally, gastrointestinal symptoms. I always expressed my anxiety in my gut. Over time, we learn to focus a microscope on our target organ symptoms. Anything you focus on becomes exaggerated. Add a bit of our ever-present scary imagination and we turn normal symptoms into possible cancers, heart attacks, brain tumors, ulcerative colitis, strokes, or insanity—obvious magnifications of organ symptoms.

You know my story. Four weeks after I began my cognitive behavioral therapy I was 95 percent better. I was constantly challenging my claustrophobia, had started my bowel accident hierarchy, and noted a dramatic decline in my daily anxiety SUDs level. For the first time in years that ever-present fist in my stomach was gone! With it went the bloating, pain, and frequent bowel movements. I didn't have IBS. I had an anxious bowel. I cured my anxiety and found I had a cast iron stomach and a dependable normal bowel. I could eat alligator, tongue, and spicy foods of any nationality and digest them all. Perhaps we are genetically endowed with biological sensitivities that determine our target organ. Nevertheless, if it is anxiety that is producing the target symptoms, then interoceptive exposures or desensitizing hierarchies are the pathway to eventual cure. Hit your target and you will learn that all phobias and obsessions can be cured.

## Trichotillomania (Hair Pulling)

A ten-year-old attended the six-week children's Phobease class with a two-year history of *hair pulling*, with resultant noticeable crown baldness. As a result, she constantly wore a camouflaging *bandana*. She was incessantly teased about her hair dress. She also feared being *called on in class*, experienced severe *separation anxiety*, and was unable to sleep outside of her home except at one close family member's house. A contributing concern was her vocal Tourette's syndrome (involuntary phonations). She was concerned that she would "bark" in her sleep and be ridiculed. This prevented her from going on *overnight school trips*.

Children love the class props: the rubber brain, the Boo monster, marshmallows, and squirt guns and readily embrace the Phobease doctrines. Most phoboc children, and this young lady particularly, can best be described as age ten going on age thirty-five. They are exceptionally bright, insightful, intelligent, creative, and eager to cure. She thoroughly enjoyed the program.

Excessive hair pulling is a normal habit that gets out of control. Some feel it's related to the repetitive grooming habits seen in animals. Far more common than previously thought, it affects 3.5 percent of the population. However, if you combine hair pulling with other human impulsive grooming habits such as nail biting, skin picking, hair twirling, and ear cleaning, it may affect as many as one in five adults.

It is virtually *never* an indication of a serious mental condition or character defect, but rather a benign neurobiological quirk. It seems to be an inborn tendency as it often runs in families. It is *not* a result of poor parenting—it may be seen in early childhood as a temporary phase or may persist into adulthood. The pulling most commonly involves scalp, eyebrows, and eyelashes, but any hairy area may be used. The resulting cosmetic defect—patchy baldness—can cause bothersome social problems. Patients often avoid social events, swimming, windy weather, intimate relationships, and even doctor visits where their hair loss might be seen. The resultant shame and guilt further complicates the situation. Doctors rarely recognize the condition and patients virtually never discuss it. Hair pulling is a zealously guarded secret lest sufferers be thought of as crazy. As a matter of fact, the most disturbing part of this condition is that patients are annoyingly *sane*. Indeed, all patients with trichotillomania share four common myths:

1. I am the only one who has this and mine is the worst case.
2. I'm crazy or will go crazy.
3. I'm weak and lack self-control.
4. I can't stop and I'll never be cured.

Nonsense. It's most important to realize the condition is common, is a benign habit, has nothing to do with willpower, and is treatable and easily cured.

Treatment is combined and includes psycho-education, cognitive behavioral and shame-reduction training, symptom awareness and antecedent behavior identification, competitive habit reversal techniques, and occasionally, medications if deemed necessary. Over 90 percent of patients show rapid and significant improvement.

## Hair Pulling Hierarchy

Begin with the classic twenty-four-hour diary—how, what, where, when, why, and antecedent behaviors. A common human endeavor involves hair of all origins: scalp, eyebrows, eyelashes, nose, ears, chest, pubis, and so forth. Often done unconsciously, hair pulling is a habit, not an indication of severe psychological problems.

### Approaches

Accept the habit without shame or guilt. It is a *normal* tension-relieving activity.

*Mechanical.* Cover affected area. Remove pulling tools (i.e., tweezers, scissors, or magnifying mirrors). Wear gloves or finger cots to eliminate sensory rewards.

1. Scalp—hat or helmet
2. Eyes—glasses or goggles
3. Chest—turtleneck
4. Ear picking—cotton plugs or ear muffs
5. Competitive behavior—When there is an urge to pull, make a fist or squeeze hands for three minutes or, in private, lift weights for brief periods, do push-ups, exercise, or take a walk.
6. Stay conscious of the act: antecedent behaviors include reading, watching TV, shirtless activities, fatigue, and stress. All are invitations to pick and pull. Be prepared with alternate strategies.

*Desensitization hierarchy.* Count and save the hair you are pulling.

1. Delay and measure delay after urge to pull, make it harder by stroking hair, but not pulling or cutting. (Continually extend delay for minutes, hours, and eventually, days.)
2. Reward yourself for each progressively longer delay—pick rewards in advance (no pun intended).

*Finally . . . Save for cosmetic effect.* There are no terrible consequences. Invariably, over time, the activity diminishes with these conscious strategies.

A key to the behavioral change is the competitive behavior. It brings the habit into consciousness and a squeezed fist can't pull. You can substitute squeezing a book or newspaper for fist clenching, but don't let go or that hand may wander. Don't berate yourself for the urge. It's normal—just squeeze your hands.

## Result

By the third week, the young girl was able to remove her bandana five minutes before the class ended. She had never done that in public before. The fourth week she informed us she had attended school without her head covering. She had volunteered to speak in school about her hair pulling and her Tourette's. On the fifth session, costume night, she sprayed her hair multi-colors to bring attention to what was once unthinkable. At brag time, she announced she had not pulled for three weeks. She attended a class sleepover for the first time and entered a school essay competition and wrote about her trichotillomania for the whole world to know. She wrote the following interpretation of her disorder and gave me permission to print it:

> Out of all the time I spent working doing my homework and practicing the work you told me to do I never totally understood. Why, how, and what is fear but now I understand deep down inside of me. *I look at fear as a brick wall blocking my path as something that's limiting my life so that I may not strive to reach my goals. Something that keeps me from doing the things that I really want to do in life. That brick wall must be broken so that I can do the things that are on the other side. Along the path there will be other obstacles that must be broken, beaten, so that I can live my life without the Boo. Without a wall of containment surrounding me so that I am not confined in the small space within. But gradually, these walls can be broken and each time that area limiting me becomes bigger and bigger until all the walls disappear.* Well, that was my description of fear and I hope that some day every one will come to understand what I know. Thanks for everything, Kristina Furukawa.

Now you understand "age ten going on age thirty-five." Her essay came in second at school but I gave her a Phobease honorary first place.

## Fear of Vomiting (Emetophobia)

A twenty-eight-year-old woman presented with a twenty-year history of fear of vomiting. Her phobia severely curtailed her social life; she *rarely dated* and virtually never went to *social events*. She stated she "would rather die than vomit." She ruminated constantly and experienced both chronic levels of *high anxiety* and occasional *panic attacks*. Her target organ for her anxiety was her stomach. She felt nauseated whenever she was stressed. Her *diet* had been *severely restricted* for the past several months. She avoided anyone who *looked ill* for fear she would get the stomach flu. She had quit several jobs during the flu season for that very reason.

Fear of vomiting (emetophobia) is a common manifestation of social phobia. This disorder involves the characteristic devastating iceberg phenomenon, impinging on every aspect of one's life. Dating and intimate relationships are severely curtailed. I have known several students who dropped out of school for fear they would vomit there.

Patients often mistake the nausea or stomach distress caused by anxiety as evidence that something is organically wrong and vomiting is imminent. Patients adopt all kinds of strategies including food restriction, safe foods, eating only easily digestible foods, and utilizing a number of medications to counter abdominal symptoms. One patient made food selections based on appearance of vomitus. She avoided red sauces because that might look like blood and be more offensive to others. Plain bread and mashed potatoes were her first choices if she had to participate in a rare social outing.

### Treatment

As always, treatment begins by identifying the avoidant and neutralizing behaviors and incorporating them into an exposure hierarchy. Patients begin by writing vomiting phrases for fifteen minutes. If you measured social concerns by the number of existing synonyms, vomiting would rank second only to dying: barfing, hurling, puking, chunking, upchucking, throwing up, urping, losing your lunch or your cookies, weak stomach, or more polite medical jargon such as retching, emesis, regurgitation, and, of course, vomiting. The second step is to say these words aloud while looking in a mirror until the person can say them without grimacing. The third level is to look at pictures of people vomiting and finally the fourth through tenth levels are to use plastic or rubber vomit, make the vomit sounds, and "throw up" in hierarchical fashion. They begin by "throwing up" on fellow Phobease classmates, then on our poor hospital volunteers manning the information desk. They have been vomited on for over twenty years. Patients then take the fake barf home and puke on family members, friends, peers, and finally strangers. Interestingly, the most common response to such shenanigans is laughter. This is especially important to emetophobics who rapidly realize the world regards vomiting as an acceptable human endeavor.

*Her hierarchy*

1. Write synonyms for fifteen minutes daily
2. Say synonyms aloud for fifteen minutes
3. Look at vomit pictures while sucking on a lollipop
4. Add yogurt and cottage cheese to diet for breakfast, lunch, and dinner
5. Add scrambled eggs and cheese for protein source
6. "Throw up" fake vomit in class
7. "Throw up" on volunteers
8. "Throw up" on family repeatedly
9. "Throw up" on peers and friends
10. "Throw up" in the hospital elevator

The patient loved throwing up and became famous among her peers for her antics. Subsequently, her dog ate some tainted food and threw up five times. She, for the first time in her life, was able to clean it up.

She eventually progressed to co-facilitating several adult Phobease classes and is now in the process of setting up her own Phobease class in a large central city.

## How to Be a Phoboc Failure

I always end the fourth session by reading a very cynical piece of literature. I invite hissing, booing, catcalls, and cynical retorts at every level; so be my guest:

1. Don't commit to cure. "Boo, hiss, I have more important things to do."
2. Don't read the chapters. "Boo, hiss, I don't like your style of writing and the Boo is stupid."
3. Don't do the homework. "Boo, hiss, I graduated from high school years ago. I don't do windows and I don't do homework."
4. Don't do your hierarchies. "Boo, hiss, my doctor put me on medication; that will cure me."
5. Don't do thought stoppage. "Boo, hiss, you said it doesn't stop initial thoughts anyway, so I'm not going to waste my time."
6. Don't practice relaxation. "Boo, hiss, again. I tried it once and it didn't work. I was born to be anxious."
7. Don't exercise. "Boo, hiss, I have a bad knee and I just don't have time to burn up adrenaline that way."
8. Eat and drink whatever you want. "Boo, hiss, I love Surge, Mountain Dew, and a cappuccino blast for breakfast—it gives me that morning lift."
9. Don't write down your victories. "Boo, hiss, and boo, I'll remember them; I've got a good memory."
10. Don't write in this book. "Hiss and boo, I remember you would get in trouble in school if you wrote in your book, so I'm not going to."

11. Don't name your Boo. "Hiss, hiss, I'm not going to spend time talking to an imaginary figure—ever!"

12. Don't commit to a cure. "Hiss, boo and enough of this non-sense—you said this already, are you daft or something?"

I hope I covered most of your retorts. I will end by simply reminding you for the eighty thousandth time—I like to be repetitious—*If you follow the program and do the work, you will cure.*

## Chapter 4 Highlights

1. Begin hierarchies by identifying all avoidant and neutralizing behaviors.

2. Practice daily in imagination the entire hierarchy and in vivo one step at a time. Write down your victories.

3. Be aware that setbacks are expected and are a normal part of healing.

4. Inundate your world with the things that make you anxious. Invite fear into your life.

5. Remember thoughts are just thoughts. They are simply spontaneous neurobiological creations that have no power unless you give power to them.

6. Accept your obsessions and resist your compulsions.

7. Remember all panic and urges go away. Stay in the cold pool, habituate, and master your fear.

8. Remind yourself that comfort is not your goal—living is. The more uncomfortable you are, the closer you are to a cure.

9. Be aware that Phobease works if you do. Make a commitment to cure.

10. Reread the first three chapters often.

# Chapter 4 Assignment

Do your daily relaxation process.

Exercise fifteen to thirty minutes daily.

Do daily diary entries.

Practice your hierarchies daily in fantasy and in vivo, as often as you can.

Find ways to start challenging your phobias.

1. Begin to put yourself in situations that are threatening to you. If you feel uncomfortable sitting near an exit, begin to sit in chairs that are farther from the exit. I now always sit in the "worst" seat—on purpose—farthest from the exit.

2. What are some of your taboos? Break some and see what happens. Sing in public or eat out alone and read a newspaper. I wouldn't go out on Saturday night alone because people would know (WPT) I didn't have a date, so I began to go out Saturday nights alone. Nobody cared.

3. Make a list of things you are shy about. Do some fantasy desensitization and then try some in vivo trials. Make a hierarchy to conquer your shy behaviors.

4. Go to school or work in an unusual state of dress or costume. See what happens if you overdress. Wear two different colored shoes or an outrageous tie. This is an exercise in dealing with WPTs.

   Anxiety is what you feel when you squirt adrenaline

   **D** = Dispute            **E** = Exaggerations

   **R** = Reframe            **A** = Appearing

   **F** = False              **R** = Real

Avoiding and ritualizing are poor ways to handle anxiety. Stay in the cold pool and habituate. Place yourself repeatedly in anxiety-producing situations and stay until your SUDs level diminishes.

## Phobease Midterm Examination

*Note:* This test counts for your entire Phobease grade, so be sure to answer all questions "all of the above."

1. How did you get to be phoboc (phobic and/or obsessive compulsive)?
   a. Born genetically neurochemically sensitive
   b. Sensitized anxious learning
   c. Exaggerated danger perceptions
   d. All of the above

2. What are the characteristics of the Boo (scare) voice?
   a. It is a consummate bully, a swine
   b. It loves to demean, deprecate, and depress
   c. It always lies, exaggerates, and catastrophizes
   d. All of the above

3. What are the only tools and weapons of the Boo?
   a. The "what ifs"—imagined catastrophes
   b. The WPTs—What will people think?
   c. The *only* weapon it has at its disposal is adrenaline
   d. All of the above (Do you notice a pattern here?)

4. Adrenaline, the most powerful drug in your body is
   a. Secreted by anxious thoughts, beliefs, negative statements, and dreams
   b. Is a normal body function and never leads to death or disease
   c. Never leads to heart attacks, strokes, or insanity
   d. All of the above including a, b, and c

5. Panic attacks
   a. Are intense anxiety episodes created by multiple doses of adrenaline
   b. Are always preceded by a thought, belief, statement, or dream
   c. Always go away
   d. Never lead to death, disease, or insanity
   e. Never prevent you from getting enough oxygen
   f. Are no more threatening than dropping marshmallows on your bare feet
   g. all of the above

6. Thought stoppage
   a. A monitoring technique used to recognize and identify your Boo
   b. Never stops the initial thought
   c. Is always followed by calmative breathing and phoboc tools
   d. Must be used immediately and every time
   e. All of the above

7. Calmative breathing
   a. Should be done immediately and every time you feel anxious
   b. Inhale through nose, pause and count to four, and exhale through pursed lips
   c. Should be abdominal, slow and deep
   d. Uh, all of the above

8. Some useful Phobease tools might be
   a. Recognize, accept, dispute, and reframe Boo voice ramblings
   b. Thought stoppage and calmative breathing
   c. Cortical shift, assess your fear level, model, mirror, neutralize the Boo, humor, worst and best case scenarios
   d. Imagined and in vivo hierarchies
   e. A wild guess—all of the above

9. Important Phobease doctrines
   a. "Face the fear correctly and it will disappear"
   b. "Comfort is not your goal—living is"
   c. "So what, I will handle it"
   d. All of the above

10. Phoboc tenets
    a. All phobias and obsessions are exaggerations of normal concerns
    b. All phobias, panics, and obsessions are curable
    c. All panics, obsessions, and phobias are curable
    d. All obsessions, phobias, and panics are curable
    e. All of the above and all of the above

Answers: 1–10: All of the above
Grade:   10 of 10 = 100 percent: A plus, you smart little rascal!
         9 of 10  = 0 percent: F minus, please reread entire manual, and do 400 push-ups

Although we present this test in a jocular fashion, it contains over forty-five tools and strategies you have learned in the first four chapters. You are now ready and trained to wage war against your nefarious Boo.

# 5

# Cognitive Therapy—Faulty Thought Processes

*Ingredients for costume night—my attire:*

1 large "Boo" hat

1 "Boo" tie

1 "Boo" vest

1 pair of "Boo" underwear (worn over pants)

1 doctor's coat with "I Killed the Boo" embroidered on the back

1 "S_ _T Happens" T-shirt

1 squeak and 1 electronic "breaking glass" hammer

1 bar of Ivory soap

*Directions:*

Wear costume to work and class to learn to deal with your WPTs. Phobocs like to fade into the woodwork and thus become invisible. Place all props in front of seventy fearful adults and children.

COGNITION IS THE SUM TOTAL of the psychic skills that you bring to bear on any psychological problem. It includes your IQ, social upbringing, vocation, self-evaluation, personal experience, religion, education, economic status, and your core beliefs. Cognition is the personal map that colors your perception of every situation you encounter. The goal of cognitive therapy is to identify the thoughts, statements, and beliefs that lead to anxiety, depression, unhappiness, and undesirable physical symptoms. Once recognized, these thoughts, repeated so frequently they often become automatic, must be challenged and changed. This process is called "cognitive restructuring." It is an essential element in eliminating the destructive beliefs that create your anxiety and discomfort.

Freud believed that feelings, emotions, and psychological problems were the result of unconscious motives and desires of which you have little or no insight. He believed it would take years of analysis or psychotherapy to recognize and deal with these unconscious desires. Then along came Drs. Beck and Ellis, the fathers of modern cognitive therapy who challenged Freud's belief. They stated that feelings, emotions, and psychological problems are the result of conscious contemporary patterns of thought. In essence, you are what you say and think. You don't have to even know how your problem began to treat it successfully. You simply have to identify how you think and what you say and challenge it if it is inaccurate and leads to psychic discomfort. By changing your conscious thought patterns, you can make dramatic changes in your life in minutes rather than years!

At this time, I announce to the class that, "it feels warm in here." I take off my wonderful huge Halloween Boo hat. "Still warm." I remove my tie that has a pattern of hundreds of "Boos," then off come the Boo underpants. I state, "it's still warm," and with the audience now caught up in the obvious striptease, they yell "more." I take off the Boo vest to reveal the famous "S_ _ T Happens" T-shirt. I walk around the class showing the message on my chest and tell them, "This stuff happens but not by accident. We create it by what we say, think, and believe, and if that is so, we can change."

You may have been wondering what that bar of Ivory soap has to do with cognitive restructuring. When I was growing up if I said a cuss word, my mother washed my mouth out with soap. It only took one time to clean up my mouth forever. It didn't taste good and its nauseating effects lasted for hours. Well, that bar of soap stays prominently displayed for the last six weeks of class. It reminds you to watch your mouth. If you create that stuff by inadvertently employing any of the faulty thought processes, I will wash out your mouth with soap. I caution the class to "Watch your mouth because your brain is listening."

## Programming Our Brain

As stated previously, the brain is a high-speed computer. It makes 100 million computations per second. But, like any computer, it must be programmed. It has the potential to do innumerable tasks but can't until you give it the information to carry out those functions. A computer is like an empty bank vault—you have to fill it before it becomes productive. The problem is computers don't challenge the accuracy of their programs. If you programmed your computer that $2 + 2 = 5$, that is the answer it will continue to give. Computers don't think. Computers with a "spell check" function are supposed to correct your spelling mistakes. However, if you type the word "for" when you meant "four," the computer won't identify it as a mistake because both words are spelled correctly. Your brain acts exactly the same way. It believes everything you tell it, it does not question the veracity of the programs you place in its confines.

The average person hears 180,000 negative personal comments by the time they reach age eighteen. In the same time, we hear 140,000 *no*'s and 25,000 hours of negative parental, authoritarian, societal, and religious messages. In essence, our "brain bag" is filled with garbage. The problem is that we are born phoboc and we don't know it. We hear this deluge of negativity through our congenital predisposed sensitivity and we feel it far more intensely than non-phobocs. We invariably embrace these destructive messages as truths and allow them to influence all future perceptions and decisions. If these negative statements are repeated often enough, they become automatic thought patterns. They act as posthypnotic suggestions.

They are unheard, yet powerful deterrents to enjoying and mastering life's many challenges.

## Negative Core Beliefs

These personal affronts lead to a series of negative core beliefs. As we grow, we are constantly searching for information that will provide a useful foundation to cope with our challenging world. We need specific survival information: look both ways before crossing the street; don't jump out of an eighteen-story window. Phobocs, born with an anxious predisposition, constantly exaggerate danger: "Beware of strangers, they will kidnap, rape, or kill you!" We hear that message once and are sensitive for life. Phobocs see things as dangerous until they are proven safe, whereas normals see things as safe until proven dangerous. The brain does not know our anxious proclivities; it accepts fully what we tell it.

But what happens when the information you embrace is inaccurate and detrimental? Your brain could care less. It files it as a set of negative core beliefs. I am ugly, stupid, uncoordinated, shy, quiet, clumsy, unworthy, and unlovable; these are examples of beliefs that, if unchallenged, will sabotage your quest for happiness and success.

It has been estimated that 50 percent of our brain programs are in place by age five. We have a tradition in our family to take our grandchildren on their first Disneyland outing whey they reach age five. Anybody know what usually happens to a five-year-old on a crowded day at Disneyland? Adults are constantly accidentally kicking them in the head with their knees. To a five-year-old, an adult is an eighteen-foot, 700-pound giant and from that lofty height comes the information that creates many early beliefs. The problem is that if your parents were phoboc, alcoholic, immature, or rage-aholic, your early messages may be inaccurate and ineffective. However, at age five, we don't question or challenge these early doctrines. We accept them as truths and carry them unchallenged forever. By age eight, we have received 80 percent of our brain programs. That means that, unless we have examined and changed many of those inaccurate, negative, or detrimental beliefs, we will use them to influence many of our adult perceptions and decisions. Would you go to an eight-year-old guru for psychological or financial counseling? Of course not. Yet, many of the conclusions you are making about your disorder are being made by an eight-year-old that you may not even like.

Probably the most destructive programs we embrace concern issues of our worthiness and lovability. Who told you that you were not worthwhile? In this society, virtually everybody—peers, siblings, parents, teachers, religious leaders—criticizes, often under the pretense that they are doing so for your own good. Sure, "how about sticking a knife in my heart?" When we receive them through our phoboc sensitive ears, they become very painful messages. They lead to an inordinate amount of shame if we accept that we are blemished, defective, unworthy, and unlovable. It is imperative that we challenge these negative core beliefs. We'll deal further with challenging such beliefs in chapter 9, "Self-Esteem."

John Bradshaw, a famous counselor, states that 96 percent of families are dysfunctional—not trained to raise children. I always ask my classes, "Do you drive?" Most everyone raises a hand. "Did you have to take a test to get your license?" Those same hands go up. "How many people here are parents?" Most raise a hand. "How many people took the test to become a parent?" Everyone giggles and puts their hand down. Most of us have had no formal training at raising children. Your parents were amateurs. They did the best they could. It is a universal rule that everyone does the best they can at that particular moment in their life. If they had known how to do it better, they would have. But if you're phoboc, it is conceivable that one or both of your parents were, too. Perhaps they were immature, rage-aholics, or addicted to drugs or alcohol. If so, then chances are they may have inadvertently helped fill your brain bag with garbage. This is not to blame them. Cognitive therapy doesn't allow blame. Blame displaces and absolves us of responsibility and cognitists demand 100 percent responsibility for our lives. So while poor dysfunctional parenting may explain *why* you are what you are, cognitists simply ask, "What are you going to do about it?"

We live in a difficult society that is highly comparative and incredibly competitive. Social psychologists have defined competition and comparison as the harshest forms of social injustice. I shudder when I watch the women's Olympic gymnastic competition. In the quest for sports domination, it is common for participants to be literally "torn from their mother's breast" (how's that for literary drama?) at a tender age and placed in gymnastics camp. There, exempted from public school, they practice and perfect skills six to eight hours a day, often seven days a week, to attain international skill levels. During the Olympic broadcast, there is invariably an interview with one of the products: a fourteen-year-old competitor, whose growth has been stunted by excessive exercise. She is swathed in bandages from prior injuries and speaking in a child's voice because her periods and secondary sexual characteristics have been delayed as a result of chronic weight restriction. She is tearful. Why? Because she just won a silver medal. Second place out of five billion people and in tears because she let her country down. She did not win gold. That's the society we have inherited. We are bombarded with the need to succeed, to excel, to be successful—tough demands if you are a born phoboc. This constant pressure may lead you to embrace a number of destructive programs. These programs then become the basis for many of your negative core beliefs. Let's examine a number of these faulty thought processes.

## Perfectionism (All or None)

Many phobocs strive for perfection. If you are perfect, you are above reproach. If you are perfect, you might bring honor to a dysfunctional family. If you are perfect, you cannot be criticized. You will be honored and regaled. The problem is that this is an incredibly destructive program. It dooms you to failure. Life is just too complex to get it all right. Therefore, you fail often and this leads to "perfection paralysis." You don't submit a term paper or work project because you fear it is not perfect. It can be an obsessive manifestation if you don't submit projects for fear they may contain a mistake. You have set such high standards for yourself and others that you often have difficulty reaching them. Here is where I use those famous Phobease squeak and electronic "breaking glass" hammers. I hit myself on the head as I say, "The house is not clean enough" (squeak). "I only got 97 percent on the test; if I had studied harder, I could have gotten 100 percent" (bash). "I ruined my whole talk because I left out one sentence" (crash, bang, squeak). Perfection-seeking phobocs wear these hammers out. They are filled with self-contempt and are constantly self deprecating with harsh, crucial internal dialogue. Perfection is always black or white. You either succeed or you fail; there is no tolerance and no gray area. It is a recipe for disaster. You must stop striving for perfection—instead, strive for excellence. Silence that critical internal voice and replace it with a supportive, nurturing one.

Begin by dividing a page in half. On one side list one negative core belief pertaining to making mistakes or being imperfect. On the other side, write as many refutations as you can. Leave it for a day and then come back and add some more. Be relentless in your challenges—see if you can come up with ten or fifteen challenges. This is the format for any cognitive restructuring. Negative core beliefs have the quality of absolute truths and that is where they become vulnerable.

By attacking them, you may not entirely eliminate them, but you weaken them and bring them into a more realistic, rational perspective. Do this exercise with every one of your negative core beliefs. Your brain bag is filled with inaccurate conclusions derived from that ocean of negativity inflicted on you. Your job is to assume that every negative belief is wrong and then prove that to be true with your cognitive challenges. You don't have to be perfect to be worthy. If it's mistakes you fear, you need to get comfortable with being imperfect. You'll soon have fun making mistakes on purpose to see whether you and the world can handle it.

## Over-Generalization

Remember that your brain is your slave and will accept and carry out any command. Over-generalization is a faulty process wherein you must truly watch your mouth because your brain is listening. Be careful of using words like "never," "always," "everybody," and "nobody." They are absolutes and very damaging because they create a closed negative brain program. "I will never get over my phobia," "Nobody likes me," "I will always be shy." If you say it, it will be so. There is no room for refutation. Over-generalizations are so dogmatic that we accept them as truths. Other similar programs are "can't" and "don't." "I can't stay on a diet," "I can't talk to people," "I can't save money." Yup, that's true.

I like to visualize the brain as a loyal, dedicated well-trained golden retriever. Sitting there in an imposed "sit and stay," poised and ready to follow its master's next command. Waiting tensely, tongue hanging out, it will carry out your commands faithfully and accurately. You say, "fetch" and you are assured that your order will be met. Your dog doesn't ask, "Do you really mean that? Do you want me to fetch it now or later?" That's not what a well-trained dog or brain does. You tell your brain you can't and your faithful golden retriever brain will comply. It is your slave.

As part of your phoboc cure, you must turn an ear inward. Capture those over-generalizing remarks on that same divided paper and then refute them. Find contradictions in your statements and then challenge and change them—that is the essence of cognitive restructuring. Ask, "What am I saying? Is it true? Is it helping?"

## Mental Filter

A mental filter is a process whereby you maintain your destructive negative beliefs by filtering out any positive information that would contradict or weaken your belief. A seventy-two-year-old man sat in my office in tears. He was, he said, a "failure." His wife said he was a wonderful husband and grandfather. He was a foreman who supervised thirty-five men. He was a machinist and held multiple patents. He had invented and built his own airplane, boat, RV, and dune buggy. So why was he a failure? His two brothers were doctors. His father told him that any man who worked with his hands was a failure. He filtered out his many wondrous accomplishments in order to maintain his negative beliefs and accepted his father's definition. "I am a failure."

A young man was convinced he had botched a presentation at work. However, several coworkers complimented him on an excellent, informative, and creative lecture. He filtered out those compliments because he had mumbled his boss's name in the introduction and that "ruined" his fifty-minute oration.

A young woman was mortified when a national TV program filmed at her house showed a piece of notebook paper lying on the steps of her staircase. She had spent hours cleaning the house in preparation for the show. Her efforts were rewarded by multiple compliments from those who had viewed the tape. She filtered out the compliments and focused on that one piece of paper, convinced the world saw her as an incompetent house cleaner. The mystery was solved when the paper turned out to be the show host's interview questions.

Challenge your negative core beliefs, on paper, and filter out the negatives instead of the positives. There are positives in any endeavor and it is your job to find them.

## Cognitive Restructuring

| Negative Core Belief | Refutations |
|---|---|
| My father said, "any man that works with his hands is a failure." I work with my hands—therefore, I am a failure. | 1. My dad was wrong. His definition of failure was far too limited. |
| | 2. He was probably just trying to steer me to another profession. |
| | 3. By his definition, all farmers, carpenters, plumbers, machinists, mechanics, and repairmen are failures. That is ridiculous. |
| | 4. You don't define human beings by their vocation alone. |
| | 5. I am a successful foreman, an accomplished inventor, a staunch supporter of my church, a great father and grandfather. |

| Negative Core Belief | Refutations |
|---|---|
| | 6. I am not on this earth to measure up to anyone's expectations, including my father's. |
| | 7. If I disappointed him, too bad. He'll have to deal with it. |
| | 8. I am worthy simply because I say so. (He read the chapter on self-esteem). |
| | 9. My dad has never called me a failure. I wonder if I took his statement out of context. |

Refutation conclusion (must be supportive, nurturing, and self-affirming): "I am a multi-talented, accomplished human being and I feel much better after this exercise."

## Automatic Discounting

Someone pays you a compliment and you reject or minimize it. This is another form of mental filtering. Someone says, "That's a nice dress you're wearing," and you answer, "It's old and only cost five dollars." By discounting, you get to maintain your negative self-image. You get to keep your unworthy and unlovable labels. In my Phobease class, participants do a compliment exercise. They turn to people on the right and left and compliment them. Most people do that fairly well. Then I ask the class to turn to the same people and tell them some nice things about themselves. You should hear the response to that request. Moans, sighs, and groans invariably precede the event. I then ask, "Which was harder, paying a compliment to someone or saying nice things about yourself?" It is always the former. Why? All of us are raised on "humble pie." We are taught not to brag, not to be the "big guy" on campus, not to be conceited. With all that propaganda, it's hard to regale ourselves.

Muhammad Ali, the great heavyweight boxing champion, began at age eight to tell everyone, "I am the greatest." Could you imagine what a useful slogan that would be for anyone? Imagine if you believe that and ask a girl out for a date and she turns you down. You think, "Poor girl, she had a chance to go out with the greatest guy in the world and she missed out. Well, there are 50,000 others just waiting in line for that opportunity." Compare that with a self-deprecating phoboc who would use that same rejection to wear out another hammer. "I knew she wouldn't go out with me" (bash). "Women don't find me appealing" (crash). "I'll never get a date," (crack). "I'm not a good conversationalist" (crash, bash, smash, clunk, and ouch).

Unfortunately, "humble pie" sucks. It does not enhance our self-worth or self-esteem; it doesn't protect us against life's many rejections and adversities. Drop the program. When someone compliments you, say, "Thank you." You'll have a homework assignment to look in a mirror and say nice things about yourself for two minutes. (That's two minutes by the clock.) Become a compliment giver. It forces you to focus on others' good points.

Did you know that humble pie is a true English culinary dish? It got its name from the fact that poor people could not afford good beef or chicken cuts so they used ground-up bird intestines to fill their meat pies. You deserve better—nothing but filet mignon. The correct response to any compliment is "Thank you."

## Mind Reading—Jumping to Conclusions

Because we are wearing out those "hammers," constantly demeaning ourselves, we assume that other people think similarly. A clever rascal once pointed out that when you assume, you make an "ass of you and me." Don't mind-read, don't guess what others are thinking—check it out. "I hope you didn't think I was terrible when I was feeling panicky and left the party early." The answer: "I didn't even know you left." We're worried about how other people perceive us and they're not even paying attention. You're worried about how they're evaluating you and they're really trying to decide whether to choose vanilla or chocolate ice cream for dessert. Don't mind-read. If you're concerned, check things out. You may be delightfully surprised to find how little people are concerned about your problems. They usually have enough problems of their own. Be aware that it is often your Boo suggesting what other people are thinking. Tell your Boo to shut up and check it out.

There is a wonderful party game in which you divide couples who have been married a long time—they should know each other well—husbands on one side and wives on the other—and ask them a series of questions. The men have to answer personally while the wives have to guess what the husbands will answer.

The results are hilarious. The wives rarely guess their husbands' answers. "If you received a $50,000 windfall, what would your husband buy?" *Wife:* "We've always talked about a cruise around the world—he'd buy that." *Husband:* "My own Corvette." If people who have shared the same roof for twenty-five years don't know what their spouses are thinking, you are not going to read the mind of a stranger or casual acquaintance.

People with a fear of vomiting (emetophobia) assume they would be hated and despised if they threw up, when in reality most people would simply offer comfort. Constantly challenge the assumptions you think others are making. We project our self-contempt and negative self-evaluations on to unsuspecting, loving, and accepting human beings. You must stop doing that. If you don't own a crystal ball, you can't mind-read.

## Magnification and Minimization

We phobocs love to magnify our defeats and minimize our victories. One of the most common ways to do so is to use the word "but." "I went to a movie for the first time in twenty years *but* I sat on the aisle." "I went across the bridge for the first time in fourteen years *but* my husband was in the backseat." But, but, but. When you use the word "but" you discount and minimize any statement that precedes it. In Phobease, we demand you become a "but" detective. When you "but" an event, you diminish the magnitude of your victory and your infamous Boo receives a point. There are no minimal victories in Phobease. Every victory is a "Rocky" moment. Do you remember when Rocky finally runs all the way to the top of the steps? He throws his arms in the air in jubilation. That's how you greet *every* Phobease victory. In class, all victories are met with whistles, cheers, foot stomping, and table banging. The "aw shucks" approach does not serve you well, either. "Yes, I won the Nobel Prize but, aw shucks, it was nothing." Wrong. It was fantastic, terrific, marvelous, and sensational, and so was crossing the bridge or going to a theater. Magnify your victories and minimize your defeats.

If you are claustrophobic and you move one seat from the aisle— that is a huge victory. In the absence of seventy supporting classmates, you have to provide the obligatory yodels, claps, table banging, and foot stomping yourself. Reward yourself—one seat deserves a new Mercedes. If you're agoraphobic and you drive one mile farther from home—you guessed it—an incredible victory—a four-carat diamond might be appropriate for such a stupendous victory. I used to accomplish hierarchy levels so I would have a victory to boast about in the next class—just to hear the applause. When we are mired in our anxiety disorders we don't get a whole lot of self approbation. In any phoboc challenge, find some nuance to magnify into a substantial victory. If your Boo hears you cheering all the time, it may get the message that its days of power are coming to an end.

Magnify your personal attributes and accomplishments and minimize your deficits. Then you can walk around honestly proclaiming, "I am the greatest."

## Emotional Reasoning

I feel bad so there must be a real reason for me to feel this way. I'm afraid that is not so. Since thoughts create emotions and feelings and thoughts, as you have learned, are often inaccurate untruths, they create inaccurate emotions. I ask people to exchange subjects for verbs. Rather than "I am depressed," say, "I depress myself with my thoughts." "I don't have panic attacks, I panic myself with my thoughts." Often trying to analyze why we are having such negative thoughts is an exercise in futility. It also gives credence and power to those neurobiological creations. At this stage, accept your emotions not as truths, but resultant products of your thoughts. Don't let them interfere with your Phobease exercises.

A patient argued that she had a right to be depressed. I never realized that I was trying to infringe on personal rights by insisting that your emotions must be a product of accurate thought processing. If you are depressed because you "feel" unworthy, when in fact you have not been taught how to assess your worthiness, then I would challenge your "right" to be depressed. If negative self-evaluations and self-comparisons are creating your depression, you need to acknowledge, challenge, and change them before you can embrace the resultant "rightful" depression. Most negative emotions result from faulty thought processing and thus are inaccurate. Don't let these unchallenged emotions prevent you from doing your Phobease exercises. You can be sad, discouraged, and anxious, but do your challenges anyway.

## Should Statements—Shame and Guilt

Shame and guilt are common destructive phoboc emotions. Guilt means, "I feel bad because I made a mistake." Shame means, "I am a mistake. I am blemished, defective, unworthy and unlovable." Guilt may be a useful strategy early in life to create conscience, but it has no positive role in adulthood. In fact, as adults, the only consideration is whether you are willing to pay the consequences for your behaviors.

Dr. Albert Ellis, one of the recognized fathers of cognitive therapy, suggests that you can reduce much of your emotional pain if you change the word "must" or its derivations "ought" and "should" to "prefer." He refers to the use of those words as "musterbation." It creates a demand that is often not met and leaves us with a sense of frustration and despair. "Everyone must accept me" is softened when you change it to, "I would prefer for people to accept me but if they don't, I will survive."

It is incredible how your life changes when you begin to substitute for that word. "I must not have an anxiety disorder" changes to "I would prefer not to have an anxiety disorder, but I will handle it." "Should" and "ought" are words that are used to control you. We suggest you change should and ought to "I could if I choose to." Ask, "What is best for me?" That's a tough question for people-pleasing phobocs to ask. We are not used to taking care of our needs first. We call it constructive selfishness—making yourself number one and then acting accordingly. If I get my needs met, I will have a lot more to give. The family Christmas party is a drunken orgy but I go because I should. Now, I choose not to go. I'm going to Hawaii instead and I am willing to deal with the possibility of family disapproval. People probably already know we are easy to coerce with guilt. Change that by reviewing any guilt-provoking request with your newfound challenge: "Am I doing it because I should or because I have chosen to do so?" I would *prefer* you do the latter.

## Labeling and Mislabeling

Negative labels are often a result of those 180,000 negative comments we purportedly hear before age eighteen. Unfortunately, self-imposed negative labels continue to erode self-confidence and self-worth until challenged and replaced. We tend to live down to our labels. You become what you say. If you are repeatedly stating you are shy, stupid, inadequate, then you will be shy, stupid, and inadequate. Again, get in your brain bag, challenge and replace those destructive labels. Get out that famous piece of paper and again, divide it in half. On one side, list one of your destructive labels and on the other side refute that label—do that for every negative label. Again, be relentless in your attack of the inaccurate designation.

| Negative Label | Refutation |
| --- | --- |
| I am shy | 1. I wasn't shy, just untrained. |
| | 2. I wasn't shy, just not experienced. |
| | 3. I now am an assertive, accomplishing adult. |
| | 4. I wasn't shy, just phobic and I have cured that and am now an adventurous, social tiger. |

You must change your destructive internal dialogue.

Begin by glorifying your imperfections. Take any one of your defects and find why it is a tremendous asset. Change "I am fat" to "I am big and powerful." Change "I'm a cry baby" to "I'm a sensitive, empathetic human being," or "I'm a people pleaser" to "I read people well and am a compatible, affable human being." If you have a destructive internal dialogue, you don't need enemies. Instead, be your own best friend. Eliminate all negative labels—they are inaccurate and destructive. Glorify your imperfections. Demand that your internal voice be embarrassingly supportive and nurturing.

## Personalization

Even though we phobocs are highly intelligent, creative, imaginative, awesomely responsible, sympathetic, and empathetic, we wrongly assume that anything bad that happens is our fault. As phoboc children, if Mom or Dad fight, it's because we didn't get good grades or forgot to clean our room. If they divorce, it's because we are bad children. If World War III were to break out, we would somehow feel responsible. This faulty belief creates untold pain and sorrow, frustration and guilt. We are 100 percent responsible for only one person and that person is ourself. We are not responsible for our parents' health or our wife's happiness. We are not responsible for our children's failure or anxiety disorders. We may choose to participate in their lives but we are not ultimately responsible. We have to learn to let other people deal with the results of their poor decisions without intervening. We can offer advice but we don't have to insist they follow it. Continue to focus on your own needs and let everyone else do the same. That will help absolve you of your misplaced responsibilities.

## Secrets

For thirty-one years, I kept my phobia a secret. For thirty-one years, I scripted all of my behaviors and responses so that no one would know I was phoboc. I went to private psychiatrists so no one would see me using our facilities. I left meetings, pretending I had been summoned for consultation, when I got anxious. I could always find a reason to be busy with a patient if I thought a scheduled meeting might be too anxiety provoking. My whole life was a carefully planned avoidance. This created an enormous amount of wasted psychic energy. I feared that if people found out I would be ridiculed, demeaned, and shunned. After my cure, I wrote an article for two million Kaiser members revealing my "terrible" secret and the world yawned. All that happened was that the universe found out I was a human being with failings. I was an imperfect physician and they couldn't care less. Thirty-one years of abject terror, fearing the consequences if my phobias were revealed, and all that happened was I got a raise! So I wrote another article for our local newspaper. Another 160,000 readers were now informed of my deficits and accepted them with aplomb. I did not get a raise for that article. Nevertheless, through the years, I have shared my anxiety disorder in classes, workshops, on TV, radio, the Internet, in magazines, books, and newspapers to let myself and others know it's nothing more than human. Self-revelation is an important part of the Phobease cure doctrine. You don't reveal so others understand. You reveal so that you desensitize to your destructive phoboc label. Through the years in my Phobease classes, I have heard innumerable secrets revealed and accepted. "I'm a CEO of a multimillion dollar corporation and I can't read," "I have a large scar on my chest," "I self-mutilate," "I'm bulimic and vomit six or seven times a day." There is a cathartic benefit from such disclosure. The world is often more accepting than you are and will embrace your deficits.

When you are ready, we strongly encourage self-revelation until the secret loses its emotional clout. It is the famous "What is so is so and so what?" Normal human beings have failings, normal human beings have fears, phobias, and obsessions and it's okay. Tell the world and get that burden off your back.

## Affirmations—A Reprogramming Tool

The most powerful tool to replace destructive programs, negative core beliefs, and labels is affirmations. These are powerful, positive, and personal defining statements of the person you would like to be. They are behavioral reminders in advance. The more unreasonable they seem, the more emotional resistance they provoke, the more likely they are something you need to hear and embrace. We live up to our affirmations and down to our labels. They are generally voiced in the first person: "I am great, I am wonderful," but are also powerful in the second person, "Howard, you are fantastic, you are sensational" because that is often how we hear our 180,000 negative putdowns. Third person can also be very powerful: "The world thinks Howard is sensational, terrific, and magnificent." You can invoke the deity, "God loves you and knows you are an outstanding human being." Affirmations are a wonderful form of positive brain washing. Have fun with them. Say those words you longed to hear when you were growing up. Have some fun with the exercise—don't limit your accolades. They should be read or spoken out loud hundreds of times per day. Pound on your chest as you voice them, tape-record them, and listen to them repeatedly, paste them on your bathroom mirror and read them every morning. Carry them with you and repeat them throughout the day. You have to undo years of negative self-talk and labeling, so persist. If you accept the cognitists' doctrine that we are what we say we are, then the dutiful use of affirmations will lead you on your path to becoming the person you would like to be.

Circle the following affirmations that seem especially opposite the person you are now. You know by now if you keep saying, "You are shy" a thousand times, then you are shy! Substitute an affirmation such as "I am socially aggressive," "I love social events," "I am friendly and affable" and repeat those before social events and you will reduce anticipatory anxiety.

## Affirmations

Pick twenty-five words from the following list and say them to yourself frequently each day, aloud, and particularly when you see yourself in the mirror. Choose the words that describe what you would really like to be. Post them on your mirror; carry them with you and voice them throughout the day.

*I AM*

| | | |
|---|---|---|
| great | energetic | enthusiastic |
| terrific | funny | fair |
| fantastic | empathetic | honest |
| wonderful | child-like | understanding |
| daring | artistic | incisive |
| strong | spirited | attractive |
| confident | humorous | independent |
| handsome | assertive | self-reliant |
| beautiful | optimistic | successful |
| selfish | caring | sexy |
| kind | considerate | sensual |
| sharing | devoted | industrious |
| happy | dynamic | responsible |
| relaxed | powerful | intelligent |
| fortunate | mature | a living legend |
| rich | a leader | vigorous |
| wealthy | dependable | analytical |
| unique | a genius | charismatic |
| healthy | strong | magnificent |
| logical | shrewd | indefatigable |
| wise | lovable | loving |
| clever | intuitive | friendly |
| cogent | discerning | affable |
| brilliant | spiritual | tolerant |
| charming | vigorous | loyal |
| flexible | forceful | sympathetic |
| adaptable | cool | relaxed |
| worthy | sensational | smart |
| brave | tactful | witty |
| courageous | imaginative | kind |
| fearless | creative | receptive |

*Note:* When you say you are fantastic, magnificent, a genius, a living legend, it is not up for discussion. It is a decision totally devoid of external input. Affirmations are mine because I choose them. What power!

It may be difficult to remember all these faulty programs but you can ask two simple questions: What am I saying to myself? Is it helping? If not, challenge, restructure, and replace with a supportive nurturing message. Use thought stoppage; when you hear them, dispute and reframe. Clean up that internal dialogue and become your own best friend. Right now, assume that everything in your brain bag should be evaluated. Continue to spring clean your bag of negative labels and programs. Remember our family Disneyland tradition? Remember those eighteen-foot giants kicking my grandson in the head? Well, you are that giant now and you are the master of your bag.

## Chapter 5 Highlights

1. Identify thoughts and beliefs that lead to unhappiness, anxiety, and depression and challenge them.

2. Avoid "all or none" perfectionist thinking—strive only for excellence.

3. Avoid over-generalizations—ever, never, always, nobody, everybody—they are invariably limiting and untrue.

4. Remember that mental filtering maintains negative destructive beliefs.

5. Don't discount compliments—it diminishes you. Just say "Thank you."

6. Don't mind-read by guessing what other people are thinking—check it out.

7. Don't personalize—you are only responsible for yourself.

8. Be aware that blame displaces responsibility—everyone does the best they can with the knowledge they have at the time.

9. Challenge all destructive labels. We live up to our affirmations and down to our labels.

10. Watch your mouth, your brain is listening—keep your Ivory soap handy.

11. Magnify your victories and minimize your defeats and deficits.

12. Review what you are saying to yourself. Is it helping?

---

## Chapter 5 Assignment

Do your daily relaxation tape.

Exercise fifteen to thirty minutes daily to burn adrenaline and make your heart more resistant to adrenaline.

Do daily diary entries and continue adding to your victory card. Write them down immediately.

Practice your hierarchies daily—in fantasy and in vivo—as often as you can.

1. Who told you that you were unworthy or unlovable?
   a.
   b.
   c.

2. What destructive "shoulds" do you follow?
   a.
   b.
   c.

3. What are some of the destructive labels or beliefs you embrace?
   a.
   b.
   c.

   Make a challenge sheet: Divide a piece of paper in half. List your negative belief or label on the left side. Refute it vigorously and relentlessly on the right side. Finish by restructuring the original label or belief to a self-affirming, nurturing conclusion.

4. Write down fifteen things that are bugging you. Concentrate on changing some of those. Learn to accept some of the things you can't change.

5. Say something nice about yourself every time you look in a mirror. Use "I am's" from this chapter. Say them aloud. Record and listen to them frequently.

6. Do you have "something" you hate? Write ten things that you like about that "something."

7. Write twenty-five personal "I am's." Voice them frequently through-out the day. Post them on your bathroom mirror and read them daily.

    Do it! Change! Take a risk!

    Face the fear without tools and it endures.

    Face the fear incorrectly and it reappears.

    Face the fear correctly and it will disappear.

    Be a "trained" phoboc.

# 6

# Cognitive Therapy: Destructive Beliefs

## THE DIRTY DOZEN

*Ingredients:*

1 large bar of Ivory soap
1 "Same S_·_T, Different Day" T-shirt
1 squeak and 1 electronic "glass breaking" hammer
1 rubber Boo monster
1 brain bag
1 large squirt gun
1 bag marshmallows
1 plastic brain with knife-blade switch

*Directions:*
Place in front of seventy interested adults and children.

OUR CRUISE SHIP docked in the azure waters of the Mediterranean. We were tendered ashore to the most beautiful of Greek Islands—Santorini. Its steep slope had been carved thousands of years ago by a huge volcanic explosion. The rim, which contained the beautiful sun-soaked town, was accessible only by tram or mule ride. We chose the mules. You've heard of how sure footed these wonderful animals are? Mine tripped and fell seconds after we mounted. I'm sure he didn't plant me on a load of mule doo on purpose. He righted himself and we continued up the mountain; my smelly stain reminded me that "stuff" does not happen by accident. As we reached the summit, we could see the classic white stucco homes with colorful doors and shutters and the ever-present explosion of geraniums. We breached the last few feet and dismounted in front of a souvenir shop. Displayed quite prominently was a T-shirt that read, "Same S _ _ T, Different Day." It was nice to know that, even in the most glorious of locales, this "stuff" still happened.

Remember from the previous chapter that it doesn't happen by accident. We create it by what we say, think, and believe. In the last chapter we discussed a number of faulty thought programs that need to be changed in order to reduce anxiety and self-deprecation. Perfectionism, over-generalization, mental filtering, automatic discounting, magnification and minimization, mind reading, emotional reasoning, personalization, and shame and guilt programs must be identified, challenged, and restructured. That is the essence of cognitive therapy. Identify those thoughts and programs that lead to anxiety, unhappiness, and depression, and restructure them.

## Deadly Dozen

This chapter presents twelve more destructive programs often embraced by phobocs. I call them the "deadly dozen" because of the pain, shame, and guilt they create.

## 1. It Is Necessary to Be Loved by Everyone and for Everything

Why are songs so powerful? If you ever end a relationship, every love song you hear for the next six months will bring you to tears. It's as if they have been written especially for you. Songs create such a powerful psychological reaction because they are dual brain stimulae. The music invokes the right side of the brain and the lyrics the left. During every armed conflict, we are bombarded with patriotic songs that reach our very soul with powerful emotional assaults. Throughout our lives, we are bombarded with a constant array of information delivered in songs. Often we unknowingly subscribe to their implied doctrine. The problem is that many messages we receive in songs are inaccurate. If unrecognized and unchallenged, they become another bit of garbage filling our brain bag. Years ago, there was a famous radio (that's television without a picture tube) program called the *Hit Parade*. It kept track of record and jukebox sales and presented the top ten songs each week, starting with the tenth and ending with the highest-rated song for the week. One particular song remained at the top of the *Hit Parade* for thirty-two weeks. For thirty-two weeks, millions of Americans heard an extremely disheartening message: "You're nobody 'til somebody loves you. You're nobody 'til somebody cares." Wow. Thirty-two weeks of a powerful dual brain message that said, "You are worthless and incomplete until you find that special person who will love you and make you somebody." What pressure, "I have to find my soul mate or I am doomed!" If you truly believe that message, then the person you find to make you whole is in deep trouble. If you "need" someone to complete your life, you will be very fearful of losing that person. You will become very protective about maintaining such an important relationship. Anything we focus on so intently in our lives is exaggerated. Our concern for that person's loss might lead to jealousy and extreme possessiveness—behaviors that might actually result in the very thing you fear—driving that person away and disrupting your relationship.

The cognitive restructuring of that song message should have been, "You're nobody until you fall in love with yourself." I'm afraid that's not as lyrical as the original, but far, far more accurate. The only person that has to love you is you! It is said that a successful psychotherapeutic program requires two things: First, it must be effective. Many people are saddled with inappropriate and ineffective programs that fail to allay their anxiety. Phobease is an effective program—if you do the work you will cure. The second and most important requirement of a successful program is that it must result in self-love. When you finish, you must be crazy about *you*. That is an expressed goal with the Phobease program. Self-love, like everything in your course, is learnable. There is a precise path that leads you to unconditional self-acceptance and self-love.

Do you know what unconditional means? It means without *any* conditions. It means loving yourself even with your faults, phobias, fears, anxieties, obsessions, weaknesses, abortions, jail time, mistakes, failings, divorces, weight, figure, build, IQ, poor grades, and on and on. Get the message? "I accept me and all my little nasty secrets." Normal human beings have failings, fears, and phobias and it's okay. Normal human beings make mistakes and it's okay. You know now that everyone in the world does the best they can at that moment in their life. That goes for any of your painful experiences and defeats. If you knew more, you would have done things differently. You did the best you could. There was a famous book titled *I'm OK and You're OK and That's OK*. Well, I'm threatening to write my own sequel called, "*I'm* Not *OK, You're* Not *OK and That's OK*." The first step toward self-acceptance and self-love begins with self-forgiveness. "I forgive me."

You don't have to be loved by anyone except yourself to be whole. Most of us phobocs are people pleasers. We have great difficulty doing otherwise. The admonition that we have to be loved for everything is simply unachievable. Life is far too complex to please everyone. Although we try mightily, there might be some people that aren't going to like us; that is their choice. You can't make people like you. You can't be loved for everything because even if you do everything perfectly, you may not meet others' definition of perfection. When you recognize that fact, you will take another step away from being controlled by the WPTs. Self-love and self-forgiveness are personal, internal decisions, totally devoid of external input.

You will have a wonderfully powerful exercise to do at the end of this chapter. You will look in the mirror, make eye contact with that human being, and for two minutes (by the clock) say, "I love you unconditionally." I have seen patients so contemptuous of themselves because of their anxiety disorders that they couldn't complete this assignment for two years. I couldn't use the word "love." I hated myself so much that I could only say "I accept you unconditionally." I didn't know I was phoboc because I was born genetically pre-dispositioned to be so. I didn't know I was phoboc because no one had taught me how to manage my anxiety effectively. I wasn't defective; I was simply untrained. You have to keep doing the exercise until you fully understand the power of that stated message. Self-love demands unconditional self-acceptance—so choose it. This is not a dress rehearsal; this is the only "you" you get.

## 2. Certain Acts Are Wicked and Awful

Is it okay to kill? From a deeply philosophical moral position, is it OK to kill? Well, of course not, if you do, you will be tried by a jury of your peers and put to death. But, what about the man who dropped the atomic bomb on Hiroshima; killed 70,000 innocent men, women, and children; and then received the Congressional Medal of Honor—this nation's highest award?

The Buddhists are pacifists. If ants invade their homes, they feed them. They never plow their fields in the dark, waiting instead until daylight and walking in front of the plow to remove insects from harm's way. These same Buddhists planted seventy million land mines in Cambodia.

There are some societies that, in times of famine and drought, practice geriatricide—killing the elderly—or infanticide—killing non-productive infants.

In the United States, if you kill one person you could get the electric chair, but societies kill thousands and are not punished and some are even rewarded with medals. How does that incongruity come about? Society simply changes the rules. You can justify killing 70,000 people because they are the enemy. You can plant seventy million land mines because the Cambodians are your enemy. You can justify that because, like the cognitists, Buddhists demand 100 percent responsibility for their lives. So, if I plant a land mine, it is your responsibility not to step on it. Geriatricide and infanticide are "practical" and necessary steps to protect productive workers in times of duress. Seems like societies can justify anything, and they do.

Now I'm not condoning any of this, but it does teach an important lesson that may help you on your path to self-acceptance and self-forgiveness. Many times we can't forgive ourselves because we have done something we deem as terrible or horrible. Well, if society can blithely change the rules to condone heinous behaviors, so can Phobease. We are going to redefine "terrible" and "horrible." From now on, killing twelve million people in gas chambers is the only definition we accept for "terrible and "horrible." Thus, unless it was you who was responsible for those deaths, then getting divorced or pregnant out of wedlock; going to jail, flunking, failing, putting a child up for adoption, having an affair, making a mistake that led to another misfortune; or being a hair puller, a nail biter, a self-mutilator, an alcoholic, a drug addict, a phobic, or an obsessive compulsive doesn't qualify as "horrible" or "terrible." It is simply human and you know a lot about human beings and their failings. With that new definition, you may be able to give up hope for a better past and now look in the mirror and say, truly and without reservations, "I love you unconditionally."

## 3. It Is Horrible When Things Are Not the Way You Want Them to Be

An amusing T-shirt I wear to class says, "This is not the life I ordered." For thirty-one years, I wished that I had not been born phoboc. It would have been so much easier to have been born perfect and normal. Unfortunately, that is not the nature of the game of life. Buddha said, "Life is suffering and the goal is to overcome." Buddha wasn't trying to be pessimistic, but realistic. I always tell my class that if we asked everyone in the room to share some of the painful events in their lives, we would be overwhelmed by the amount of human misery expressed. Virtually no one escapes unscathed. It's no accident that many in a room of anxious people are there because of early traumatic life experiences.

Someone once suggested that I was phobic for thirty-one years because it was God's plan. Now the God I talk to is a lot like Mel Brooks. With my personality, my God has to have a perverse sense of humor. If God is a loving God, He's not going to torture a poor phoboc doctor for thirty-one years just to make him an effective teacher. Ten years would have done the job very well. The truth is, God didn't give me my phobia, Mother Nature and her nefarious genes did the deed and Mother Nature has no conscience or plan.

Though we can't control how things are, we can control how we perceive and choose to react to them. We can accept our disorders and make a decision to commit ourselves to a cure. If you educate yourself, utilize your tools, dedicate yourself to completing your hierarchies and cognitive restructuring your brain bag contents, you will overcome your sufferings. When you have cured your anxiety disorder, you will receive a well-deserved gift. You will have gained the confidence from your multiple victories to realize that you will be able to handle whatever future crises befall you. What a wonderful way to wake up each morning.

## 4. Human Misery Is Externally Caused

As a matter of fact, it is never the event, but always your perception of it. Do you remember what happened on October 19, 1987? It was the day of the modern stock market crash. The market lost 25 percent of its value in one day! In the days following the event, forty-seven people committed suicide, leaving notes that their lives were over—they were financially devastated. The next day, I called my sister, an active stock market investor. You would like her. She is even more phobic than I am. (Did I mention this phobia stuff runs in families?) She is an animal hoarder. At the time, she had twenty-six cats. At 5:00 P.M. every day, three large neighborhood dogs appear on her doorstep.

She takes these three and eleven of her cats for a walk. She walks the entire menagerie down the middle of her street to spare her neighbors' lawns. She is affectionately known as the Cat Lady of Sherman Oaks. I give you this background information so you understand that if you want a unique interpretation of any situation, call my sister. I asked her what she thought of the stock market crash. She said, "White Flower Day Sale." "What do you mean?" I asked. "Stocks went on sale yesterday at a 25 percent discount! Would you have bought Bank of America, IBM, AT&T the day before if you could have gotten them wholesale? Go in your dresser drawers and take out your money stash, take money out of your back account and wife's purse (just kidding, dear), take back the deposit bottles in your garage, and buy stocks." Forty-seven people commit suicide and Sis says this is a unique stock-buying opportunity. It is never the event, but your perception of it. How would you like to be one of those suicide victims who never knew that the stock market has since quadrupled and they would have reaped a fortune had they stayed the course.

A mother suffered a horrible misfortune when her daughter was run down and killed by a drunken driver. Out of this tragedy came MADD—Mothers Against Drunk Driving—now a vast international organization that has been responsible for stricter policing and harsher penalties for drunken drivers. Thousands of lives have been spared as a result of their efforts. It is never the event, but how you choose to perceive and react to it.

A gondola slipped off its main cable. The safety cable remained intact and the occupants were assured by firemen operating a rescuing cherry picker that they were perfectly safe. Within an hour, they were safely on the ground. One young lady professed that this was the most horrible hour of her life. Despite the reassurance, she was convinced she would die and if she didn't, vowed she would never go in a gondola again. She had actually written a farewell note. The young man rescued last, twenty minutes after the young lady, said it was the best ride he had ever taken. He believed the firemen and never felt threatened. He had been on the short gondola ride before but had never had a chance to enjoy the beautiful topography so thoroughly. It was great! Have I mentioned it is never the event, but how you choose to perceive it?

A Chinese peasant was regaled in his community because he owned the only horse—a marvelous asset for farming and hauling produce. One day his horse disappeared. His neighbors offered their condolences for his loss. The peasant responded, "Let's wait and see." Days later, his horse returned with a wild horse. His riches had doubled. His son tried to break the new horse, was thrown, and suffered a broken leg. Again, the townsfolk dropped by to commiserate with the father. "Let's wait and see," he said. The next day, the local recruiting officer appeared to conscript all able-bodied men to fight in the war. The son was deemed unfit because of his broken leg. Whenever you are facing a crisis, simply ask, "What good can come from this?"

As chief of an inpatient rehabilitation center, I took care of patients who had suffered catastrophic medical conditions, strokes, amputations, paralysis, or multiple sclerosis. They would frequently ask, "Why did this happen to me?" I always told them, "You can't ask that question." If something bad has happened to you, what kind of answer are you going to get? "You were rendered a paraplegic because you were a wonderful gracious man?" Nonsense. You are more likely to get a negative conclusion: "You are being punished because you sinned." Instead, the question you must ask is, "What good can come of this?"

There is a wonderful recipe for a long life—get a medical disease and take care of it. You suffer a heart attack. What good can come from that? You have been overweight for years, smoke a pack of cigarettes a day, haven't exercised in eons, and you're working sixteen hours, six days a week. As a result of the heart attack, you stop smoking, go on a low-fat, low-calorie diet, and shed thirty pounds; you start a daily jogging program and reduce your work schedule. Heart attacks are not a death sentence, but an invitation to live a healthier life. Disease creates an urgency to live and enjoy an expansive life.

You throw a piece of meat, wax, wood, sand, and steel into a fire. The meat cooks, the wax melts, the wood burns, the sand turns to glass, and the steel is unchanged—all different responses to the flame. It is not the event but how you choose to perceive and interpret it.

Ask, "What good can come of this?" What good can come from your anxiety disorder? As you proceed down your path to cure, you will gain an admiration for your expressed courage. As you improve, you will doubly enjoy your newfound world. Every time I go on a new cruise, I revel in the fact that there was a time I couldn't do it. I now appreciate every day I awaken—a feeling I lacked for thirty-one years. What good can come from your phobia? Not much changes when things are going well, but when we're challenged, we are forced to grow and change. I hope someday you will thank your phobias and obsessions for providing you with the challenge you need to create a magnificent, fear-free future. When you awaken one morning knowing that you will be able to handle whatever happens, you will know what good came from your anxiety disorder.

## 5. One Should Be Upset When Things Are Dangerous and Fearsome

Phobocs always want assurance that things are safe. Unfortunately, safety is an illusion. If you want to be safe, don't be born. There is no safety. There is a risk to living. I have a perverse habit of collecting stories of annoying ways to die. A couple was killed in their bed when a wheel fell off an airplane and crashed through their roof. A German locomotive derailed and the front wheels rolled a mile and a half into a town and crashed through a house wall, killing the occupants. Those are definitely disturbing ways to ruin an afternoon.

Okay, let's get statistical. Do you know how many people were killed in domestic commercial airline crashes in 1998 and 2002? None. Zero. Nada! Unfortunately, during those same two years, 100,000 people were killed in highway accidents—so don't drive to the airport. Stay home. Amazingly, 16,000 people died in home accidents during those same two years, so get out of the house and take a walk. You guessed it, 12,000 pedestrians were killed during those two years. Incredibly, the safest place you can be is in a domestic commercial airplane. So the next time the door of the plane shuts say, "Thank God, I'm safe now."

The essence of a phoboc cure demands that you accept the inherent risk in living. There cannot be a 100 percent guarantee. What if the pilot wants to commit suicide and crashes the plane into a mountain? As we always say in Phobease, if that happens and you die at any time during the course, you don't have to do that week's homework. You have to put your faith in God, waitresses, pilots, and doctors, or you can never live that expansive life you are seeking.

I travel extensively now. People ask me a contemporary "what if" question these days. "What if a terrorist commandeers your plane?" Terrorized by a terrorist? I was terrorized by a Boo voice for thirty-one years. No terrorist threat will stop me. I was limited for so many years that I refuse to be limited by such an improbable threat. Death can hold us all hostage. Remember that the two things your brain doesn't want to do are die and be embarrassed. Until you accept your own mortality, you will never be free. I have accepted mine.

## 6. It Is Easier to Avoid Life's Difficulties and Responsibilities

You know now "avoid" is a dirty Phobease word. Avoidance is the disease and non-avoidance is the cure. The first step is to recognize any avoidant behavior, record it, and challenge it. Are you avoiding difficulties or shirking responsibilities? Sometimes it's because we are blaming others. Blame displaces responsibility. "It's not my fault—it's theirs." No way. You are 100 percent responsible for your life. Avoidance and neutralization of anxiety always represent negative reinforcement and perpetuate phobias and obsessions.

Dedicate your life to non-avoidance. Listen carefully to your Boo and do the opposite. When things seem hard—do them. When the Boo tells you not to—do it. "On purpose" and "repeatedly" should be your daily mantras as you relentlessly pursue your exposures. It is easier to avoid life's responsibilities but easy does not define your pathway to cure.

## 7. One Needs Something Other or Stronger or Greater on Which to Rely

This is where we invoke the deity. There is a famous saying that "God never gives you anything more than you can handle." I've always viewed God as a loving being. God is not a sadist sitting in heaven plucking pieces off a butterfly's wings until it can just barely fly. God did not give you your phobia or obsession to give you a meaningful challenge. Nature gave you your phobia and nature, as you have heard, has no conscience. I like the existential view—the universe is totally indifferent to your suffering. There is no plan. You're phoboc because you were born to be phoboc. God is not a punisher. God is up there hoping you cure. The bad news is that God does not do hierarchies or homework. God gives you the strength and faith but you have to do the work. I have worked with many devout religionists who are angry at their god for not providing deliverance from their anxiety disorders. If you really believed and practiced and put your life in God's hands, you would be cured. Unfortunately, only experiential victories cure phobias—not faith. So pray for faith, courage, and strength to do the work necessary to cure.

John is plowing his field. When finished, his neighbor comes by and says, "You and God did a wonderful job on that field." John says, "You should have seen it when God was doing it alone." If you are keeping track, God does not do hierarchies, homework, or plow fields. God gives you a toll-free 800 number called "prayer." Use it any time to enhance your motivation to do those activities necessary to cure.

Sam looks out his window to see the flood waters rapidly rising. He climbs to the roof of his house as the water reaches the eaves. A motorboat passes and the driver says, "Come on, jump in." Sam says, "No thanks, God will save me." The river continues to rise and now he is ankle deep. A rowboat comes by. "Jump in." Sam says, "No thanks, God will save me." The water rises to his chin as a helicopter hovers above him. "Grab the safety harness." Sam says, "No thanks, God will save me." Sam drowns and goes to heaven. He meets God at the Pearly Gates and asks, "You know I've served you faithfully every minute of my waking life. How could you let me drown?" God says, "Are you kidding? I sent you a motorboat, a rowboat, and a helicopter." If you believe, you know that God works in many wondrous ways. For me, just a small suggestion to watch the 10 o'clock news is what saved my life. Perhaps for you it was whatever it took for you to come upon this book.

God gives you the strength but not the skills. Prayers alone won't make you a concert pianist or a Phobease expert. If you're a believer, fine, you have an ally. If not, you and you alone are enough to effect your phoboc cure.

## 8. One Should Be Thoroughly Competent, Intelligent, and Achieving in All Respects

Ptoocy! I accent each of the words "thoroughly," "competent," "intelligent," and "achieving" by smacking myself over the head with my squeak hammer. That's societal nonsense. That's a perfectionist's creed and absolutely unattainable. You are not on earth to meet anybody's expectations or excessively high standards including your own! Never accept anyone else's goal for you. It is okay to lower your standards and expectations. When you set excessively high standards, you set yourself up to fail. If you believe you have to be perfect to be accepted or feel worthwhile, then constant failing will undermine your goals.

A young mother of six sat in my office in tears. Her forty-two-year-old husband had suffered a severe stroke. Why the tears? Her house was a mess. Her impeccable standards gave her no leeway. Even if you have six children and a young husband disabled by a massive stroke, you still should be able to maintain a perfect house? It is okay to fail and make mistakes. You reward the unremitting effort and not the accomplishments. Who did you disappoint? Too bad—they'll just have to deal with it.

Remember, you are the giant now and you alone can decide on career choices, marital partners, sexual orientation, and personal preferences completely independent of external input. Those lofty goals are often foisted upon us when we are too young to voice our protestations. Well, you are old enough now. Cast away your shame and guilt and redefine those imposed goals. You now know the spiel: You don't have to be thoroughly competent or intelligent or achieving to be thoroughly worthy. We are worthy simply because we exist. We are worthy simply because we strive and persist. We don't define ourselves by any accomplishments. If you haven't accomplished all your goals—lower them.

## 9. Because Something Once Affected You Strongly, It Will Do So Forever

(Do you notice the over-generalization?) Nonsense. The reason your anxiety disorder persisted was because you were not "trained." (You didn't know how to juggle.) Like most phobocs, you may have had years of inappropriate therapy, which led you to make an inappropriate conclusion (i.e., myth number 3). "My case is so severe, so chronic, so unique, that I am incurable." If you do the work, you will cure. You are not biologically doomed. You now know you have a highly treatable disorder. Even after thirty-one years, which certainly seemed like forever, I was dramatically changed after eight hours of appropriate instruction. If you have not previously received a psycho-educational, cognitive behavioral, experiential desensitization program, then you were not appropriately treated. Thus, you have no basis to make a future pessimistic conclusion. When you cure, you will find that your phoboc disorder becomes a distant powerless memory. Incredibly, there is a large body of research that suggests that the longer you have had your phobia or obsession, the *better* the prognosis for cure. This has been my personal experience.

The longer you've restricted yourself the more motivated you are to change. When you are sick and tired of the limitations imposed by your disorder you are more likely to stay highly motivated and make the commitment to cure. I wear my thirty-one phoboc years as a badge of honor in light of my cure. However, I have treated patients with durations far, far longer than mine—fifty, sixty, and seventy years—who have gone on to cure. It is never too late to learn how to juggle and to cure an anxiety disorder. When I learned that there was a path and a cure, I dedicated every waking moment of my life to that effort and proved that my phobia would not affect me strongly forever. I invite you to do the same. This might be an appropriate time to mention that all phobias and obsessions are curable and the cure lasts forever.

## 10. One Must Have Certain and Perfect Control over Things

Unfortunately, you never will. To a phoboc, this is bad news indeed. We are always trying to be in control. I was relatively comfortable if

I was driving my car, if I was in charge. I could stop anywhere without asking permission. If someone else was driving, I felt I was at their mercy. I would have to ask if I needed a bathroom stop. How degrading and difficult for me. My solution (how clever we phobocs are) was to declare early and loudly that I would not drink and thus, I would be the designated driver. One of my worst panic attacks occurred when another person, probably phoboc, absolutely demanded to be the driver. I was forced to give up control, sit in the backseat of a two-door car, and experience intolerable anxiety symptoms.

A local newspaper editor enrolled in my Phobease class. He was a licensed pilot, could fly comfortably in his own plane, but would not fly in a commercial airline because he was not in control. That famous "what if" question: "What if the pilot is suicidal and decides to deliberately fly the plane into a mountain?" "What if the pilot is inebriated or under the influence of drugs and misses the runway?" He took the class and cured. He realized that to live an expansive life, one must relinquish control. Part of curing is accepting uncertainty. You will be forced to put your faith in pilots, dentists, surgeons, engineers, and many others and utter those famous words, "Whatever comes along, I will handle it."

Annoyingly, another area we can't control is our death. Much avoidant phoboc behavior is to keep us safe. Unfortunately, the safer we are, the more constricted our lives become. I do like that wonderful coffee cup inscribed with the admonition, "Eat right, exercise, and die anyway." Even in this most important life event, we have virtually little or no control.

I love having other people drive me now. I feel I am being chauffeured and pampered. I have found I am able to look about at my leisure and take in all of the scenery when someone else steers. If I need to stop, I simply request it and they comply. They don't want their back seat soiled. Paradoxically, the more control you give up, the freer you are to live your expansive existence.

## 11. Human Happiness Can Be Achieved by Inertia and Inaction

It cannot. Life is an action game. The best-kept secret of success for writers is to write 1,000 words per day. If you are tired, you write 1,000 words per day. Bored, unmotivated, sick with the flu, or eleven months pregnant, you write 1,000 words per day. To cure a phobia or obsession, you follow the same doctrine. Your 1,000 words per day are your exposure hierarchies. Every day you do your hierarchies in imagination and in vivo. Every day you identify, confront, and challenge your Boo. Tired, bored, sick with the flu, or eleven months pregnant, you do your hierarchies and faithfully practice the Phobease doctrines.

Five frogs are sitting on a log and one decides to jump off. How many are left? Most people say four, when of course the answer is five. Deciding, thinking, wishing, praying, hoping, or planning are not doing. Just do it, you'll have a victory to brag about and write down. When participants say they are planning to ride the elevator or drive across the bridge next week, I roll my eyes and smirk. Nothing is going to happen. The brain is programmed to reply to direct, specific action commands. You don't see signs that say, "Think about not walking on the grass." More important, the brain does not differentiate between negative and positive commands. It blindly carries them out. The following examples may inadvertently lead to many of our destructive behaviors.

**I can't/don't.**   "I can't stay on a diet. I can't stop eating. I can't resist buying pastries or snacks. I can't stop smoking. I can't talk to anyone. I can't talk to groups. I will never be able to fly in an airplane. I can't drive on freeways. I can't dance—I have no rhythm. I can't eat anywhere but my home. I can't use a public restroom. I can't save money," and on and on. These typical statements will generate avoidant or unproductive failure behaviors.

**I should/need to (but I won't).**   "I need to lose weight. I need to stop smoking, drinking, smoking marijuana. I need to see my dentist. I need to get a medical checkup. I need to write my hierarchies. I need to stop procrastinating. I need to get started on that term paper. I need to start my exposure therapy," and so forth. When phrased as such, nothing is going to happen. These are not action commands to your brain. Brain commands must be precise and specific.

**Hate programs.**   "I hate work, school, homework, my boss, my teacher, getting up in the morning, commuting, standing in line, rain, cloudy mornings, hot days, exercising, my figure, my breasts, my thighs, my weight, my hair, my skin, my nose, my mouth, my brother, my sister, my parents, organized religion and me," and so on. Hate programs will create destructive beliefs with predictable negative consequences. Hating makes life more difficult.

**Negative labels.** "I am stupid, clumsy, shy, phobic, dumb, gangly, fat, unworthy, slow, humorless, inarticulate, sloppy, cheap, uninteresting, unfriendly, a perfectionist, hard to live with, short tempered, spoiled, vain, poor, lazy, undisciplined, jealous, dependent, and I lack talent." If you say it, your brain will accept it as truth and will guide your behaviors to fulfill your label.

**Brain commands.** "I always get sick when the kids go back to school, I look at food and I gain weight, I get hurt all the time, I am the unluckiest person in the world, I never win anything, I will never find another, with my luck the plane will probably crash." The brain and you will accept these as absolute truths and you pay the emotional price as if they indeed were true.

To cure your phobias and obsessions you must now carefully identify which of these destructive belief programs you embrace. Regard all your beliefs as theories or hypotheses, not truths. They must be held up to scrutiny and challenged. If they are untrue—and most are—use affirmations and precise specific brain commands to change those destructive programs: "I don't smoke." "I save 10 percent of each paycheck." "I eat small bites of small portions from small plates." *The brain's main job is to prove that what you say and believe are truths, so watch your mouth because your brain is listening.* Improve your self-talk and you will immediately change your life for the better.

## 12. One Has Virtually No Control over One's Emotions and Responses

This is a common belief in people who are not trained in thought dynamics. You will often read that panic attacks "come out of the blue." That is a frightening and inaccurate concept. Thoughts create moods, feelings, and emotions. All thoughts have an instant biochemical concomitant. We don't have panic attacks; we create them with our thoughts, beliefs, or dreams. I have mentioned before that we don't have depression; rather we depress ourselves with our thoughts. For the past two chapters I have talked about the importance of monitoring your thoughts and beliefs because they are the determinants of your feelings and emotions.

Your brain is a thought machine, that famous high-speed computer that makes one hundred million computations per second and thinks of everything and expresses it in thoughts. You can't control initial thoughts, but you can control your interpretation and reaction to them. You must avoid robotic reactions that create unnecessary anxiety. Your brain is at your command and not vice versa. You have tremendous power in choosing your responses. You can thought stop, calmative breathe, reassess, react non-emotionally; you can dispute and reframe. When you reprogram, it will be with precise brain commands and positive core beliefs. That gives us tremendous control over our emotions and responses.

Most of us possess an internal voice that sounds like a harsh boot camp Marine sergeant. It constantly deprecates, demeans, and screams negative epithets at us. You don't need any enemies with a voice like that. Well, it's time to change that internal voice to a supportive, nurturing, friendly counselor. No more destructive self-talk. Instead, say, "Howie, you are wonderful, a genius, a living legend, a magnificent teacher and writer." When you talk that way, your instant biochemical reaction is calming. Create your own "governing affirmation"—a powerful phrase that allows you to make life changing steps toward conquering your most limiting fears.

I was shy. For years, I turned down any social invitation—a wonderful negative reinforcement of my social ineptitude. To change that response, I created the following governing affirmation: "I am socially bold and adventuresome." Any invitation generated that internal message and I said "yes" to all situations. In a short time, I gained confidence with my positive successful social experiences. Only victories cure phobias and governing affirmations often open the door to those victories.

When you have to jump out of an airplane and parachute down 12,000 feet, you don't get out by reciting paragraphs—a simple motivating phrase, "Okay, what the hell," or a word, "Geronimo," works better. Try these for initiating actions:

- *Fearful and timid:* "Things are hard for me" becomes "I love new challenges," or "I do hard things well."
- *Dirt and contamination fears:* "I love germs," "I eat germs for breakfast," or "I love being dirty."
- *Clutter and hoarding:* "I love being organized," or "I love throwing things out."

## Summing Up

Remember, you are the adult giant with a goal of reprogramming a brain bag filled with garbage. We've covered a lot of ground in these past two chapters, but two simple questions will guide you along a constructive path:

"What am I saying to myself? Is it helping?"

If not, challenge, refute, and reframe. You must forgive yourself; you were doing the best that you could at that time in your life. If you knew better, you would have done things differently. You'll have a homework assignment to identify all of your negative beliefs and negative labels and replace every one of them with supportive nurturing doctrines.

Finally, ask, "What is best for me?"

Now there is a strange concept for people-pleasing phobocs. We are used to taking care of everyone in the world save one person—me! In Phobease, we insist on adopting a concept of "constructive selfishness." You make yourself number one! Your needs get met first. Is this heresy? No, this is the time to start taking care of yourself. When you get your needs taken care of, you have more to give to others. As that famous commercial says, "You're worth it!"

## Spring Cleaning

Continue to spring-clean your brain bag and replace it with the positive affirmations, labels, and beliefs of a "trained" phoboc.

## Chapter 6 Highlights

1. The only person you have to love is you. Your love must be unconditional self-acceptance and self-love.

2. The only definition for "horrible" and "terrible" is killing twelve million people in concentration camps.

3. We cannot be in control of everything and never will.

4. It is never the event, but your perception of it. In that we have great power and choice. Ask, "What good can come from this?"

5. There is a risk to living. There are no guarantees. If you wish to be safe, don't be born.

6. Avoidance is the disease. Non-avoidance is the path to cure.

7. God did not give you your anxiety disorder. While there for support, He does not do hierarchies.

8. You are not on earth to measure up to anyone's high expectations, including your own.

9. All phobias and obsessions are curable. You won't be like this forever.

10. Life is an action game. This is not a dress rehearsal.

## Chapter 6 Assignment

Do daily relaxation.

Exercise fifteen to thirty minutes daily.

Do daily diary entries.

Practice your hierarchies.

1. Practice your goals alone. Be independent; run your own errands; make your own phone calls. If you have trouble phoning, make a hierarchy; start by calling businesses and asking how late they stay open.

2. Separate from your support person for longer periods of time.

3. Listen to your thoughts and Boo voice messages. Continue to use thought stoppage, thought recognition, disputation, and positive self-talk.

4. What kinds of destructive messages do you use to drive yourself? Write them down. Can they be made more supportive? Use a challenge sheet: Divide a page in half. On one side write your destructive message and labels. On the other side, list at least five disputations and end with a nurturing restructure. Do this for all your destructive messages and labels.

5. What are five things that you would like changed? Discuss each with the appropriate person. Be assertive.
   1. _____.
   2. _____.
   3. _____.
   4. _____.
   5. _____.

6. List at least three destructive programs that apply to you. Recognizing them is the first step to change. Challenge every one of them.
   1. _____.
   2. _____.
   3. _____.

Comfort is not your goal, living is your goal!

If you can't, you must. If you must, you can!

Watch your mouth, your brain is listening!

# 7

# Life Skills: Assertiveness

***Ingredients*** *(the usual):*

1 brain bag
1 rubber Boo monster
3 squirt guns
1 bag large marshmallows
1 fake red rose

***Directions:***

Display all but the red rose before seventy well-trained Boo killers.

## Assertiveness

I define assertiveness as getting what you want. It is not the same as aggressiveness. I always ask my class participants to put their hands in the prayer position and then instruct them to push with their right hand, harder and harder. Most people wind up with both hands still in the same starting position in front of them because they reflexively resisted with their left hand. I never told them to do anything with their left hand. If they had done the exercise correctly, they would have finished with their right hand all the way over on the left. If you aggress against people, they will resist and not give you what you want. Assertiveness, on the other hand, is an honest, straightforward approach to letting people know what you want.

So, why don't we get what we want? There are a number of reasons but the most important one is that we simply don't ask. So the next logical question is, why don't we ask? The primary reason is that we fear rejection. Early in life, we may have asked our parents for a pony. "You can't have a pony, they're too expensive; you can't have one in this apartment because they mess the rugs." The words don't count; what you feel is unloved and rejected. "If they loved me, then they would give me what I want; I feel terrible; I'm never going to ask for anything again." Another reason we don't ask is because we feel we don't deserve anything. Us phobocs are often filled with self-contempt because of our disorders. We feel unworthy and have difficulty rewarding ourselves. Thus, we simply talk ourselves out of asking. Another reason is that we might not know how to fulfill our needs. Families often fail to teach assertive asking skills and so we end up not knowing how to ask. Furthermore, in this independent society, we receive subtle messages like needing help is a sign of weakness. "Real men don't ask for anything." Often we limit our potential by asking for only what we think we can get. You can try playing the "mind reading game": "I don't have to ask because people should know what I want," but unfortunately, they don't.

Rejection is the equivalent of death to human beings. When a colt or calf is born, it is on its feet in seconds, seeking food. When human beings are born, we lay in a crib for eighteen months. Intuitively, we know if we don't please those parental giants, they may not provide the shelter and sustenance we need and we could die. It is far safer not to ask than to risk starving to death. We will find out later that rejection of a request is not rejection of self. In addition, we will learn that no one can reject us without our permission.

So, here's the cardinal rule of assertiveness: *You can ask for anything you want—anything*. Now you know, you can't be rejected; it's not a matter of being loved; don't talk yourself out of anything; people don't know what you want—so ask.

Here's an important tip. People have difficulty saying no. Do you have curb number painters in your neighborhood? They know people have trouble saying no. Thus, they knock on your door and ask for $10.00 because they have provided this absurd service. I once asked why I needed the number painted since I already had a large clearly visible number on my house. The painter explained, "If your house was on fire, the smoke might hide the number." I imagined the fireman desperately looking for my house number on the curb because the flames pouring out of the house had burned away the house numbers. Each year, I get to practice my assertive skills by saying no to the painters' request.

Most of us have heard 140,000 *no*'s by age eighteen and we have all felt the sting of not getting what we want. When you ask for something, it forces the other person to deal with their own guilt if they have to say no to you. So ask, and ask again. If you don't ask, your chances of getting what you want are zero. At least if you ask, you have a fifty-fifty chance of getting a yes. By the time you finish this chapter, you will have raised your odds to ninety-ten or more of getting what you want.

There are some important rules for asking correctly that will increase your odds of having your requests met.

1. *Ask at a good time.* Remember, it's a question of getting a yes answer. So, ask when the person is well fed, relaxed, and unencumbered.

2. *Make eye contact.* It is much harder to say no if you are looking directly into the other person's eyes.

3. *Maintain a good, confident posture.* It is simply more empowering. If you cower, people may use your implied weakness as an excuse to say no.

4. *Ask in a voice consistent with your request.* Write and practice your request, tape it, then listen and critique it. Practice it in front of friends and get their feedback on your presentation.

5. *Dress for it.* If wearing boots or a business suit makes you feel more assertive, then wear them.

6. *Offer no qualifying statements*. You know now that people have trouble saying no. Qualifying statements invite and facilitate "No" answers.

If you approach making an assertive request in a bowed, humble posture, avoiding eye contact, speaking in a subdued quiet voice, you are reducing your prospects for a positive response. If you begin by stating, "I know this is a bad time to ask, I know we can't afford it, and I know I don't deserve it," you will have created a nineteen-foot giant waiting to reject any and all of your requests. If they had trouble saying no, you just gave them three excuses to do so—use no qualifying statements.

If you go into your boss's office to ask for a raise, don't start with: "I know this is a bad time to ask," or "I know the economy is bad," or "I know we didn't have a profitable year." You're giving your boss three good excuses to say no and he or she is now ready to squash you like a bug. Instead, start with: "I am a loyal, dedicated, and responsible employee. I have contributed greatly to this firm and I need a 6 percent raise this year." That's power.

Finally, and this is so powerful it is almost unfair: make eye contact and tell them, "This is really important to me." People intuitively want to help people get things they deem important. So tell them how important this is, and then ask.

A young lady shared that she had been married for thirteen years to a wonderful husband but had never received birthday, anniversary, or Christmas presents from him. Why would a loving husband not give his wife presents? His reasons were simple. In his family, it was not considered manly to give women gifts. His wife had studied her Phobease assertiveness training well. She remembered that you have to be very specific, so she asked her husband for a one-carat synthetic Chatham emerald ring with two diamond baguettes, in yellow gold, size six, on sale for $399 at their local department store. He agreed to purchase it for her and asked, jokingly, "I suppose you want me to take you out to dinner, too?" He needn't have asked. She told him the restaurant and the phone number and asked him to make reservations for 7:00 P.M. That's the way to ask.

Her revelation led to an interesting class discussion. Is it worth getting things if you have to ask for them? It was answered with a resounding, "Yes!" If you leave the choice of gifts to the whims of our capitalistic society, you might conclude that what women want on Mother's Day is washing machines, toasters, and irons. You might want to inform your husband that those are necessities—not gifts. Ask for what you want and be specific or you risk disappointment. One young man in the class had purchased a diamond stickpin for his wife months in advance to commemorate their twentieth anniversary. His wife, however, assertively untrained, had hinted—not asked—for diamond earrings. When they window-shopped, she admired earrings but never asked for them. When the day arrived, her husband handed her the wonderful black velvet box. He smiled in anticipation of her response. She slowly opened the lid and viewed the diamond stickpin with tears of disappointment. Hinting, whining, complaining, suggesting, hoping, or praying are not asking. You want diamond earrings? You ask for one-carat total weight diamond earrings, yellow gold, with a six-prong setting, hypoallergenic posts available at Sam's jewelry store at 321 Maple Street, open 9 A.M. to 9 P.M. on weekends. That's how you ask.

## Ask for Anything

You have a right to ask for anything. You may not get everything and you probably won't, but you may not get anything if you don't ask. You don't even have to get over your fear of asking—just ask. You can ask for money, tutoring, help around the house, sex, hugs, kisses, time, attention, grants, advice, coaching, guidance, instructions, feedback, and anything else.

At this time in every Phobease class, I make an unusual offer: "We will pay $1,000 cash to anyone who can hit the target." There is a moment of hushed silence until someone asks the appropriate question: "What's the target?" "Of course, we're not going to tell you because we don't want to have to pay the money." But in truth, your universe is a target-seeking industry. Put it out there, and the universe will trip over its own feet to fulfill your request. Once the wheels are in motion, hundreds will gather to form a coalition just to meet your wants. You would like a $200,000 purple Lamborghini? Tell everyone; post a picture of it on your refrigerator and someone in your neighborhood will soon be knocking on your door with your prize—well, almost.

A young woman was to celebrate her fiftieth birthday at the next Phobease class. She explained that she had never received a rose on any occasion and would like some for her birthday. Her universe and her Phobease classmates met her request. Cameras at the ready, she walked into a classroom filled with roses—hundreds and hundreds. She asked and she gloriously received. To this day, I always place a red rose on the table on the day I give my assertiveness lecture to remind me of this wonderful story. The world takes extra pleasure in giving people what their hearts really desire.

A young lady attended the Phobease classes for several reasons. She was extremely agoraphobic. She could barely get to the class from her house, four miles away. She was studying to be a professional clown but was so shy she couldn't attend her own clown class graduation because it entailed going up on stage to receive her diploma. In a short time she cured both disorders and that opened the possibility of fulfilling her lifelong dream to live and work in Hawaii. The problem was that she didn't have any money. At the conclusion of the assertiveness lecture, she decided to ask for, not borrow, money to live her dream. She asked friends, family, and Phobease classmates. Again, that famous universe tripped over its clumsy feet, rushing to fill her request. Money poured in, people had a wonderful personal cause and they embraced it. She sold all of her possessions and with the donated funds flew 2,500 miles—not bad for an agoraphobic—and found a job, an apartment, and happiness for many years on the big island of Hawaii. So what is it you haven't asked for? Need I remind you to ask?

There is a built-in failure rate for most endeavors. One famous "door to door" sales company created an interesting contest. The salesperson who got the most *no*'s in one month would win a substantial prize. Statistically, if you make seven cold calls (i.e., knock on seven doors unannounced) you will average one sale. If you're good at math, 14 doors would be 2 sales, 70 doors would be 10 sales, and

700 doors would be an incredible 100 sales. Now, of course that means that 600 patrons said no. That's a lot of *no*'s if you didn't know you were right on target. If you had knocked on the first door and received a vociferous "No," you might have quit—perhaps muttering to yourself that you are a lousy salesperson, in the wrong profession. Had you done that, you would have missed out on 100 subsequent sales.

Do you know who Alex Rodriguez is? He's the highest-paid baseball player in America, earning more than $25 million a year. His batting average is over .300. If you're not familiar with such calculations, in English, that means he gets 30 hits for every 100 times he comes to the plate. Another way to look at that figure is that 70 times out of 100, he *fails* to get a hit. Someone is paying him $25 million, for a six-month job, to fail 70 percent of the time! How about this analogy: "How would you like to go to a doctor who missed the diagnosis 70 percent of the time?" You would have to climb over a mountain of dead bodies to get to him. Why would anyone pay someone so much to fail so often? It is because of that built-in failure rate. No professional baseball player has ever batted 1,000 over a full season. No player has ever gotten a hit 100 percent of the time. Good players get 25 to 28 hits out of 100 and great players get 30 to 35 hits. Well, you also have an acceptable failure rate. To find it, you have to start asking for everything you want. It is your right. Accept your *no*'s and press on.

Many years ago, I was invited to Toronto to present a lecture at the Million Dollar Round Table—a collection of the most successful insurance salespersons in the world. To be invited, you must sell more individual insurance policies than 99.5 percent of other salespersons around the world. In a group meeting, it was revealed that even in that group, 90 percent of participants were still uncomfortable making cold calls. The secret? They made them anyway. *They got comfortable being uncomfortable*. They got comfortable with "No."

Remember, I'm sure you do by now, the brain doesn't want to die or be embarrassed. "Cold" can freeze you to death; "cold" can give you frostbite. People can reject you and give you the "cold" shoulder. "Cold" is dangerous. Many discussed their personal strategies for getting out the door and challenging—daily—such a dangerous climate.

Some listened to motivational tapes and others made their own inspirational tapes—one for each day of the week. (Motivation is temporary and has to be repeatedly stoked.) By the time you listen to those messages, you leave your house charging out the front door. After ten minutes of listening, you tell yourself: "I'm a genius of a salesperson, a member of the elite Million Dollar Club, there's no sale I can't close, no argument I can't refute, I am a living legend, persistent, dedicated, persevering, knowledgeable, affable, and loveable. They have no choice but to buy." I have such tapes—they are fun to listen to. Others use the twenty-five-bean technique. Start with twenty-five beans in your right pocket. With each call, transfer one bean to the other pocket. You are finished when all twenty-five beans have found their way into your left pocket. Sales or no sales, you've got twenty-five beans to move. Some use the four "SW's"—"Some will buy, some won't, so what, someone's waiting—Next." Many regard "no solicitor" signs as a personal invitation to visit an organization that must be starving to see a salesperson. Get in the front door and start moving beans.

My son's initial vocational choice was to be an actor. You think selling is difficult? An aspiring actor has to go to fifty auditions to get one call-back. That means they are rejected forty-nine times. That would be a lot of emotional pain if one took rejection personally. The strategy is simple. Attend every single audition no matter what they are seeking. Attend singing auditions even if your voice is not appropriate. Attend dance auditions even if that is not your forte. Get comfortable with "No." It was of interest that my son often received offers for parts that were not part of the audition. You can practice the same strategy with job interviews. Apply to numerous jobs, even some you would not consider, to get comfortable with and knowledgeable about the process. Then, when a desirable position is offered, you will be well prepared. The more comfortable you are with "No," the more likely you are to get a "Yes."

## Failing Is Not Failure

Many phobocs are very concerned about failure. I assure them that they can't be judged a failure until the day after they die. Human beings fail often. Life is just too complex to get 100 percent. Some sage stated, "If you want to be twice as successful, you have to fail twice as much." Normal human beings make mistakes, normal human beings fail and it's okay. Failing is not failure. Failing sets up a phenomenon called "successful approximation." Every time you fail, you find out what doesn't work. Edison experimented with more than 900 filaments before he found the one that worked. Did he fail 900 times? Of course not; he simply found out what didn't work 900 times and that eventually led to the solution. All of life is about learning. Thus, there is no right or wrong because any result teaches you something. Accept that failing is not failure but the path to greater accomplishment.

There are some notable examples of famous failings: Do you know who Michael Jordan is? He is reputed to be the greatest basketball player in the history of the game. Do you know what happened to Michael in high school? His coach cut him from the team. Bob Cousey, the greatest ball handler in the National Basketball Association suffered a similar fate. Edison was told he was too stupid to learn anything. Beethoven was told he was a failure as a composer. Walt Disney was fired by a newspaper editor because he lacked imagination. The judgment at one of Fred Astaire's movie auditions was, "He can't act, can't sing, but can dance a little." Winston Churchill failed the sixth grade and had to repeat it. Then there was a young man who failed twice in business and declared bankruptcy at ages twenty-two and twenty-four. At twenty-three he ran for the legislature, was defeated, and suffered a nervous breakdown at age twenty-seven. At twenty-nine he was defeated for Speaker of the House. He ran for Congress at age thirty-four and thirty-nine and was defeated both times. He ran for the Senate at ages forty-six and forty-nine and was defeated. He ran for the vice presidency at age forty-seven and was defeated. At age fifty-one, he was elected president of the United States. That man was Abraham Lincoln.

Each used their failing as a motivation to eventually succeed. Persist in the pursuit of your goals—don't let defeats or others' opinions deter you—risk and accept failings as a badge of growth.

## Broken Record

A powerful tool, when dealing with stores and corporations, is the "broken record." Those of you who are old enough might remember those large vinyl records. Over time, they would get worn and scratched and when the needle hit that area, it would keep bouncing back and replaying the last words. Unattended, it could do so for hours. The broken record technique does just that. You keep repeating your request, irrelevant of the negative response. My wife purchased a dress in Hawaii and told the clerk she wanted to take it up to her hotel room to try it on with the proper shoes and jewelry. She didn't like the fit and brought the dress down and asked for a refund. The clerk pointed to a sign that said "No Refunds." Besides being furious, Carol remembered the "broken record" technique. "I just purchased the dress, it does not fit me well, and I would like my money back." The clerk repeated that the store did not give refunds. Carol invoked another powerful strategy called "progressive complaining." She went up the chain of command and repeated her request. People at higher levels can demonstrate their power by reversing policy and contradicting their subordinates. "I want to talk to your manager." Now she tightened the screws. "I am Governor of Soroptomists, an international women's service organization and I'm here with 1,500 of them. I will certainly let them know of your policy. I bought this dress hours ago, it doesn't fit me well, and I would like my money back." She got it!

Although not an endearing approach, its power lies in the fact that it wears people down. Keep repeating your request and invariably people will grant your annoying wish.

## Fogging

Fogging is a wonderful tool to protect you from insulting and demeaning remarks. Do you have someone in your life who constantly berates and criticizes you? He or she is the perfect person with whom to employ the fogging technique. Do you remember some of those early laughable B sci-fi movies? In one particular drama, the evil monster was a fog cloud. The problem, as you can imagine, is how do you kill a fog? If you shoot at it, the bullets pass through. You can't kill it with an arrow and you can't stab it with a sword. Fogging employs those same characteristics. You decide in advance, when dealing with critical people, to become a fog. You accept demeaning, deprecating remarks and allow them to pass through you without emotional reaction.

I demonstrate this in the Phobease class with the following offer: "I will give you $1 million if you allow me to say nasty things about your family for two minutes without you responding emotionally." Of course they accept. They decide instantly that they will ignore anything I say. I begin with, "Your dog is ugly, your cat is clumsy, and your husband dresses funny." For $1 million we hum a happy tune and let the remarks simply pass through. That is the essence of fogging.

We had a young lady report that every Tuesday she called her sister in New York and her sister would make her cry. In truth, your sister can't make you cry every Tuesday unless you permit it. Armed with her fogging strategy, she decided in advance that she would ignore her sister's vindictive remarks. It worked like a charm. She would have collected the million dollars with ease. There were no Tuesday tears that week or any subsequent week.

Finally, there is one more wonderful piece of advice. The best time to use fogging is when you are dealing with your most persistent adversary—your Boo; especially when dealing with your Boo and its ruminative worries, lies, exaggerations, obsessive thoughts, and threatened catastrophes. Fog them all. Accept them non-emotionally and they and the Boo will quickly lose their power.

## Chapter 7 Highlights

1. Know what you want and ask for it.
2. Risk a "No" answer—it is a rejection of your request, not of you. Don't take rejections personally.
3. *Ask for anything, it is your right. You won't get it if you don't ask.*
4. Do not mind-read or assume that people know what you want—instead, tell them and be specific.

5. Ask non-emotionally at a good time for both of you. Remember, there is no perfect time.

6. Do not make qualifying statements. People have trouble saying no, so don't make it easy for them to do so.

7. Make eye contact—it's harder for people to say no to you when you do so.

8. Your voice and posture should be consistent with your request.

9. Tell the individual it's very important to you.

10. Use "I" statements to personalize your request.

11. Be non-aggressive. Aggression doesn't work well. People won't give you what you want if you tick them off.

12. Use your fogging and "broken record" techniques. Most important, fog your Boo.

13. Write out a precise script and practice it in front of a mirror or record it on tape and critique it.

14. Ask for anything you want. (I think I already said that.)

---

## Chapter 7 Assignment

Do daily relaxation tape.

Exercise fifteen to thirty minutes daily to burn adrenaline and make your heart more resistant to adrenaline.

Do daily diary entries and continue adding to your victory card.

Write victories down immediately.

Practice your hierarchies absolutely daily—in fantasy and in vivo—as often as you can.

1. Practice being assertive—not aggressive. Ask for something you want. What happens?

2. Ask yourself are there simple things you don't do? Ask for a bath-room, change of a dollar, a glass of water, or return an item for a refund? Do it. What happens?

3. Do something unconventional. Sing or whistle in a store. Dress dif-ferently. Call attention to yourself on purpose.

4. Make an assertive list of your wants—things that you have never asked for. Make a script and a timetable for asking.

5. If you have trouble saying no, set aside five minutes a day to say "No" out loud or to imagined requests. A phone or door sales-man makes a request—practice saying "No."

   Get comfortable with "No."

   Don't take rejection personally.

   Successful people fail frequently.

   Failing is not failure.

# 8

# Life Skills: Public Speaking, Conversing, and Arguing

*Ingredients (the usual):*

1 brain in bag
1 Boo monster
3 squirt guns
1 bag large marshmallows
1 large standing microphone

*Directions:*

Place before seventy well-trained adults and children

———

THE NUMBER ONE PHOBIA in the world is the fear of public speaking. The risk of being negatively evaluated and failing with the spotlight on you instills intolerable fear in two-thirds of people. It's very hard to hide behind a podium. It's extremely harder to hide when a microphone you are holding might exaggerate your tremulous faults. The language of comedians personifies the threat. A bad performance is known as "bombing," "dying," or "going down in flames." A great performance is described as having "killed," "murdered," or "slayed" the audience. There is obviously a significant risk to standing up and speaking.

Remember the two things your brain doesn't want to do? Die and be embarrassed. You can do both every time you speak out. The amount of anxiety experienced in any social-speaking situation is dependent on three fear factors:

1. Your prediction of failure
2. The size and composition of the audience
3. Your perceived importance of the event

I can definitely relate to all three. In my first year of college I had a choice to take English or Speech 1A. My friend said, "If you take English, you'll be reading a ton of books and writing endless book reports. Take speech—it's a cinch A." So I took speech, not knowing my phoboc destiny. I embraced all three fear factors. Just thinking about giving a talk terrorized me. I couldn't remember the text in practice and was sure I would fail. Second, the Korean War had ended and there were many "older" students (ages twenty-one to twenty-five) in the class. I was seventeen and scared of older authority figures. Third, if I failed, I wouldn't get into medical school.

My turn came after a sleepless night. The teacher called my name. I could feel the blood pounding in my head. I was nearly breathless. I stared at the sea of critical faces, opened my mouth, and not a sound came out. I didn't know about target organ paralysis but I had just experienced it. Some people can't urinate in public and some can't speak. What a humble beginning for someone who fifty years later would make his living as an invited speaker. I sat down, devastated and humiliated. I had predicted failing and of course, I did. Fortunately, we were called on frequently and in a short time I presented well, my anxiety declined; I gained confidence and experienced victories. With the help of a very understanding teacher, I became an outstanding creative speaker. More important, I earned the all-important three units of "A."

## Public-Speaking Hierarchies

So how are you going to find a venue for becoming a fearless public speaker? In Phobease classes, students have a unique opportunity to practice a hierarchical approach to speaking in public. With their permission, I call on them repeatedly to give a "presidential" wave while seated. When comfortable, they progress to the next step—becoming more visible. When called on, they do a standing "presidential" wave. Then a standing wave with a vocal uttering: "Hi." When ready, they bring an interesting object from home and describe it to the class. They can focus on the object, not the audience, which is somewhat easier. From there, they may read a passage or discuss their weekly victories. The students are instructed to speak up at any public gathering. They commit to asking questions or making comments at school, business, or community events. Phobease instructors strongly encourage joining the local Toastmasters, an organization that teaches people how to become effective public speakers. They offer a progressive approach to more challenging presentations that eventuate in overcoming the fear of public speaking.

If you do not have an available Phobease class, you must make the commitment to find venues where you can speak in public. You can begin by asking questions or making comments at work or community events or presentations. Many patients who have enrolled in community classes or forums are able to speak out in public. However, if you need to cure your public speaking fear, again, I suggest Toastmasters or public speaking courses.

## Presentation Preparation

Here are some suggestions to minimize anxiety at your next presentation. Be prepared to deal with your Boo in advance. Anticipatory anxiety is always worse than the actual event because there is no limit to our own destructive imagination. Challenge the three fear factors on paper:

1. *Challenge your failure predictions.* "I will probably forget my whole speech." Nonsense. "I will practice repeatedly and bring

some keynote phrases to guide me." "I don't have to be perfect." "If I leave something out, no one will know." Be on guard and refute every failure message generated by your Boo. I always ask, "How much are they paying me?" Usually, it's nothing and therefore, they are going to get their money's worth. Or use affirmations: "I'm extremely well prepared and will present a terrific paper."

2. *Find the language to neutralize the size and composition of your audience.* "It doesn't matter the size, they're not going to gang up on me." I once received $3,500 to make a presentation to an audience of 2,500 people. That was the most I had ever received and my Boo was saying, "Howie, you're not worth $3,500." But I did some quick calculations and realized that if I divide 2,500 people by $3,500, they were paying less than $2 to hear my great "brain in the bag" talk. With that kind of math, I thought I was underpaid! Get innovative and challenge your scare programs.

3. *Dispute your perceived importance of the event.* I would bet that neither your life, your job, nor even your wife is on the line. The world won't end if your performance is under par. Get creative and find several reasons why it is not that important.

The day of the event, keep your Boo in check. Let it know you will handle it. Make sure you have prepared well. Practice the way you will present. If it's out loud and standing, then rehearse that way. Don't memorize; instead, learn the material thoroughly. If you memorize and forget a line, it often disrupts the flow. If you learn it, you will be able to carry on even if you leave out segments. Have readable notes, a key word outline, or cue cards.

## Presentation Day

Get there early and take some calmative breaths. Review your notes. I have found it useful to review my talks as close to presentation time as possible. Keep a close rein on your Boo. It will be loud and vociferous. Answer any failure messages it raises with your affirmation, "I am a confident, well-prepared speaker." Accept your pre-anxiety. It is normal and expected; just don't add to it with unwarranted failure predictions. Check all the equipment: make sure you know how to turn on the microphone and practice adjusting its stand. Stand at the podium and get comfortable with the environment. Say a few words to "hear" your voice. Often that squirts a little adrenaline that will rapidly dissolve.

If people are trickling in, welcome them from the podium. If you befriend the audience, they are far less likely to "attack." Check your notes and slides or overheads, make sure they are all there and in proper order. It's very disconcerting and unnerving to find your slides are upside down or your note pages are missing or out of order. I always write how many pages of notes I have on the front page so I can check completeness. If you're not the first speaker, try to ask questions or make comments about the preceding presentations. These are preliminary mini-speeches that can allay anxiety when your turn comes. Dress well for your presentation, it adds to your self-confidence. I tend to overdress for speaking engagements. If you've traveled out of town, make sure you press your clothes if they have become wrinkled.

When it's your turn, stride to the podium, calmative breathe, accept and use your anxiety to energize your presentation. Spend extra time to make sure your opening remarks are potent. Capture your audience with an appropriate humorous statement, challenge them with a provocative question, or bond with them with a self-revelation. Realize, even if you are anxious at the start, that it will rapidly fade because speaking is a powerful, effective form of cortical shifting and thus will shut off adrenaline. Never focus on how you're doing, but rather on what you are doing. The more intensely you focus on the task at hand, the faster your anxiety will fade. Critical self-analysis during a talk raises anxiety. If people fall asleep, it's because they are tired, not because you are boring. If they leave, it's because they have to be somewhere; it's not a criticism of your talk. Again, spend extra time to send your audience home with a powerful final message.

When you finish, utilize the famous National Speakers Association's "LBNT." Write down that which you *liked best* about your presentation and what you can do "*next time*" to improve. Continue to speak at every occasion and soon you will enjoy the rewards of fearless public speaking.

## Becoming a Gifted Conversationalist

Like many life skills, becoming a good conversationalist is a learnable skill. Many shy and lonely people are that way because they were never trained in conversational skills. There is often a great deal of anxiety involved in talking to another human being. You might recall the number one phobia in the world is fear of public speaking. Conversation is "public" speaking to an audience of one. So why do you think so many of us are anxious about this form of communication? I remember when my grandson said his first word. We called Grandma, CNN, and we told the whole world. That first word is such an extolled event. But unfortunately, many of those 180,000 negative comments you heard growing up referred to the dangers of opening your mouth. As phobocs with anxious perceptions, we probably paid a lot of attention to the following remarks:

"Children should be seen and not heard."
"Don't talk to strangers."
"Mind your own business."
"Think twice and talk once."
"Better to be silent and be thought a fool than to open your
    mouth and remove all doubt." (You can thank Abraham
    Lincoln for that one.)
"Don't put your foot in your mouth."
"That was really dumb, stupid."
"Boys don't make passes at girls who wear glasses."
"Boys don't like smart girls."
"Don't talk back; don't talk in class or church."
"Don't speak until you have been spoken to."
"Don't interrupt; be quiet; you're talking too loud."
"Your grammar is terrible."
"Who do you think you're talking to?"

"I don't like the tone of your voice."

"You don't know what you're talking about."

"Get your facts straight."

"Watch your mouth, young man."

That's a lot to remember. Instead, just remember you've been taught: There is a risk to opening your mouth. Better to adopt a protective label. "I'm quiet or shy or a good listener." That protects you from fears of being rejected or negatively evaluated on a very personal level.

So, if you're not a gifted communicator, how do you become one? There are three things you must do:

1. Prepare

2. Prepare

3. You guessed it: Prepare!

Incredible? You have to prepare. An opera singer or classical pianist would not consider giving a recital without practicing and preparing. It is reputed that Barbara Walters might spend four months preparing for an important interview. She reads her subjects' books, watches their videos, reviews their speeches and personal history, and brings extensive notes to the forum. If you researched topics for four months for an upcoming social conversation, you would find yourself well prepared.

Shy people often complain that they don't know what to say and they don't know how to make small talk. So, what precisely do you do? Here are five suggestions that will provide you with a wealth of topical information that you can then contribute to a conversation. It's like preparing for a final exam:

1. Read a newspaper cover to cover. If you're not particularly interested in certain areas (e.g., sports), at least read the headlines.

2. Collect interesting articles from newspapers or magazines or pertinent topics from radio and TV shows and review them prior to the event.

3. List three topics that you can easily talk about for five minutes without formal preparation. Your favorite vacation, most exciting adventure, an unusual hobby of yours, or your vocation are good examples. I could talk about my phobias for six hours!

4. Collect jokes. I'm a joke collector and teller. Before a social event I go to my files and find twenty pertinent jokes. I write down twenty punch lines and then practice my delivery. At the event, I wait for an appropriate moment and tell one. I might excuse myself after a while and review my list to see what's left.

5. Finally, create alphabetized topic lists. For each letter, list three or four examples. Since I cured my phobia and have traveled to over fifty countries, I use a geographical list:

A. Argentina, Abu Simbel, Amazon River, Alaska, Athens, Acropolis

B. Brazil, Bruges, Britain, Brussels

C. California, Canary Islands, Copenhagen, Costa Rica, China, Colombia, Canada, Casablanca

D. Denmark, Denali

E. Europe, Egypt

F. France

G. Germany, Golan Heights, Greece

(It's definitely worth it to cure your travel phobia!)

For my alphabetized topic list I use:

A. acupuncture, abortions

B. body building

C. computers

D. diamonds: real and man-made, Dharma

So, what do you do with all this information? The brain is an associative marvel. All memory recalls use "pegs," a system that allows you to readily remember and access information. Pegs are known entities that allow you to tie the information you wish to recall. The most basic is the alphabet. You tie recall information to each letter that then gives you an associative recall peg. The Phobease class uses joints and body parts. You have three things to buy at the store: hot dogs, mustard, and hot dog buns. Visualize hot dogs sticking between your toes, mustard slathered all over your knees, and a hot dog bun sticking out of your belly button. You can throw away your grocery list because you won't forget visualizations. The more absurd, the better the recall, so have fun with your orifices.

You can also use words as pegs. One famous system starts with "tea" for the number one. Vowels don't count and the consonant "T" looks like the number one with an umbrella on top. Thus if you are trying to remember your first grocery item, you would picture some hot dogs floating in your tea. The letter "N" has two down strokes and represents the number two. The peg word is Noah. You visualize a gray bearded man covered with yellow mustard. The third letter with three down strokes is "M"; the word "Ma." Visualize your mother with hot dog buns in every crevice and orifice. You memorize 100 peg words and can recall huge lists of data when you relate them to your known pegs.

The goal of your five approaches is to provide you with a huge reservoir of usable material.

An elderly couple is discussing the fact that they are both taking a memory class. "What's the teacher's name?" The elderly husband looked stumped. His wife said, "Associate, dear." He smiled and asked, "What is the name of the flower that smells nice and has sharp thorns?" His wife smiled and answered, "Rose." The man turned to his wife and said, "Rose, what is the name of our teacher?"

Now that you have the information, what do you do with it? One of my "five-minute topics" was about when I accompanied my daughter on a trip she won to Europe in 1984. I look for things that remind me of that event. If I see someone with bottled water, I might say, "Your bottled water reminds me of a trip to Europe my daughter won in 1984 and that was the first time I ever saw bottled water." I can then talk about some of the sites we visited. If someone has a dog, I might say, "My daughter won a trip to Europe in 1984 and in Paris we found out you can take your dog into markets and restaurants." Then I can launch into other details about my trip. *When you have the information, your associative brain will find ways to enter the conversation.*

Another facet of good conversationalists is that they are good listeners. I always thought if the two greatest conversationalists got together, neither would speak because they would both be listening. So, what do they listen for? They listen for topics or subjects. Immediately upon hearing one, they formulate a number of questions about the topic. If I tell you I'm a doctor, what kind of questions could you ask? What kind of doctor are you? How did you decide to become a doctor? How did you feel when you saw your first autopsy? What's the most interesting patient you ever had? What's the hardest patient you ever treated? Get in the habit of listening for topics and then formulating penetrating questions. The answers lead you to some of your accumulated materials. For instance, I might be able to tell them that in 1984, my daughter won a trip and . . .

## Closed and Open Questions

There are two types of questions you can ask. Closed questions ask for brief, specific answers and limited information. Where were you born? How old are you? When did you first go to Europe? What is your favorite color? How much do you weigh? The only problem is that you have to ask a lot of them for very little information. Open-ended questions ask for opinions, insights, feelings, and beliefs. Open-ended questions ask why? What? What if? If you were? Tell me about. How do you feel about? Notice (I hope you're not salivating) that open questions call for expansive answers. Expansive answers are sure to remind you of many topics, jokes, and stories you have assembled. Thus, if you ask good open questions of good conversationalists, you will have multiple opportunities to display your newfound associative and conversational skills.

## Meeting People

Now you know how to converse, but how do you meet people? In these days of e-mail, ATM machines, and voice mail, you can go days without speaking to a live human being. People are yearning to meet others. Sometimes we build walls around us, but to bridge that gap you smile, make eye contact, hold out your hand, and introduce yourself. If you have trouble doing that, practice in front of a mirror and perfect that winning smile.

Students in a Phobease class must formulate a ten-word personal introduction containing one or two topics. With this you give the other person an opportunity to formulate several questions. Compare that with what happens when two strangers are introduced by name alone. "Hi Carol, this is Howard." Now you have two total strangers desperately trying to come up with an opening remark. Compare that with "Hi, Howard, I'd like to introduce Carol, a retired bank manager, Governor of Soroptomists, tap dancer, and Phobease teacher." Wow. You could generate twenty inquiring questions:

*Bank manager:* How did you get to be manager? Were you ever held up? Any FBI stings? Anybody ever embezzle money?

*Governor Soroptomist:* What are soroptomists? What was your territory? What were some of your social projects?

*Tap dance teacher:* How long have you taught? Did you ever teach children? Ever have your own studio? Did you really meet your husband in one of your classes?

*Phobease teacher:* What is Phobease? How long have you taught? Did you have phobias of your own? Are you the originator of the support group?

On cruises, I start with, "Hi, I'm Howard Liebgold, the infamous Dr. Fear *(topic)* from San Francisco *(topic)*. With two topics they have ample opportunity to generate expansive answers that will remind them of their favorite vacation, which will remind me, did I tell you that in 1984 my daughter and I . . .

Now, if you have initiated the meeting, what do you do after you shake hands? You begin by asking an open question. Do you know what people like to talk about most? Themselves, of course. Thus, the best question is about the person or the situation. It could be about something you observe. If you are in their house, it might be a picture, or a piece of jewelry they're wearing. Listen for topical answers and jump in when appropriate. One important secret, everyone has a unique skill, hobby, or story to tell—your job is to find it. We were on a cruise and met the quietest man in the world. He barely spoke. I happened to mention that my first car was a 1938 Ford. All of a sudden, this sleeping giant sprang to life. He, too, had purchased a '38 Ford and spent $20,000 refurbishing it. He had pictures of his creation in his wallet. From then on, I couldn't shut him up. He designed and built his own airplane that he dismantled and now stores in his house and garage. The wing is tied above his bed. He invented a sail-driven desert dune buggy and his own RV. He maintained all his motor vehicles and boasted that they had over 600,000 miles on them. He designed insulation for his house and windows using reflective shields. As a result, he never needed to use air conditioning even though the average summer temperatures were 110°F. We uncovered treasure just because of a 1938 Ford. Find their passion and unlock their communicative genius.

## Mingleaphobia

Mingleaphobia is a contrived humorous designation of the common fear we have of meeting people at social events. Your brain was programmed early to beware of "strangers" because they might kidnap, rape, or kill you. Thus, it's not uncommon when facing an upcoming event to experience fear because there will be "strangers" there. Be assured that everyone has a little bit of mingleaphobia. Well, here are suggestions for dealing with unfamiliar people and settings:

1. Your major goal should be to meet people and have fun. In fact, meet as many people as you can.
2. Limit contact to five to ten minutes per group and move on. Shop around to see which group you may want to dine with.
3. Make sure you have done your five information assignments and you are prepared.
4. Review your ten word topical self-introduction. Don't wait to be introduced, the hostess may not be available.

5. Take a calmative breath and begin by selecting the least threat-ening group. Uncomfortable looking lost souls or groups marked by frivolous laughter are good places to start.

6. Avoid two-person groups in intense intimate conversations.

7. Have a reason for joining in:

   a. *Honest:* "I don't know a soul, mind if I join you?"

   b. *Personal mission:* "The hostess said I must meet everyone here tonight."

   c. *Humorous:* "I'm running for president and I'm starting my campaign here tonight. Mind if I join you?"

   d. *Quiet:* Just blend into the group, listen to their dialogue, and when appropriate, tell them about some exciting life event. Continue to use your prepared material as indicated.

After a few minutes, excuse yourself to get some food or a drink and then meet the next group. Use your open-ended questioning skills and their expansive answers will provide multiple opportunities for you to utilize your prepared material. If you sit, immediately introduce yourself to all. Another secret of mine is to take out a pen and write down names when they are offered in return. People are always com-plimented and then you don't have to deal with your embarrassment if you forget a name two seconds after you heard it. Another trick is to write names in the order people are sitting so you always know who is who.

So, let's review:

1. Prepare, prepare, and prepare—did I mention prepare?

2. Complete five assignments: newspapers, interesting articles, three five-minute stories, jokes, and alphabetized memory pegs.

3. Listen for topics and contribute where appropriate.

4. Master the art of open-ended questions—ask and listen for topics.

5. Mingle—accept every social invitation so you can practice your newfound skills.

There you have it. When Barbara Walters or Larry King retires, you'll be ready to take over and collect their royal salary.

## Arguing

Arguing is a very important communicative skill. At best, it is an effective form of negotiation. Indeed, if you are in a significant relationship, there are hundreds of issues to negotiate. Some have suggested this process takes approximately seven years to complete. It is of interest that the average marriage in the United States ends in divorce by the third year. The unfortunate problem with arguing is that most of us are untrained in the art.

Do you know what the Marquis of Queensbury Rules are? Boxing rules. They dictate that you cannot hit below the belt, that you cannot fight if you are intoxicated or under the influence of drugs. You can't bite, kick, or hit after the bell rings. You can kill your opponent, but you must do it fairly. You can't hold or punch in the kidneys. Rules make it a civilized, governable sport.

The problem with arguing is that most people have no rules and no protective standards. If you are going to argue correctly and effectively, you need a set of rules, agreed upon by both participants. Here are some you might consider:

1. *Never argue if one of you is under the influence of alcohol or drugs.* Intoxicated fighters don't follow the rules and someone may get hurt.

2. *Define your personal "belt line."* Which topics do you not want to argue about? These are topics that cannot be raised in arguments. My wife and I have agreed not to discuss our previous marriages. I'm Jewish and my wife is Catholic—we don't argue about religion. We don't argue about politics. I have asked not to discuss how I handle money issues with my children. Carol has asked me not to discuss her weight. If any forbidden topics are raised during an argument, the violation is

pointed out and must be stopped. Hitting below the belt is usually hurtful and no one must ever be hurt in negotiations.

3. *Never argue when you're angry.* That sounds like a contradiction, but anger interferes with rule compliance. Boxing matches tend to be very controlled, scientific, and restrained. If one combatant hits the other after the bell rings, that is a clear violation and suddenly all science, sportsmanship, and Marquis of Queensbury Rules fly out the window. They'll wrestle, bite, kick, and hit each other with their corner stools. The same thing happens in personal arguments. If one or both of you is angry, take a time out, do some calmative breathing, write down your feelings, or take a slow walk. You may have heard that it's good to discharge your anger by hitting a punching bag or going in a closet and screaming. Instead of calming, these behaviors actually rehearse aggression and should be avoided. Instead, calmative breathe, lower your voice, pet your dog or cat, meditate, and slow down.

Is anger good or bad? Anger is a normal emotion that has two main purposes. It helps you blow off steam and it incites change. We often confuse angry behaviors with the angry emotions. Angry behavior equals yelling, breaking things, slamming doors, and so forth, actions that are threatening and intimidating and against the rules. No one can justifiably hurt another person in an argument. Phobocs tend to be angerophobics and thus avoid conflicts and confrontations. Often, because combatants have never been taught to argue correctly, we don't learn that this activity is safe.

4. *You can't raise your voice during an argument.* Yelling is threatening and intimidating. It represents age regression. Yellers are now discussing the issues at a four-year-old's level. All arguments must be held at conversational voice levels. If they rise above that, ring the bell and declare another time-out.

5. *You must communicate openly.* My mother, all 4 feet 7 inches of her, was a rage-aholic. She screamed loudly and threw lamps and other objects, resulting in police being summoned. I

remember at age eight, sitting outside while the police resolved an issue. I vowed to myself that when I got married, I would never raise my voice or argue; in twenty-five years of marriage, I never did. I was a classic passive aggressive male. I would simply leave the scene and not discuss the issues. I might be fuming, but I was a phoboc "good guy." Years later, I found out that "good guys" suck! It's unfair to your partner when you fail to communicate your resentments. An old psychological truism is that all unexpressed anger will eventually be expressed. If you're angry, your partner will pay one way or another. So express it but remember that expression is not an explosion of rage and anger. The belief that it must be dispensed that way or one would suffer physical harm is incorrect. You express anger by communicating or writing and only in the acceptable manner designated by your rules.

Passive aggressive arguers "gunnysack." That is, they carefully collect and keep track of every bothersome event, disagreement, and annoying behavior. If your partner says, "That's the last straw" and explodes over some minuscule occurrence, you know their bag has overflowed. I'm always impressed when the neighbors of mass murderers are interviewed. "He was such a quiet, nice, kind man." Sure, quiet and nice while he is categorizing every annoyance until he explodes in a fit of rage. While anger is relatively controlled, rage represents a total loss of civil inhibitions. If someone is in a rage, leave immediately and notify authorities if warranted or if the behavior escalates. Enraged people hurt others.

The number one topic that leads to fights is money. Money issues carry tremendous unresolved emotional baggage. The most common day to argue is Wednesday. There is little hope for the day labeled "hump day." The weekend and escape from the working world is still three days away. Thus, to ease the boredom and create a little excitement, we argue. Finally, arguments tend to be more common at the end of the month because that's when people have less money. So, if the last day of the month is Wednesday and you're broke—watch out.

## Battering

This is an appropriate place to discuss the delicate topic of battering. Batterers are sick. Seventy-five percent of people that batter have been victims of physical or psychological abuse. It is not your fault. You never make anyone mad enough to hit you. That is their personal choice and they do their heinous deeds behind closed doors, not in public where they may be observed. It is a progressive disorder that involves three phases:

1. *Escalation phase:* Batterers are often gunnysackers who handle early anger poorly. As tension rises, they seek a discharge and find it in physical violence. Eventually, they come to believe that this is the only way to get rid of their inner tensions.

2. *Battering phase:* This is manifested by explosive rage, often out of proportion to the perceived insult. The behavior often results in feelings of shame and guilt on the part of the batterer and leads to the third stage.

3. *Honeymoon phase:* This is the apologetic and loving phase. Flowers and candy complete the seduction, which often convinces the abused to stay in the relationship.

Unfortunately, untreated, the disorder persists and over time, escalates. The phases shorten and the battering becomes more severe.

It is imperative that you report battering to the authorities. Batterers often deny the extent of their actions. Local agencies will counsel you on your rights and alternatives. Batterers need intensive and prolonged therapy—often one to two years. Battering always affects children, even if they are not the recipients of direct assaults. For their sake and yours, get help; it is not going to get better by itself. Batterers often have difficulty recognizing early symptoms of their frustrations and anger. They go from upset to rage in milliseconds because they ignore early anger cues. Part of their therapy is to recognize and deal immediately with early discomforts. Over time, they learn more effective and acceptable ways to discharge escalating tensions. Only after therapy is complete and deemed successful should you risk reconstructing the relationship.

## Preparing to Argue

1. Know what you want.

2. Set up a good time to discuss your desires. A full stomach and no pressing demands are good considerations. Decide which time is best for both of you. The first argument my wife and I had was at 7:00 A.M. Now, my wife gets out of bed at 6:00 A.M., but her brain isn't fully functioning until that second cup of coffee, so early discussions are out. We brought up the next dispute just before sleep and then stayed up all night. We agreed that our best time is after dinner when we have both calmed down from our daily work challenges.

3. Discuss the problem within two to four hours of its onset if possible. Don't let the sun set on a conflict. You'll both sleep poorly if you delay.

4. Never argue when mad. Use your tools to gain composure.

5. Announce in advance what you wish to discuss so both of you can prepare.

6. State the problem with "I" statements. Never use the word "you." It is accusatory and means the jury has already returned a guilty verdict. "You" statements are often countered with accusatory "you" statements. "I" is a personal feeling or opinion and is an honest expression of heartfelt emotions. Argue in the present tense as often as you can.

7. Propose your desired change and only argue about one topic at a time.

8. Outline the benefits and the consequences. Don't put the relationship on the line.

9. Other's responses:
   a. "I'll do it."
   b. "I'll do it with these conditions."

    c. "I will not do it but I'll do this instead."

    d. "I need some time to think about it." (Set a specific time period.)

10. Set a trial period to see if there is compliance.

11. Write agreements down: if participants tend to "forget" or procrastinate, write it down and give a copy to each partner.

12. Strive for a win/win.

13. Fight often, but follow the rules—you do have those hundreds of issues to negotiate.

14. Face it with style and use humor to diffuse anger. Try wearing clown noses to put arguments in perspective.

15. Finally, I repeat: strive for a win/win. It's not a war but an important relationship you wish to enhance.

## Chapter 8 Highlights

1. Remember that your anxiety in speaking situations is related to your prediction of failure, the size and composition of your audience, and your perceived importance of the event.

2. Find venues for speaking in public and do so. Join Toastmasters.

3. Note: good conversationalists and public speakers prepare.

4. Listen with "big ears" for topics and generate open-ended questions.

5. Read a newspaper cover to cover; find interesting articles; prepare three topics you can talk about extensively; collect and practice jokes; make associative alphabetized lists.

6. Meet people with your topical self-introduction.

7. Make eye contact, smile, and shake hands to introduce yourself.

8. Remember: people like to talk most about themselves.

9. Be aware that everyone has a unique personal story—find it. What is the most interesting thing you would want people to know about you?

10. Argue fairly and often—it is an effective form of negotiation.

11. Strive only for a win/win.

---

## Chapter 8 Assignment

Do daily relaxation.

Exercise fifteen to thirty minutes daily.

Continue your diary and your victory card.

Keep working on your hierarchies.

1. Introduce yourself to one new person per day. Use your hierarchy skills and start with the "safest" people.

2. Create in ten words or less a self-introduction phrase with at least one or two topics (e.g., "Hi, I'm Carol, the best tap dancing banker in California").

3. Introduce yourself to a series of people using your ten-word self-introduction. Follow it with an open-ended question about the person, the place, or the situation.

4. Write ten open-ended questions you could ask anyone:

1. _____?
2. _____?
3. _____?
4. _____?
5. _____?
6. _____?
7. _____?
8. _____?
9. _____?
10. _____?

5. What are some of your emotional "Achilles' heels"? Topics that you are sensitive about and do not wish to have brought up in fights:

1._____?

2._____?

3._____?

*Prepare, prepare, practice, practice, practice, and practice.*

You want guidance? Listen carefully to your Boo and do the opposite!

# 9

# Self-Esteem: Where It Went and How to Get It Back

*Ingredients:*

1 rubber monster
1 brain in bag
3 squirt guns
1 bag large marshmallows
1 large brass bucket with large coins
2 hammers—squeak and electronic—in good working order

*Directions:*

Place before seventy relaxed adults and children

---

## Where It Went

The estimation of your self-worth and self-esteem is probably one of the most important life decisions you will ever make. Unfortunately, it is the rare individual who was formally instructed and coached in making that evaluation. Low self-worth and -esteem sabotage us at every level of our functioning existence. Various authors have suggested definitions for self-worth and self-esteem:

1. How great you think you are
2. How much you love and value yourself
3. How you feel about you—the reputation you have with yourself
4. Your feelings of competence and efficaciousness

It is difficult for people to love themselves in our highly competitive, comparative, and demanding society. We spend much of our early life trying to please parents, teachers, coaches, and religious leaders. We wrongly conclude that when we "earn" their approval, we are esteemed and valued. Unfortunately, that is quite temporary because we have to do it again and again to maintain our concept of worthiness. We are thus bound by others' external opinions. If they don't approve of us, if we don't meet their demands and expectations, we are devastated.

Who told you you were not worthy, not lovable? In today's society—everyone! Parents, peers, siblings, teachers, and religionists contributed those 180,000 negative personal comments. As phobocs—confirmed people pleasers—the early formative years can be exquisitely painful. There is frightfully little stability and continuity in our society:

- 50 percent of children live in separated, divorced, or remarried families.
- 68 percent have both parents working and largely unavailable.
- In 1890, 90 percent of grandmothers lived in the home. In 1990, only 7 percent did. There is virtually no generational continuity.
- 24 percent of us are born out of wedlock.
- 24 percent of us are born to drug- or alcohol-addicted parents.
- 25 percent of women and 16 percent of men will be sexually, psychologically, or physically abused by age eighteen.

- 50 percent of high school seniors have contemplated suicide.

- 30 percent of us are living in substandard conditions.

- 41 percent of young adults drink heavily every two to three weeks. 80 percent of college students do likewise.

- 10 percent of girls will become pregnant before they graduate from high school.

Combine these statistics with 180,000 derogatory topics and put-downs, a critical demanding society, and our phoboc personalities and it is little wonder that self-acceptance and self-love are lacking in many adults.

Despite being a physician, board-certified specialist, chief of the Kaiser Foundation Rehabilitation Center, and California Physician of the Year, I despised myself. If you had asked me to rate my self-esteem on a level of 1 to 10, I would have been a minus 14. I was a phobic. I defined myself entirely by my disorder. I viewed myself as defective and blemished, not as the perfect impeccable physician I thought I needed to be. I was filled with self-contempt. If I had won the Nobel Prize, the Pulitzer, and the Congressional Medal of Honor, it would not have helped. I knew that 97 percent of me was good stuff. I was an accomplished, dedicated, sympathetic physician, a devoted husband and father, but 3 percent of me was phoboc and 97 percent was a failing grade. Nobody had taught me differently. I love this chapter and my lecture on the topic because it was something I desperately needed to know.

Low self-esteem sabotages happiness and every other endeavor. It influences our vocational, financial, social, and marital choices, and yet no one teaches us how to make these all-important decisions. Low self-esteem increases the potential for destructive behaviors such as addiction, depression, sociopathy, eating disorders, jail time, school failure, divorce, and suicide. Societal platitudes do little to ease our distorted perceptions. Leo Buscaglia's message to love and hug everyone falls on deaf ears when you are battling restrictive phobias, obsessions, and destructive core beliefs. Bobby McFerrin's message to "Don't worry, be happy" doesn't seem to help either.

There are an estimated 170 million addicts in the United States—addicted to tobacco, alcohol, drugs, gambling, food, work, the Internet, and sex. Social psychologists have defined addictions as a *functional* form of self-medication to ease the pain we feel as incomplete human beings, to bring some sense of order to what we perceive as a chaotic world, or to soften our negative self-evaluations. Incredibly, there are approximately 170 million adults in the United States. That means that virtually every one of us has had or is currently dealing with a destructive addiction.

## The Empty Bucket

It all begins at birth. Most of us embrace what I call the empty bucket theory (i.e., we enter this world with an empty bucket). We then proceed to please the surrounding adults in order to get a token to fill our bucket. We wrongly conclude that tokens come from achievements, awards, and genetic endowments. You get a coin for getting an "A." (I demonstrate this in the Phobcase class by throwing oversized coins loudly into a brass kettle.) You receive a coin for being rich, good looking, strong, fast, and smart—a coin for driving an expensive car, being thin, having a good complexion, straight white teeth. But then you get a pimple and you have to take a coin out of the bucket. A little overweight and you lose another coin. Then you get a "C" in geometry and another coin comes out. We spend our whole lives trying to fill that ever-demanding bucket. Now, newborns don't know about buckets. They intuitively know that they are the center of the universe. They are not worried about designer diapers or cellulite on their thighs. They can satisfy those adoring adults by filling up a diaper: "Wow, look at that load—what a guy!"

But then, the destructive process begins. John Bradshaw, a famous counselor, calls it "soul murder"—an endless tirade of destructive, disparaging, demanding remarks; rejections; criticisms; sighs; and raised eyebrows that gradually undermine our self-worth. Were you wanted at birth? Were you an accident? Were you the desired sex? "We wanted a boy, but we were glad you came along." Were you put up for adoption at birth? If you were, it wasn't because your mother didn't agree with your philosophical beliefs. It wasn't anything personal. However, we may feel it as rejection. It is felt we bond in utero and thus, with adoption, there is a disturbance of that bond and a psychological scarring that may persist for years.

The onslaught continues in school. Teasing and put-downs are universal. Cruelty in school is an art form. If I feel badly about me, I will put you down and that elevates me. We pray to be average. Anything distinctive is fair game. You'll rapidly find out if your ears, nose, knees, calves, figure, skin, voice, hair, religion, or ethnicity are worthy of negative distinction. You are unmercifully compared to a 100 percentile, graded, and judged on everything you do or don't do.

Those 180,000 negative comments, 140,000 "no's," and 25,000 hours of negative tapes constantly contribute to our individual soul murder. Over time, we incorporate all that negativity into our self-talk. We no longer need enemies or adversaries. We become our own worst enemy, repeatedly voicing a myriad of negative labels. (I demonstrate this by bashing myself over the head with my infamous squeak or "breaking glass" electronic hammer for each deprecating remark. "I am stupid, shy, clumsy, worthless, blemished, fat, short, scrawny, weak, slow, inept; I can't dance; nobody likes me; I'm a failure" (bash, crash, smash).

Parents have a particular dilemma. If you compliment your child, they discount it. Parents are supposed to say, "You're the most beautiful, handsome, brightest child that was ever born." But, if they are human, they may say, on occasion, "You are a stupid moron, don't you ever do anything right? You're going to drive me insane; you're going to put me in an early grave; you are selfish, ungrateful, and a rotten punk." Negative parental remarks are four times more hurtful because they are coming from a supposedly nurturing, supportive source.

But, even if you have perfect parents, the moment you leave your doorstep, you will be exposed to a harsh, greedy society whose goal is to make you feel "less than" so you will buy more products. It begins with our obsession about weight. Thirty percent of seventh-graders have dieted. We have a $15 billion a year weight loss industry with a failure rate of 97 percent. Women are judged on looks and weight and not competence. Girls lose 80 percent of their self-esteem going from junior high to high school. In junior high, girls are superior to boys in math and science. In high school, that is reversed. Girls learn early that boys don't like smart girls and if you wish to be popular it's best to remain silent.

## Weight

There is a general belief that if you eat a low-fat vegetarian diet and exercise vigorously, you will be thin. There is a species that follows those dietary requirements, runs fourteen miles a day, and weighs six tons—elephants! There are 1,200 diet articles published every month in this country. In 1950, Miss America averaged 5 feet 7 inches and 150 pounds. In 1990, the contestants averaged 5 feet 10 inches and weighed 111 pounds—21 percent under ideal body weight. Thirty percent admit to eating disorders, especially induced vomiting, and 70 percent have had plastic surgery. Though Miss America and *Playboy* centerfolds decreased in weight, the average American woman's weight increased from 125 pounds in 1950 to 143 pounds today. It's very hard to compare favorably when the discrepancy is so large. (No pun intended.)

Today, 60 percent of Americans are overweight. Now, if you read beauty magazines (and what girl doesn't?), you will come to two very painful conclusions: you are ugly and you are fat. The average age of skin models is thirteen years. If you compare your skin at age sixteen you will already notice nature's toll—better buy those facial moisturizers. Mirrors are hell. Ninety percent of women and 70 percent of men hate their bodies, figures, or physiques. Remember, we are judging ourselves more critically through our phoboc predisposition. We are diminished at every turn and become contemptuous of our intellectual, psychological, social, and sexual adaptation. Someone once suggested if one morning every woman woke up satisfied with herself, the entire American economy would be devastated.

## Put-Downs

Then we get to school where passive aggressive put-downs become an art form. "Cruel and cool" is the order of the day. Teasing is universal.

If you were unaware of your flaws, your irreverent peers will gleefully and repeatedly point them out to you. I put you down and I feel better. But again, our sensitivity fares poorly against that ceaseless persistent barrage. Over time, we embrace a distorted self-image. Forty percent of adults felt that junior high and high school were the worst time of their lives whereas only 1 percent felt it was the best. Unfortunately, at that age, we haven't developed mature coping skills; we have an intense need to be accepted and an exaggerated concern for the WPTs. Being phoboc does not help, indeed, it increases our vulnerability.

School is where our judging begins. The focus is primarily on grades. We don't know that IQ is genetic or that a higher IQ allows one to process information rapidly. We begin to label and define ourselves as "smart" or "dumb" or as "A" or "D" students. We don't know that IQ and grades contribute less than 20 percent to the prediction of success, that personality traits, persistence, perseverance, empathy, optimism, motivation, diligence, responsibility, and our ability to read and work with people are far more important. Phobocs rate high in humanistic categories. We are not "C" people because we get "C" grades. It is reputed that President George Bush and Secretary of State Colin Powell had "C" averages in college. Those are not average men. As young students, we don't know that and it leads to low grades and more self-deprecation and destructive self-labeling. The process of soul murder continues unabated.

Finally, in our quest for love and affection, we may give up our self and our childhood. Our empathetic responsible inclination may lead us to prematurely assume adult family roles. We may raise mother's babies or take over managing the family finances. We may get jobs at an early age to supplement family income. I always had jobs, beginning at age ten, delivering newspapers, selling newspapers and magazines, cutting lawns, and becoming bottle wiper supreme in the local liquor store. I became the little man when I gladly contributed my meager earnings to the family coffers. Little wonder that years later I would find myself a workaholic, often with three jobs even while going to medical school. Surviving childhood is not necessarily good preparation for adulthood. Out of all this negativity comes a destructive internal dialogue. We no longer need external enemies. We now translate those 180,000 negative *you*'s into *I*'s. The lower our self-esteem, the more fuel for our Boo and the louder our destructive internal voice becomes. Many of us end up with utter self-contempt. The process of soul murder is complete—we hate ourselves.

## How to Get It Back: Correcting Soul Murder

What if I told you that everything you learned about self-worth and self-esteem was probably wrong? What if I told you that we were born with a full bucket that cannot be diminished? What if I told you that you don't have to accomplish anything to be deemed worthy? We are not human doings; we are human beings. What if I told you that there is no universal standard for worth? While we need a Mr. Trump in our modern society to create jobs with his massive projects, his lack of training in blowguns would greatly diminish his worth in a primitive jungle setting. What if I told you that worth cannot be based on genetic endowments or possessions? So it cannot be based on beauty, figure, strength, speed, IQ; your bank account, stock holdings, house size or location; or the clothes you wear. What if I told you that true human worth is impossible to determine?

You have to invoke the concept of karma—everyone has an important role in society. Why do we need criminals? Well, if we didn't have crooks, an awful lot of people would be out of work. The entire judicial system, drug and law enforcement, jailors, parole officers, bail bondsmen, and social workers would be standing in the unemployment line. If we didn't have garbage men, our cities would be overrun by rats feeding on the decaying waste.

A young woman wrote to Dear Abby that her husband, a gas station attendant, wasn't going to his twenty-fifth high school reunion because of what he saw as his lowly occupation. His wife described him as a loving father and a wonderful husband and provider. I always ask my class how many people it took for each of them to get there on a given night. With pride in their independent spirit, they always answer "one!" As a matter of fact, it has been estimated to take closer to 10,000! (Unless you grow your own food, manufacture your own clothes, mine the ore to make the steel to build your car, drill for the oil to make the gasoline to run it, manufacture the 27,000 parts that make up a modern car, build the roads and bridges that allowed you to get here, construct the building you're in, make the chair you're sitting on, and the table supporting your notebook.) We are totally and inescapably dependent, including the lowly fellow who might pump your gasoline for you to get here. Let's hope he goes to the reunion.

Finally, what if I told you that self-worth cannot be diminished? Let's embrace the existentialist concept that we are worthy simply because we were born—simply because we exist. Fifty-five million sperm competed to be you and only one succeeded. You are a winner. Of all the fifty-five billion people that were ever born, there has only been one you. You can prove that by your DNA. If that is so, except for Dolly the cloned sheep, it proves that you are unique. Unique means incomparable. You cannot be compared with anyone. You don't earn worth. Worth means something of value—if you were born, exist, and are unique, then you are worthy. Someone said when Lucille Ball died, there would never be another one of her and that is so. When Sammy Davis Jr. died, they said the same thing. Well, you're in a very elite group. There will never be another you. We don't earn worth— we *claim it*.

Now is the time to declare your freedom from all those who shamed and tried to diminish you, including your siblings, peers, parents, teachers, authority figures, and religionists. We often wrongly believe if we are not deemed worthy in the eyes of our parents or loved ones that we are not worthy. Nonsense! They were wrong. You alone determine self-worth. You are worthy because you exist. You don't have to be perfect to be worthy. You can fail, make mistakes, weigh too much, be a fallible human being, and still be worthy. Worth cannot be diminished. Your bucket is full.

## Saving F.A.C.E.

The first step is to forgive ourselves. When we forgive ourselves, we heal our guilt. More important is to accept ourselves. When we accept ourselves, we heal our shame. That acceptance has to be unconditional and you now know what that means. I accept me with my faults, mistakes, failings, phobias; my looks, breasts, or penis size; my obsessions—weight, figure, or physique—etc without conditions. I say this daily, aloud, looking in the mirror, making eye contact with that unique, worthy reflection I see. Further, I vow to be self-caring, to practice "constructive selfishness," to take care of my needs and to make me number one. That is a tough concept for us people-pleasing phobocs. We take care of everyone in our universe with the exception of one person—"us." That has to stop. If I get my needs met, I will have a lot more to give. Ask, "What is best for me?" Cough. In this society, a woman has to have a temperature of 103°F to be excused from her family responsibilities. However, if her temperature is only 102.8°F, and her pneumonia involves only one lung, she is still expected to make dinner, do the dishes, bathe the children, and clean out the cat box before she collapses in bed. I wish I were kidding. Get in the new habit of including your needs at the top of the list. Finally, when you F.A.C.E. yourself, you Forgive, Accept, and Care for you, and you will Esteem yourself. I call it saving F.A.C.E.

## Embellishing Esteem

If self-esteem is not based on accomplishments, genetic endowments, or possessions, how do we assess it? Self-esteem is based on conscious volitional traits. It is based on integrity, morality, honesty, sympathy, empathy, responsibility, loyalty, dedication, perseverance, courage, dependability, motivation, persistence, effort, caring, trustworthiness, kindness, commitment, loving, and optimism. Since these are conscious, chosen acts, we can enhance our self-esteem daily by doing commendable acts. It is based on perceived efficaciousness, a feeling of self-competence and self-confidence: "I can handle it." These are all characteristic phoboc traits. We are good, worthy human beings and as such we have a right to esteem ourselves highly. It is an internal evaluation only, innate and undeniable, completely devoid of external impact. "I am great, fantastic, terrific, sensational, a genius, and a living legend and it's not up for discussion." You are the final judge. "I am worthy because I say so." Wouldn't you have loved to hear these acclamations when you were growing up? Well, you can voice them now. What wonderful power. My evaluation is noncompetitive; the competition is only with me. It is noncomparative. Someone said comparison is the harshest form of social injustice. When you constantly compare yourself with everyone superior, you reinforce your ineptitude. Everyone's successes will reinforce your failures and everyone's accomplishments will cast a negative shadow on your life. Stop comparing! Depression is reinforced by negative self-evaluation and destructive self-comparisons. Recognize these behaviors and stop them. Use your thought stoppage and challenge sheet exercises. Continuously monitor your internal dialogue; make sure it is nurturing and supportive. Challenge any destructive programs and restructure them to enhance your feelings of worth and esteem. Continue to voice your personal affirmations. We become what we say, so say them daily, tape-record them, say them out loud. Challenge and change all your destructive labels and beliefs. You are the giant now and you are the master of your bag. Continually ask, "What am I saying to myself, is it helping?" If it is not helpful then challenge it on paper and refute it. Recognize and continually challenge your Boo. The higher you esteem yourself the quieter the Boo voice becomes. Challenge others' expectations of you. You are not on earth to meet anyone's expectations, including your own. If you haven't achieved all of your goals—lower them.

Self-esteem and self-worth are not permanently set in childhood. They can be enhanced anytime you choose. It is a lifetime process. You are the giant now and the master of your bag. You are worthy simply because you were born—simply because you exist.

Know thyself.
Accept thyself.
Esteem thyself.
Love thyself.

*Self-esteeming affirmations*

I am a unique, special individual.
I am intelligent, creative, warm, compassionate, dedicated, loyal, and responsible.

I accept and love myself unconditionally.

I am positive, energetic, and indefatigable.

I love life and I love my special talents.

I am worthy simply because I was born.

I like people and they like me.

I am so unique that there will never be another me.

I am worthy and lovable.

I am a genius and a living legend.

I am somebody and I am the person I choose to be.

I am my own best friend.

I am crazy about me.

## Chapter 9 Highlights

1. You are worthy simply because you were born—simply because you exist.

2. You don't earn worthiness; you claim it.

3. We are not human doings; we are human beings. Never value yourself on your accomplishments.

4. Rather reward your persistent effort.

5. To be twice as successful, you have to fail twice as often.

6. Self-esteem is purely an internal decision and completely devoid of external input.

7. Never judge worth on the basis of genetic endowments or acquisitions.

8. Worth is based on conscious, voluntary traits and can be enhanced daily.

9. You are genetically unique and thus incomparable. Stop comparing and competing. The only competition is with yourself.

10. Love and accept yourself unconditionally. There will never be another you.

## **Chapter 9 Assignment**

Do relaxation exercise fifteen to thirty minutes daily.

Continue your phobia diary.

Update your victory card.

Practice your hierarchies.

1. Mirror exercise: Make eye contact for two minutes daily; say nice things about yourself. Forgive yourself for all transgressions by saying, "I love you unconditionally."

2. Write down, ten to a card, fifty things you like about yourself, nice things you've done, things you've accomplished. Tape a card on your bathroom mirror and read it each day. Change the card weekly and keep writing more things.

3. Write a list of ten "shoulds" that might not be true for you now. Change them to "I could if I choose to."

4. Call a friend once a week. Make one new friend per month.

5. Find a way to be of service—volunteer.

6. Make a "balance calendar." Include work, play, growth, and spiritual pursuits. Try to get your life more in balance. How much time do you spend on each category?

7. Write a letter to yourself as a three- or four-year-old child telling what you've accomplished as an adult. Tell about how big you are, how much money you have, your credit line, your cat or dog, your marriage or children. At four, did you know you would be a powerful huge adult? Of course not!

Self-worth is a choice, a process, and a journey. Invest in yourself by taking human growth/development courses. Join supportive, nurturing groups and seek professional help.

You are a human being and not a human doing.

Don't compete. Don't compare. *You are great because you say so! You are worthy just because you were born.*

# 10

# Codependency and How to Cure Any Psychological Disorder

***Ingredients*** *(the usual):*

1 rubber Boo monster
1 squirt gun
1 brain in bag
1 bag large marshmallows
1 squeak and 1 "breaking glass" electronic hammer
(reminders of basic Phobease principles)

***Directions:***

Place before seventy bold, assured, fearless adults and children.

## Codependency

Many years ago my wife was studying for her psychology degree. She invited me to attend a weekend workshop on codependency. I had read several books on the subject but never studied the topic intensely and thought that it might be an interesting class. I wasn't aware of any particular relationship to phoboc patients but I would soon find I was wrong. Phobocs, because of their people pleasing focus, are extremely likely to manifest codependent tendencies.

Authors have proposed a number of definitions:

1. An excess focus on others

2. A person who chronically neglects himself or herself in favor of a sick, needy other

3. Someone who finds his or her identity exclusively in caring for others

4. One who organizes his or her life around another person

5. A loss of self in favor of a sick, needy other

6. An excessive attraction to exciting, addicted, unhealthy, needy people

There is a codependent tendency in all of us but it becomes a problem when the degree of self-abandonment is excessive. I needed to take a class to find out that I had strong issues of codependency myself and, in fact, they were instrumental in my decision to become a physician. It is not an accident that the helping professions have the second highest incidence of anxiety disorders. It is those same personality traits—sensitivity, empathy, sympathy—and an awesome sense of responsibility that are characteristics found in codependent persons. It often has a shame-based origin. Decreased self-worth and self-esteem fuels co-enabling tendencies. Disruptive, dysfunctional, and non-nurturing family settings foster the belief that one can be redeemed by taking care of needy human beings. If I feel that I am blemished, defective, incompetent, or unworthy, I can restore my worth by choosing a noble profession—what better one than nursing or medicine? As a young man, when I told people I was going to be a doctor, I received instant adulation and acceptance. Sick patients likewise glorify their attending physician. Medicine is the guaranteed road to acceptance. I recognized the perversion of my vocational choice when I returned from vacation. Standing at morning rounds, tanned and relaxed, while the nurse gave my patient reports: "Mr. Smith has a temperature of 104 degrees," "Mrs. Smith threw up a pint of blood," "Mr. Jones had two seizures." I was struck that first day back that I had made a strange choice. Days later, the emotional impact of such human misery faded into the emotional numbness that allowed me to continue in my chosen field for over forty-five years.

## Codependent Beliefs

All codependents embrace three beliefs that perpetuate their disorder:

1. "I don't deserve better. I am not worthy and will be lucky if I find anybody."

2. "I only deserve second best." A recent article described a young lady who was shot twice in the head and once in the shoulder by her boyfriend. She spent four months in the hospital but still vowed that she loved him and would marry him when he got out of jail in twenty years. She said, "My friends told me I'm crazy, but they don't pay my bills. I love him and I'm going to marry him." Perhaps going on to the third belief might explain her behavior.

3. "I can't survive alone and I won't find another. I will buy your alcohol and drugs, I will call in work excuses to give you time to recover from your excess—anything to maintain our relationship." Sure he shot her three times, but that's better than not having anybody.

Codependent "love" is desperately needy love. It is love at any price. It is described as smothering, enmeshed, judgmental, conditional, undisciplined, unbalanced, dependent, manipulative, suspicious, jealous, exploitative, irresponsible, controlling, and restrictive. There are no clearly defined boundaries. The energies of the relationship are tilted toward one sick individual. It is the opposite of a mature love relationship that is supportive, nurturing, trusting, and balanced—where the needs of both individuals are the primary consideration.

Codependents can't end destructive relationships. They are trapped by their destructive beliefs. The relationship is doomed from the onset and predictably leads to financial and psychological devastation. This reaffirms the codependent's feelings of self-worthlessness and further erodes their self-esteem. Since there is little self-caring, I view your problem as my problem. All my energies are directed outward. That external focus serves to distract me from my own personal problems; thus, I can maintain my destructive behavior. The eventual failure of the relationships adds to my shame. It is the most destructive emotion. Shame is the pervasive premise that I am flawed, defective, inadequate, totally unworthy, blemished, unacceptable, undeserving, a fake, a fraud, and absolutely unlovable. Shame means I am a mistake; it is a sickness of the soul. It robs us of joy, often leads to seeking solace in drugs and alcohol and frequently leads to depression.

Yet the cycle is frequently repeated. Why would anyone make the mistake of marrying three alcoholics? Why don't they learn from their poor choices? The answer is simply that codependents need and seek out those sick, needy people. The cycle consists of three stages:

1. *Rescuer:* "I feel worth only when I abandon myself in favor of that desperately compromised other. The martyr role suits me well. I crave it."

2. *Victim:* "As a result of my poor choice I become victimized. I suffer psychic, physical, and financial ruin. I resent it intensely. After all I've done for you, I then become the . . ."

3. *Persecutor:* "I direct my anger at my hapless partner. If the relationship ends, I must find another very soon to fulfill my obligations to rescue and the cycle beings anew."

Codependents tend to be crisis addicts; often they have been victims of physical and/or psychological abandonment by their families. Family dissension and turmoil are common in co-dependents and lead to what is dubbed, "the excited miseries." Codependents are emotional overreactors and they seek out partners who fulfill their requirements. It often leads to psychic exhaustion and destructive addictions. One pays a high price for constantly assuming the role of rescuer.

Women in our society are often subtly trained to become codependent. Snow White entered the messy house of the seven dwarves and the first thing she did was clean it. Tammy Wynette suggested you should "stand by your man." Ptooey. Let him take care of himself. Certainly the rigid feminine roles have softened in succeeding generations but still remain ensconced in many societies. Codependency is the dependent rescued by the dependent. An admixture that is doomed to fail. The deficits of each partner become magnified in relationships that demand maturity and responsibility. Codependents are often indecisive and have difficulty solving problems.

## Sick Families—Sick Secrets

Codependents are often brought up in "sick," dysfunctional families. Such families often fail to resolve conflicts and issues because solving them demands facing problems. Instead, a child in that environment learns to keep the secret. If one or both parents are alcoholic, children learn not to bring friends home, lest they find Mom and Dad passed out, covered with their own vomit. Early codependent training begins when children invent excuses for Mom or Dad's absence from school plays, teacher conferences, or PTA meetings. They learn early to live the lie, though never directly spoken, they learn to keep the family's sick secret. They lie about family dynamics and create a dysfunctional family fantasy. "My family is loving and wonderful." In truth, Mother is addicted to prescription drugs and Dad has had multiple affairs and is abusive to his wife and children. However, at Thanksgiving, Mother makes the best turkey and stuffing. We learn to deal with these early family crises by "numbing" out. We learn not to feel—it's too painful. We survive by adopting a protective emotional trance—a state that often persists into adulthood. We learn not to get too enthusiastic or to plan too far in to the future because the chance for canceled dreams is high. Over time, we may detach and dissociate. The early environment robs us of joy and often leads to depression and sometimes thoughts of suicide. We often personalize the parental dilemma and feel our behaviors have contributed heavily to the situation.

Phobocs become masters at reading people, finding out their needs and attempting to resolve them. We are often better at taking care of others' needs than our own. Self-caring is often non-existent. We learn early that people will love and accept us if we please them, so we do. As a result, we give, give, give, and ask for nothing in return. Remember, I can't ask for anything because I don't believe I deserve it. I feel uncomfortable if I receive anything and so the giving imbalance persists. We become loving martyrs. Even if my partner beats me, fails to contribute emotionally or financially, steals from me, refuses to work or help in any way, I can't leave him because he needs me and I love him. The three destructive codependent beliefs are in full command here.

Codependents feel worthy only when they are needed. If I'm not needed, I can worry. Worry feels like caring, but in essence is a painful, unproductive habit. Worry is an epidemic of hidden "what if" questions. When you worry, you pay the emotional price as if the event were happening now. If worry does not lead to constructive behaviors, it serves no other purpose than to make you feel badly. Worry does nothing to solve tomorrow's problems, but robs today of its joy.

## Worry Tools

1. Capture them on paper.

2. Rearrange according to "SUDs" level.

3. Write worst fears for fifteen minutes or tape-record and listen for fifteen minutes.

4. Create worst case scenarios and read for forty-five minutes daily until you diffuse the anxiety that accompanies those thoughts.

5. Get in the "here and now." Is it happening now? If not, then say, "I will handle it."

"Worry is an old man with bent head, carrying a load of feathers and thinking it is lead." The result of all this turmoil is frustration and anger. Frustration because I am trapped; I see no solution to my dilemma. I become angry—angry with everyone and everything. I behave codependently because it makes me feel good. It doesn't work well, but it works. The incredible part is that we don't know why. We don't know we were born with a vulnerable phoboc predisposition that leads us inexorably to our codependency. Your upbringing provided you with little effective problem solving or effective coping skills and you don't know that either. Like everyone else, you just do the best that you can with what little tools you possess.

## Recovering from Codependency

The first step in healing codependency or, indeed any psychological problem, is to come out of denial—to acknowledge and accept it. Healing begins when you end up with both feet in the proverbial gutter. You see no way out. The day my feet slipped off the curb and I ended up gutter-bound was the day I received those two tickets to the Olympic games. I knew I couldn't handle the claustrophobic challenge. I knew I would have a severe panic attack and be found out. I knew if I didn't go, it would be a horrible disappointment for my son. I was trapped. I thought very seriously about that pistol I had purchased. Perhaps that possibility helped me acknowledge the true depth of my restrictive disorder. That night, as you recall, a local TV news program presented a segment about an organization that was having phenomenal success treating phobias. It was an easy choice. From the gutter, I made the call that changed my life. I was out of denial.

Over the years, I have come to understand the myth of Phoenix. Human beings, in their despair, often rise from those proverbial ashes. I was about to make my flight. We come out of denial when we give up, when we hit bottom. I can recall literally hundreds of crisis calls from patients whose very livelihood, marriage, relationship, or life was compromised by their anxiety, and they, like me, made a decision to do whatever it took to cure. When the pain of staying in the gutter is greater than the fear of change, good things will happen. I always advise support persons or family to help their anxious loved ones skip gently into the gutter. Don't do anything that would delay the venture. In the gutter you show a willingness to face yourself and accept your deficits. Remember, "accept" does not mean liking or condoning. You are willing to examine and challenge your core issues and beliefs. For codependents, it revolves around those three destructive beliefs:

1. "I don't deserve better"—Yes you do.
2. "I only deserve second best"—No you don't.
3. "I need to take care of the needy human because I will never find another"—No, you need to take care of yourself and then you will find many others.

From the gutter comes the all-important commitment to cure. I am now prepared to follow any path that shows promise. I will seek professional help, whether individual, group, insight, or cognitive behavioral therapy. I will persist until I cure. I will additionally seek help for my addiction I now recognize. They are often self-medicating, avoidant behaviors and I know now that avoidance is the basis of all anxiety disorders. I will join a twelve-step program. I will persist until I cure.

If I'm in a current destructive relationship, I can identify it with one question. Is this relationship balanced? I must stop rescuing. I must realize if a new suitor "rings my chimes," I should run. I might choose a "buddy conservator" whom I trust to counsel me on my partner choices. It might be that my fourth alcoholic, wife-beating parolee might not be a wise choice at this time of my life. I must learn to help others only if they ask and then only if I choose. I must be aware of the dangers of being attracted to the "excited miseries" and look, instead, initially for the boring and mundane. Stop looking for happiness in other people. This is the time to "FACE" yourself. *Forgive*— you did the best you could with the tools you had at the time. *Accept* yourself unconditionally with your faults, blemishes, phobias, or weight. We are all fallible people. It is human to fail and make mistakes and it is okay. It is time to *Care* for myself. It is important that I declare myself number one and start asking, "What is best for me?" Look in that mirror and say, "I love you unconditionally" and keep saying it until you mean it. Finally, *Esteem* yourself. You are worthy simply because you were born. You are worthy, independent of your accomplishments, and worthy because you claim it. You are worthy because you continue to strive and persevere. I don't need anyone to give me permission to esteem myself highly. It is my decision alone and I choose it.

I need to define and establish boundaries and relationship requirements on paper. I have to learn to be comfortable alone. I need to recognize the triggers that have gotten me into trouble in the past and find alternative ways to deal with my neediness. I have to deal with my indecisiveness. I have to make choices and be willing to accept the fact that others will probably make poor decisions. That's all right now. I know human beings fail and make mistakes and it's okay. I have to trust in my choices. All of life is learning and any results I get will teach me something. There is no right or wrong—only learning. If you don't make choices, someone else will make them for you. If you constantly look for answers from partners, therapists, counselors, even cults, you will never practice the internal process of making mature decisions.

## Self-Improvement

Part of the commitment to cure requires improving the self. You need to learn life skills—assertiveness so you can honestly ask for what you want and need and conversational skills to allow you to be more comfortable in social settings and to expand your ability to meet a more diverse selection of possible partners. Mastering the art of arguing will allow you to negotiate effectively and safely and diffuse hostile encounters. Risk and grow. Remember comfort is not your goal. Conquer your phobias and obsessions. Practice disciplined non-avoidance. Become independent. What things have you delegated to others? As chief of rehabilitation, I frequently dealt with family crises brought on when the primary wage earner suffered a debilitating stroke. Often the wife of many years had no knowledge of family finances or investments. She had never dealt with checking accounts, never lubricated the family car, and never programmed the VCR. Make a conscious decision to do everything you don't do. Find out if you have a will or trust and their specific contents. Ask what stocks, bonds, or debts you have incurred. Learn the location of safe deposit boxes and important documents.

Embrace selfish self-caring. Make yourself number one. Take care of your needs. Ask what is best for you. Demand balance in giving and receiving in your relationships. Ask assertively for what you need to achieve equal distribution of responsibilities. Your new governing affirmation might be, "I deserve the best." Say that a few hundred times and then demand it. Seek serenity, slow down, meditate, master your relaxation skills, and just mellow out. Challenge your low frustration tolerance. Stay behind slower drivers, choose the longest checkout line on purpose, and calmative breathe. Study yoga, chi gong, or tai chi. Learn to feel your feelings. If you have trouble identifying them, start a feelings diary. There are only four basic feelings: mad, glad, sad, and scared. Identify them when you are experiencing emotions. I had learned in my upbringing to discount anger. When frustrating or annoying situations arose, my wife would ask if I was mad. I told her honestly, "I don't know." Using a diary, I often decided twenty-four hours later that I was really "ticked off." Over time, with the use of the diary, I began to recognize earlier manifestations of discord and gave myself permission to express my new-felt feelings.

## Goals

Set specific goals. Rudderless ships have difficulty staying on course. Goals should be short, mid, and long term. They must be written down and assigned completion dates. They should be behavioral, personal, and important. Consider rewards for accomplishing them. Make yourself more interesting. Take martial arts classes, look at night school catalogs and attend some courses. Start or restart a unique hobby. Take a weight lifting or boxing class. Go to a carnival and take some challenging rides. Carnivals are safe places to challenge fears. Do it. Learn new skills—get proficient in computers or learn a musical instrument. Volunteer and find a service project. Interesting people attract interesting people.

Redefine your self-worth and self-esteem. Use your newly learned definitions: "I am worthy because I was born and exist." "I am not what I do." "I refuse to define who I am by my disorder." "I am not a phoboc but a loving father, lecturer, author, speaker, grandfather, tap dancer, gardener, marathon runner, and championship ballroom dancer who has a phobia." Make sure you remain noncomparative. Compete only with yourself and be your own best nurturing friend. Finally, commit to a cure and then commit to a cure and if I forgot to mention it, commit to a cure. You deserve it.

Know thyself.
Esteem thyself.
Heal thyself.
Love thyself.

## Chapter 10 Highlights

1. Make yourself number one; you deserve it.
2. Avoid the excited miseries. Have a trusted friend prescreen your companions.
3. Seek serenity; slow down and mellow out.
4. Don't look outside of yourself to find happiness.
5. Stop rescuing sick, needy others.
6. Be independent and make yourself more interesting.
7. Constructive selfishness means taking care of yourself.
8. Establish protective boundaries.
9. Demand that relationships be balanced.
10. There are many pathways. Follow any that lead you to peace of mind.
11. Help only if asked and then only if you choose to do so.
12. Love yourself unconditionally.

## Chapter 10 Assignment

Do your daily relaxation.

Exercise fifteen to thirty minutes daily.

Continue your phobia diary.

Update your victory card.

1. Write down the positive self-talk statements that appeal to you; keep several copies in strategic places (e.g., car, home, work, wallet, purse). Read them before you face a phobic challenge. Read your victory card too.

2. Continue your hierarchies until you have climbed to the top of each ladder. Write down every victory and reward yourself.

3. Brag about your phoboc victories. Your brain loves to hear it. Mail me a victory post card—or ten.

4. Identify and list family things you don't do or know little about. Do them.

5. Define your personal boundaries in a relationship.

6. Commit to a cure.

7. Re-read important chapters.

   Face the fear correctly and it will disappear. Good luck!

# 11

# How to Be Happy
# Though Phoboc

**Ingredients:**

An assortment of hats:

    1 wizard

    1 collapsible top hat

    1 jester

    1 Pair Mickey Mouse ears

    1 Mad Hatter

1 "Eat Right" mug

1 hourglass

1 brain in bag

**Directions:**

Place before seventy dynamic, confident, victorious Boo-killing adults and children.

# Happy

I always tell my class that to give this lecture, you need to be a wizard or a guru. I am neither, but I own a magnificent tall wizard hat and with a flourish, I produce it and put it on. I promise them that this won't be "If God gives you lemons, make lemonade." God is not in the citrus business. As I told you previously, God did not give you your phobia or obsession; Mother Nature did and as you recall, Mother Nature has no conscience. You could invoke the existentialist view that the universe is totally indifferent to your plight. We are 100 percent responsible for our own happiness. The nice part is that creating happy, like other Phobease doctrines, is a learnable skill. I will give you three powerful rules that will immediately enhance the pleasure in your life.

You recall I was severely phobic for thirty-one difficult years. I achieved my phoboc cure in August of 1984. For the first time in my adult life, I could attend movies, fly, bus, camel, and cruise without fear. Seven months later I was diagnosed with a malignant melanoma and was advised I would have to undergo a massive radical surgical procedure. I had a mole on my back for years. Twenty-five years previously, I showed it to a professor of dermatology in medical school. He said, "Don't worry, it's a junctional naevus and they never become malignant." He was wrong. It started to itch and one day in the hospital cafeteria, where most doctors get their consultations, I showed it to our chief of dermatology. He said, "I don't like the looks of that. Come to my office this afternoon and we'll perform a biopsy." The next day, he appeared at my office pale and ashen. He said, "The test shows a grade four invasive melanoma." In hours, I changed from a complacent phobic into a patient. I endured endless blood tests, radioactive uptake studies, and multiple CT scans. (I'm glad I had cured my claustrophobia!) The verdict was in. The tumor site drained into my right axilla (armpit) and I needed immediate dual site surgery. The primary lesion was removed with a large chunk of my back and I underwent the same procedure performed on women with breast cancer. The surgeon removed my entire right axilla. As I lay in recovery, I decided life was not fair. As a matter of fact, that's true.

Life just "is." I thought this really "sucks." After thirty-one years I cure my phobia and now I have this. I asked my surgeon if I would be alive to attend my son's college graduation in July—four months hence. He said, "Yes, if the tumor doesn't spread to your brain." Every phoboc physician needs to hear something like that.

For the first time in my life, I had to deal with my own mortality. I had been in practice for twenty-five years at that time and I had never missed one day of work for illness. Even though severely phoboc, I got up every day and went to work. When you treat sick people every day and you're never ill, you come to the conclusion that patients get diseases but doctors don't. I believe that people learn best when you drop a piano on their head and I don't mean the flat part, I'm talking about the sharp corner. That piano on my head was a subtle reminder that life is finite, including mine. I began to ask some important philosophical questions and in turn searched for the profound answers. What are you doing here on earth? Do you have a purpose? How do you bring happiness into your world in the face of a potentially life-threatening illness? I began to research the subject extensively. I studied the Eastern beliefs about reincarnation. I liked the idea of coming back and seeing how things worked out. I read a wonderful best-selling book by Harold Kushner called *When Bad Things Happen to Good People*. It was the rehabilitation "bible." When patients asked, "Why did this stroke or heart attack happen to me?" I recommended reading that book. Harold Kushner is a rabbi. Rabbi simply means "teacher." A rabbi is not a divine position and thus they are permitted to marry. Kushner married and had one child. That boy was born with a strange disease called progyeria, a peculiar disorder where the child ages rapidly and at age thirteen resembles a 100-year-old man. Rabbi Kushner's child died. Kushner, who had devotedly served God his entire life asked Him "Why?" In his search, he realized that God didn't cause his son's premature death. His son was the victim of Mother Nature's impersonal wrath. He came to realize his loving God was not the cause of his son's death. God was not putting bullet holes in eight-year-olds' heads to punish parents or teach them a lesson. Bad things happen to good people because of that risk we tacitly assume when we are born. It is up to us to find important meanings in tragic events.

## Happy When

However, Kushner, like me, began to investigate the question of happy in American society. He wrote another book, not as well known, called *When All You Have Is Not Enough*. He pondered why people with a nice house, a three-car garage, and good jobs were not happy. He realized in America, we frequently practice what he calls, "happy when." "I will be happy when the baby is toilet trained." "I'll be happy when the children are in school." "I'll be happy when they leave the nest." "I'll be happy when my pain is gone." "I'll be happy when I cure my phobia." "When I retire." "When I find my soul mate." I'll be happy then.

The problem with "happy when" is that it negates the present moment. It delays a positive moment in favor of a larger future event. Three thousand Americans never got to practice "happy when" when terrorists snuffed out their lives on September 11, 2001. Fifty thousand Armenians were killed in a massive earthquake; 7,000 Hondurans were killed by mudslides; and 15,000 Colombians were suffocated when a volcano that had been dormant for over 300 years suddenly exploded and buried them under fifteen feet of mud, silt, and lava. The problem with "happy when" is that there is no guarantee that there will be a tomorrow "when."

The Constitution guarantees you the right to the pursuit of happiness. Unfortunately, it is a rare individual indeed who has been taught how to be happy. The best definition I've read of happy is by Barry Kaufman who said, "Happiness is the feeling you have when you are not unhappy." Doesn't sound too profound but it most certainly is. Kaufman was saying that we create unhappy with ill-chosen negative thoughts. When we eliminate those destructive creations, we arrive at the empty unencumbered basic mind that is the essence of happiness and contentment. We are asked to pay attention to our thought processing and challenge and eliminate thoughts that lead to unhappy. Sound familiar? CBT at its finest. He doesn't require you to think happy or utter positive statements because that creates pressure to constantly create "good" thoughts. Rather, by just emptying the mind of intrusive thoughts we are led to our empty brain, our basic happy state.

Some people promote suggestive platitudes. As stated previously, Leo Buscaglia suggested we love and hug everybody. Bobby McFerrin sang, "Don't Worry, Be Happy." It is difficult to follow such advice when your phobias and obsessions are strangling your very existence. It is hard when you are dealing with unresolved personal issues. Rather than simple aphorisms, you must start on page one and do the healing work that comes from effective psycho-educational, cognitive behavioral, and experiential desensitization programs. There are no shortcuts.

## Our Harsh Society

This is a difficult society in which to be happy. It is highly individualistic, comparative, and competitive. As previously mentioned, it has been estimated that there are 170 million addicts in the United States—addicted to cigarettes, alcohol, drugs, gambling, work, food, sex, bingo, and the Internet. Social psychologists have defined addictions as a "functional" form of self-medication to ease the pain we feel as incomplete human beings, a method to soften our negative self-evaluations and a way to bring a sense of order to our chaotic world. What if I told you that there are approximately 170 million adults in the United States? That means that every one of us has embraced or currently is embracing at least one destructive addiction. This society doesn't actively promote happiness. We are constantly bombarded with negative messages. "No pain, no gain." "It's a jungle out there." Ninety-five percent of what you read or hear on the news is negative. Our brain bags are filled with garbage. My grandmother told me when I was five that "If you whistle in the morning, you will cry at night." That's an interesting message to a young phoboc who's trying to fill his bag with useful information. Conclusion: if I am happy in the morning, I will have to pay with sadness in the evening. "A whistling boy and clucking hen come to no good end." "If you sing on Friday, you will cry on Monday." You better beware of happy in this society because you have to pay a hefty price. Other sayings we hear are just as disturbing: "Happy as an idiot"—implication: if you want to be happy, you have to be mentally compromised. "Let's go down to the bar for a few laughs"—implication: you have to be drunk to be happy. "Okay, put away your toys, that's enough play time." Now happy is being rationed. Ours has been labeled "a hurry-up society." We get rushed through childhood so we can get a job and start paying taxes. Add the 180,000 personal negative comments, the 140,000 no's and the 25,000 hours of negative tapes and you have a preponderance of negative joyless messages crammed into your bag.

One interesting study followed four-year-olds for a day to count the number of times they laughed and giggled. In a twenty-four-hour period, they averaged 325 laughs and giggles. The same study followed adults for a day and counted an average of 15 laughs and giggles. So where did the 310 laughs and giggles go? In this society, they may be beaten out, cynicized out, matured out, raped out, teased out, shamed out, or compared out. The goal of this chapter and course is to figure out how to get those 310 laughs and giggles back.

### $1,000 Seminar

When I cured my claustrophobia I became a seminar junkie. In the past I couldn't attend such classes because they had an annoying habit of closing doors, and I couldn't tolerate that. I took a series of three human growth development courses that were in vogue at that time. They began with the basic principles and progressed to a more intense session on important personal relationships. The final course was titled "Success and Leadership." As the title implied, it was about becoming a successful leader. It was a seven-day workshop, eighteen hours a day, with a tuition of $1,000. The first thing the leader did was take a huge hourglass—it contained an hour's worth of sand— and turned it over. He announced that if at any time in the next week, the sand ran out, the seminar was over and all of us would forfeit our $1,000 tuition. Now, to a prudent physician, that sounded like a significant threat. Now there was a problem. The first three days of the seminar there was no talking to anyone except the leader, whether in the room or out there was a total restriction of interaction. They wanted three days of self-reflection. No TV, no newspapers, no phone calls, and no strategizing over how to handle the hourglass challenge. The rules were simple: if you felt the sand was running low, you got up without asking and turned the hourglass over. What was the intended lesson? Why did they place so much importance on this exercise? It raised several issues. Responsibility—someone was going to have to pay attention to the diminishing sand and take the initiative. Awareness—we were intensely focused on the presentation and you had to be cognizant of the status of the sand. Getting more philosophical—the sand, which represents our lives, is ceaselessly draining. It never slows down. There is no room for "happy when." What about the sand that had already fallen? What does that represent in a life? The past, of course. The lesson of the spent sand is that you cannot change the past. Even God can't change the past. All you can do is learn from it. We are all creating our own autobiographies. Consider that yours is written in indelible ink and thus cannot be erased or changed. As it is completed, each chapter is sealed. Cognitive therapy suggests that it is time to give up hope for a better past. It is unfortunate if you were victimized by your early experiences, but what are you going to do about it now? You do not have to be crippled by your past forever. It is your obligation to resolve these issues.

The sand that has yet to fall represents the future. The trouble with the future is that we view it through the negative contents of our proverbial bag. There is an interesting yearly contest held by our local newspaper. Participants are asked to guess the Dow Jones average at the end of the year. To those of you who are not familiar with the stock market, the Dow Jones is an average of thirty select stocks. If they increase in value, the Dow Jones goes up and vice versa. Let me give you some history of this important average. Since its inception it has always gone up. With recessions or depressions, it goes down, but it always recovers and inches ever upward. However, 83 percent of the participants guessed that it would be lower at year's end. How can that be? I just told you it always goes up and yet a large majority of participants predicted otherwise. It is simply because of the preponderance of negativity in our brain bags. When we look to the future, we look with an imposed pessimism. When you embark on future endeavors or relationships, you will be deluged with failure messages from your bag. Your Boo will contribute its own vicious diatribe. Don't despair—here is a future guarantee. The future is free! You will win the lottery, you will find the woman or man of your dreams, your business venture will be successful, your daughter will get married, and you will cure your phobia or obsession. Counter the engrained pessimism of your bag with conscious optimism.

But the purpose of the hourglass exercise was to teach you that the way to bring happiness into your life is to deal with the grains of sand passing through the neck of the hourglass. You are basically as happy as your last thought—as your last grain of sand. If you worry for three seconds, those grains of sand are lost and they become the wasted refuse of the past. An old proverb says: "The past is history, the future is a mystery, but today is a gift—that's why they call it the present." If you are to be happy, you have to choreograph your sand. As Kaufman suggested, you are only as happy as your last thought, belief, or statement. What were they?

## Death

At this time I always bring up what appears to be a contradiction in a chapter about happiness—death. I always ask, "What is important about today?" "It's the only time we have," the bumper sticker answers. "It's the first day of the rest of my life." I shock them with the Phobease guarantee. At the conclusion of today, you will be one day closer to your death. That usually provokes some thoughtful groans and comments like, "Thanks, Doc. I thought we were talking about happy." Most people live a lizard's existence. We waste days. We sleep under a rock, go out and get a worm, come back under the rock, and tear another day off our calendar of life. We pretend that our life is infinite. Well, death is not an enemy; it creates an urgency to live that expansive life. It forces us to deal with our finite questions. It is a powerful motivator; it gives importance to every minute of every day.

If we lived an infinite existence, we would change our priorities. When your wife says, "Dear, let's go to Paris this year." "No dear, why don't we wait two or three hundred years until the children leave home." (Wouldn't that be a real "happy when.") Death forces us to deal with our own mortality. Remember the two things your brain doesn't want to do? Die and be embarrassed. If you don't accept your own mortality, your Boo will hold you hostage. Trying to be safe will severely constrict your life. As I said, I prominently display a mug with the cheerful message: "Eat Right, Exercise, and Die Anyway." Embrace your mortality and make plans today to consciously bring happy into your life. Don't waste any more sand.

## Ninety-Day Guarantee

What would you do if I could guarantee that three months from today you would die? (Thanks again, Howie.) Even the best doctors in the world can't save you—you've got ninety days. When I found out about my cancer, I did what any overly responsible phoboc would do—I made sure my estate was in order—awwgh. If you knew you would die, you might want to patch up family quarrels and make amends. You might want to travel to a cherished destination. You might want to make a terminal video and tell significant others that you love them. You might want to give away some possessions and see the joy they bring to the recipients, rather than leaving them in your estate. You might want to start dressing up for the occasion; wear your finest threads and your best jewelry. Do you remember the first thing you did as a kid when you came back from church or synagogue? You took off your good clothes. The next time you wore them, they were four inches too short. Many people wear their best clothes once, hang them in the closet, where they either go out of fashion or "shrink." When we die and get dressed in our finery, everyone says, "He never looked better." Wear those good clothes now. Indeed, if you had a limited time to live you might want to overdress for the upcoming event. You might find that small things that bothered you in the past might not seem so important. You would probably rearrange your priorities. You might take time to enjoy nature's beauties. My wife and I have a favorite mountaintop we love to jog to. We've done it for years. The summit offers a beautiful panoramic view of the entire Bay Area. After my diagnosis, we would run the same trail but now would stop and spend time studying the beauty of the moment. In the past, we had always jogged on as if there was a hurry to be nowhere. Why didn't we stop before? We never thought about it. Accepting our finite reality might be an invitation for you to stop and truly smell the roses. To this day, I do that. On our daily run, I make sure that I focus on the sounds and sights of our trail excursion. With three months to live, you might decide to risk a bit more. Perhaps this is a good time to parachute from an airplane or bungee jump. If you know you're going to die soon it removes some of the safety issues and mortality concerns. Some people smile and say that they would "max" out their credit cards, give cocaine or heroin a try. I'm not condoning either but it's your ninety days. One fellow said he would get a tattoo. Most say they would treasure every moment and they would spend extra time with loved ones. There would be no "lizard days." Every one would be precious.

Well, if this exercise gave you a new perspective of your life or a future outline for you to follow, it has served its purpose. The bad news, though, is I can't guarantee you ninety days. I can't even guarantee you tomorrow. All I can do is remind you that you have only the present moment. Now is the time to recognize the danger of practicing "happy when." Now is the time to decide to maximize pleasure in your every day existence.

## The Ty-D-Bol Man

(I put on my top hat.) Here comes some more bad news. Do you remember the Ty-D-Bol Man commercial? A fellow dressed in a full-length tuxedo and a top hat knocks on your door. He comes in your house and makes your toilet bowl smell clean. The bad news? The Ty-D-Bol Man is not coming to your house. If you want to make your toilet smell good or bring happiness into your life, you are going to have to do it yourself. Don't wait for anyone else to bring happy into your life. It's your responsibility.

## Choreographing Your Sand

Do you remember the grains of sand running through the neck of that infamous hourglass? If you are as happy as your last thought, then you are as happy as your last grain of sand. As such, the first step to increasing pleasure in your life is to choreograph your sand for "happy." Do that by identifying things you like to do. Become selective about what TV, movies, and plays you choose to watch. I don't see movies like *Silence of the Lambs*. I don't need to waste two hours of sand dealing with an intense psychological cannibalistic drama—I had all the intense drama I needed with my years of phobias. Instead, I see movies like *Dumb and Dumber*, *Robin Hood: Men in Tights*, or *Hot Shots II*; *The Naked Gun* series, *Happy Gilmore*, *American Pie*, *Dr. Doolittle*, *Grease*, *Chicago*, *Moulin Rouge*, *Rush Hour*—basically any comedy that gets two thumbs down. I choreograph my sand with comedy and musicals. I don't see plays with deep profound messages. I attend only musicals. If I leave a theater without whistling, I consider it a waste of money, time, and sand. I am very selective about the TV shows I watch. I avoid programs that dwell on human misery, mass murderers, or natural disasters. I don't need to be that well informed. I used to watch the late news. As part of our quest for happy, we had to outline topics covered on the 11 o'clock news. Death, destruction, and natural disasters are featured. Ninety-five percent of what you read in newspapers or see on TV news is negative. Why waste thirty minutes of what could be your last day on earth watching human misery? Observing human horrors is a poor way of choreographing your sand. Instead, for the same thirty minutes preceding your nightly sleep, listen to beautiful music, spend time with your loved one, play with your pet, play your favorite instrument, or spend time enjoying your hobby. Fill your day with "happy" on purpose.

## 14,000 Things to Be Happy About

Barbara Ann Kipfer wrote a wonderfully unique book titled, *14,000 Things to Be Happy About*. Barbara didn't attend my Success and Leadership seminar, but she knew how to choreograph sand. She actually lists 14,000 separate things that you can do to enhance your pleasure. All the foods, candies, and desserts you like; your favorite music; your favorite TV shows; pets and hobbies. She invites you to focus on simple pleasures like going to the bathroom in the middle of the night and finding ample toilet paper. Your cat lying, purring on your chest when you awaken in the morning, or a tube of toothpaste squeezed from the bottom. In the Persian Gulf War, the United States and the coalition forces in days of strategic bombing eliminated pleasures we take for granted. Turning on a faucet and having drinkable water; dependable electricity; TV; radio; or refrigeration. When I grew up, we had an icebox (I can't believe I'm that old!). My job was to take my red wagon, walk two miles (awwgh) and buy a two-day block of ice. Iceboxes are not efficient cooling factories. Frequently, I would take out a container of milk, invert it, and after a four second delay, out would come one glob of putrescent spoiled milk. To this day I am thankful for the cold, nonspoiled refrigerated milk that I use for my morning breakfast. Read the book to get ideas of what you can do to add more happy sand to your life. Get in touch with your four-year-old self. Children know how to have fun. My recovery included several assignments. Buy a toy I wanted as a child but couldn't afford. I bought a large electric train with tracks so big I didn't even need glasses to put them together. I even got extra track—what a luxury—so I could fill a whole room. What a train; it puffed "real" smoke and made real engine sounds. I enjoyed endless minutes of delightful play and I invite you to do the same. Buy a yo-yo and "walk the dog"; master the hula hoop; get some pick-up sticks, jacks, or an etch-a-sketch. You can't play with these and not be happy. If this seems frivolous, let me tell you about some interesting research. There is no scientific evidence that life is serious. There are events in life, of course, that can't be taken lightly, but life in general can be. You might begin by finding evidence that this world really doesn't work. If you look at man's futile and endless search for brotherly love and peace in the face of forty-seven armed conflicts, you get the idea. Political indiscretions, lies, subterfuge, and fights at weddings make it a little easier to accept man's fallibility. So avoid "terminal seriousness." Take you, others, and the world lightly. Be childlike but not childish. The

Tidy Bowl Man may not come but you won't need him after you finish this chapter.

## The Three Golden Paths to Happy

(I put on my jester's hat.) There are three things you need to know to bring happy into your life:

1. Endorphin moments
2. The activity rule: the activity precedes the emotion
3. Look for the color blue

### Endorphin Moments

What do you like to do? You ever notice that when you engage in enjoyable activities, there is an inner smile and a time warp? Time passes by rapidly. Biochemically, when you do what you like to do, you secrete a drug in your body called endorphin. It is 200 times more powerful than morphine. It produces a delectable euphoric state; it is your happy juice. It was discovered that soldiers who had been severely injured in battle didn't require as much pain medication as civilians who suffered comparable wounds. The soldiers with significant wounds were sent from the battlefield to safe hospital settings. Severe wounds were their ticket back home. That mental state was accompanied by an outpouring of internal analgesic: endorphin. Morphine and Demerol were unnecessary. So the simple question if you want frequent endorphin moments is, are you doing what you like to do? I recently attended a Christmas Dance with my stepdaughter and her thirty-year-old friends. They all professed that they loved to dance. When I asked them the last time they had danced, it had been more than two years. That is not a lot of endorphin moments. I give this lecture frequently at retirement homes. Unfortunately, we men are a lot more fragile than women. Because of the differences in life expectancy, the audience is often predominantly female. There is a noticeable absence of male representatives. Many of the widows recount how they loved to dance and how much they missed their partners. I point out, if you have a pillow, you have a partner; put on some of your favorite dance music, grab a pillow, and dance. That's how you get your endorphin "fix." Retirement home dances, no men? Grab a female partner, decide who leads, and generate some more instant happy juice. If you love to play the piano or any other instrument, but haven't played in years, select a specific time, sit down, and play up some endorphins. Identify carefully what you used to do for pleasure and incorporate it again in your life.

## The Activity Rule

(I put on my Mickey Mouse hat here.) The activity precedes the emotion. Thus, do not wait to be happy to do happy things—that's backward. Do happy things and you will become happy. It is very difficult to sing, yodel, whistle, or tap-dance and feel unhappy. I have followed this morning routine for years. Because of my busy schedule, I get up thirty minutes early, and after breakfast and e-mail, I go to my weight room and for the next half hour I sing, yodel, tap-dance, lift weights, juggle, do the hula hoop, play drumsticks on the floor, the spoons, or a banjuke—(a cross between a banjo and a ukelele). God have mercy on anyone sleeping in the guestroom next to the weight room. When I want to study or read, I listen to opera, but in the morning, I want loud, uplifting music—drum solos, Austrian Alp yodelers. I have created thirty minutes of smiles and giggles—thirty minutes of endorphins to launch my morning commute. In the car I sing, whistle, or yodel for the entire twenty-minute trip and end up in the hospital parking lot still whistling. People always ask, "What are you so happy about??" I tell them, "I'm happy because I'm whistling." The activity precedes the emotion. Do happy things and you'll feel happy. What is your happy day? How do you dress for what could be your best day on earth? Before the $1,000 seminar, I wore blue pants, blue shirt, and a black tie—I was a smurf. I didn't wear nice clothes or jewelry because I didn't want to flaunt my monetary success in front of my patients. I thought they would be impressed with a nondescript dresser driving an old car. I was wrong. That $1,000 seminar cost me a lot of money. The self-contempt and feelings of worthlessness I felt because of my phobia were effectively discharged. I fell in love with me and celebrated by buying a new wardrobe and a new expensive car. I sold my one-bedroom condo and put a down payment on a five-bedroom home. Nice digs for a smurf. When you dress well, people notice and compliment you and that creates additional endorphin moments. What activities and things could you do to prove to yourself that the activity precedes the emotions?

## Look for Blue

(I put on my Mad Hatter's hat.) A simple exercise asks people to look for the color blue. Guess what happens? They find it everywhere. Well, I'm not going to ask you to find blue; I'm going to ask you to find humor. Guess what happens when you look for "funny"? You guessed right. You find it everywhere—at work, on TV, the movies, in the newspaper. For instance, there was a news item about twenty-five students caught cheating in a college course. Do you know what the course was? Ethics! That's funny. Here's a challenge—look hard and find five funny things in today's newspaper. There are jokes everywhere: *Reader's Digest*, the backside of the *Playboy* centerfold (pun intended), monthly humor newsletters and, of course, politics. Learn to tell jokes and people will return the favor. When you tell jokes, you are practicing an activity that precedes the happy emotion you are seeking.

The family patriarch is dying. The children gather around to ask where he would like to be buried. "Do you want to be buried with your ex-wife in Ohio, your mistress in New York, or your current girlfriend here in California?" The old man takes one more breath and says, "Surprise me."

Another man is also on his deathbed. He smells the unmistakable aroma of his wife's world-renowned chocolate chip cookies—his absolute favorite. He is too weak to stand, but crawls out of bed and on hands and knees drags himself into the kitchen. As he reaches up to grab a cookie off the kitchen table, his wife slaps his hand and says, "Don't take those—they're for your funeral."

A man fatally injured in a motorcycle accident lays dying on the sidewalk. Someone in the crowd asks, "Is there a priest present who could give him last rites?" No response. However, a disheveled homeless man steps forward and says, "I'm not a priest but for the past two years I have lived in a dumpster outside of a church. I have heard what goes on there and perhaps I could say a few words to him." "Sure, go ahead." He kneels down beside the doomed man and says, "B-13, N-32, O-64."

Fill your draining sand with large doses of fun. The happy state is simply an absence of negative thoughts and evaluations. You can crowd them out with a dedicated quest for laughter.

## Aging and Death

An elderly woman is complaining to her physician about numerous physical symptoms. The doctor reminds her that she isn't getting any younger. She tells him she's not paying him to get her younger. We pay doctors to get us older. Old is a privilege that not everyone gets to enjoy. Satchel Paige, a famous African American pitcher, once asked, "How old would you be if you didn't know how old you were?" Most of us feel twenty years younger. While we can't change our chronological age, we can reduce our physiological age with exercise, good nutrition, and healthy habits. We can stop smoking, reduce weight, wear sunscreen, floss daily, and get a yearly physical. Heart attacks and strokes are not death sentences. In fact, if you want to live a long time, get a medical disease and take care of it. Ask Dick Cheney, the U.S. vice president—he has had four heart attacks and sports an implanted automatic defibrillator. Life is an action game and you'll be dead for five or six million years—you can rest then.

Finally, don't plan for your death, it should come, as the patriarch in my joke suggested, as a surprise. Keep buying green bananas and hope you'll die with a closet full of things you bought the day before. Accept your mortality and use it as a motivator to live that expansive life.

There you have it—do what you like to do, do activities that lead to happy feelings, and continually look for humor. Celebrate each day and live it as if it were your last because one day, you'll be right. Accept your mortality, avoid "happy when," choreograph your sand wisely, and you'll get those 310 laughs and giggles back.

## Setbacks and Relapses

Setbacks and relapses are common and expected for several reasons:

### Expanding Challenges

As you continue to improve, you begin to pursue loftier, previously unattainable goals. Paris replaces the grocery store two miles away. With these jumps, you'll hear from your Boo. Tell it, "I was expecting you," read it your 500 victories, and tell it to shut up.

### Future Crises

Cure does not make you an emotional zombie. Born phoboc, die phoboc. Future crises—good or bad—will probably rejuvenate your Boo. Deaths or births, divorces or marriages, job loss or promotions—any may add new fuel to a lethargic Boo. When you hear from it, boss it back.

### Disconcerting Medications

You may experience physical or psychological withdrawal. You may even get a recurrence of symptoms. When the Boo speaks up, try the "two-word cure."

### Waning of Skills

Over time, you may experience a waning of your Phobease skills. Go back to page one and reread the book or take a Phobease class or workshop. Step back on the neck of your Boo.

## A Final Word

Continue to practice and refine your skills and you will continue to improve and grow. Be a "*trained*" phoboc killer. Follow your Phobease principles and don't forget to write to me about your victories! Improvement continues for years. Remember, the Boo is always looking for vulnerability. If you are stressed, fatigued, ill, challenged, depressed, or hormonal, you may hear from your Boo. Be prepared and handle it!

Make a commitment to cure! Remember, Phobease works if you do.

All phobias and obsessions are curable.

## Chapter 11 Highlights

1. Happy is the feeling you have when you don't create unhappy thoughts.
2. Your goal is to get your 310 laughs and giggles back.
3. The Ty-D-Bol Man is not coming. You have to choreograph your own sand to be happy.
4. Don't practice "happy when," practice "happy now."
5. Death is not an enemy but a great motivator. It creates urgency and gives meaning to life.
6. Don't live the lizard's life—celebrate each day and don't forget to dress for it.
7. Do what you like to do and you'll secrete endorphins—your happy juice.
8. The activity precedes the emotion—don't wait to be happy to do happy things.
9. Don't look for blue—instead, search for humor and find it.
10. Live each day as if it were your last because one day it will be.
11. Setbacks are normal and expected.

## Chapter 11 Assignment

Do daily relaxation.

Exercise fifteen to thirty minutes daily.

Continue your diary and your victory card.

Keep working on your hierarchies.

1. Make a list of ten things that you could do or buy to bring more pleasure and fun into your life and then do them or buy them.

2. Gratitude exercise: For two minutes upon awakening in the morning, give thanks for every body part that works or doesn't hurt. Give thanks for awakening alive. That's a good day.

3. List 100 things you are happy about. Get real basic (e.g., favorite TV program, song, singer, your pet, peanut butter). Keep writing ten per week. Read Barbara Ann Kipfer's book, *14,000 Things to Be Happy About.*

4. Write a letter of commendation about yourself for an imagined important ambassador position. List all of your attributes.

5. Buy some fun kid toys and relearn those skills. Maybe a yo-yo, a hula hoop, a harmonica, a tambourine, a kazoo, a jump rope, juggling balls, jacks, or pick-up sticks.

6. Write your obituary. How do you think your life will turn out? If you believe it's going to turn out okay, then realize that everything you're going through right now is leading to that okay outcome.

7. Make a pleasure calendar. Take any yearly calendar and write in an approximate date for everything you ever did that was fun, exciting, and memorable. Include vacations, rewards, first dates, first car, and births, and read it at your breakfast table.

Commit to cure.

Comfort is not your goal—living is your goal.

All phobocs can be cured.

# Epilogue

I JUST RETURNED from my thirty-sixth cruise—a beautiful fall foliage excursion. I revisited one of my fifty foreign countries on that voyage. I want to remind you that prior to my phoboc cure, the number of cruises this claustrophobic doctor had taken was zero.

I now travel anywhere, sit anywhere, and allow people to drive me anywhere. I fly in jets, helicopters, one- or two-engine private planes, and, on one occasion, an Otis Spunkmeyer sixty-year-old propeller-driven antique. I awaken each morning at an anxiety level of zero, confident that whatever happens that day, "I will handle it." I am still that wonderful, empathetic phoboc who cries at Lassie movies and any situation where the underdog triumphs.

The good news—you can do the same. I don't care how long you have been phoboc, how many therapists you have seen, or how much medication you have taken. If you have not had a psychoeducational, cognitive behavioral, experiential desensitization program, you have not been appropriately treated. If you have read this book and done the exercises, you are a trained phoboc on the path to cure. Phobease works if you do. If you face your fear correctly and purposefully, and repeatedly experience your fear, you will eventually habituate and master your fear. You will be able to share those fearless mornings with me and truly live that expansive life you have always dreamed about. Remember, all phobias and obsessions are curable.

Good luck,
Dr. Liebgold

# APPENDIX A

# Suggested Reading:
# Phobease Books and Tapes

## Suggested Reading

*The Secret Life of Eating Disorders* by Peggy Claude Pierre (Random House)

*Healing the Shame That Binds You* by John Bradshaw (Health Communications, Inc.)

*You Are Not Alone—Compulsive Hair Pulling* by Cheryn Salazar (Rophe Press)

*Talking to Yourself* by Pamela E. Butler (Harper & Row, San Francisco)

*Self Assertion for Women* by Pamela E. Butler (Harper & Row, San Francisco)

*The Boy Who Couldn't Stop Washing* by Judith L. Rapoport (Penguin Books)

*Journey from Anxiety to Freedom* by Mani Feniger (Prima Publishing)

*The Sky Is Falling (OCD)* by Reann Dumont (W.W. Norton & Co.)

*Dying of Embarrassment* (Social Phobia) by Barbara Markway (New Harbinger)

*Self-Esteem* by Matthew McKay & Patrick Fanning (New Harbinger)

*The Broken Mirror* (BDD) by Katherine A. Phillips (Oxford University Press)

*14,000 Things to Be Happy About* by Barbara Ann Kipfer

*When Once Is Not Enough* (OCD) by Gail Steketee & Kerrin White (New Harbinger)

*You Can't Afford the Luxury of a Negative Thought* by John-Roger and Peter McWilliams (Prelude Press)

If you fear flying, public speaking, crowds, animals, bridges, freeways, or social situations, or have any other fears, *you can conquer them!*

Dr. Fear, also known as Dr. Liebgold, has had a medical career spanning thirty-five years, including being the chief of Kaiser's Rehabilitation Program and being chosen as California's Physician of the Year in 1991. He has appeared on *Evening Magazine*, the *Oprah Winfrey Show*, and PBS, and has dedicated his life to helping people with their fears. Through his books and tapes, or his classes, you can learn the techniques he has used to help over 15,000 people conquer their fears!

More information online at www.angelnet.com/fear.html, or call Angelnet at (707) 318-7631 for a brochure.

## Books and Audiotapes by Dr. Liebgold

### Audio Tapes

101. *Self Esteem*—two tapes

    An in-depth look at where your self-love, self-worth, and self-esteem went and how to get them back.

102. *Overcoming Shyness*

    Specific tools for becoming a comfortable and gifted conversationalist.

103. *How to Be Happy*

    Specific tools for choreographing happiness into your life.

*104. *Overcoming Phobias*—two tapes

    A condensed version of all ten lectures given at the Phobease classes.

105. *Overcoming Stage Fright*

    How to conquer America's number one phobia: fear of public speaking.

106. *Assertiveness*

Understanding and acquiring the skills so you can get what you want.

107. *Codependency*

Understanding its origin and its devastating consequences and how to overcome it.

108. *OCD Workshops*—four tapes

An in-depth look at the origin, dynamics, and treatment of obsessive compulsive disorders. Includes hoarding, BDD, scrupulosity, and hair pulling.

109. *Phobease Relaxation Tape*

A combination of progressive relaxation, autogenics, and imaginal desensitization.

110. *Fearless Flying the Phobease Way*

Learn how to effectively manage your anxiety so that you can comfortably fly anywhere.

## Books

*B1. *Curing Anxiety, Phobias, Shyness, and OCD*

A ten-chapter, ten-week manual used in the Phobease classes, but also designed to be used at home for non-attendees. (174 pages)

*B2. *Phobease Revisited*

A compilation of twenty-five articles on important phobia and OCD topics written for national newsletters. A supplement to Phobease class manual. (56 pages)

*B3. *More Phobease Revisited*

Thirty powerful articles to further enhance your knowledge about the origin and treatment of phobias, anxieties, and obsessions. (70 pages)

*B4. *Even More Phobease Revisited*

Twenty-nine articles covering the spectrum from eating disorders, OCD, BDD, PTSD, school phobias, and self-mutilation. (72 pages)

B5. *The Last Phobease Revisited*

Twenty-five articles including hypochondriasis, fear of bowel accident, paruresis, selective mutism, and hoarding. (58 pages)

B6. *Children's Manual*

Curing anxiety, phobias, shyness, and OCD. A six-chapter, six-week manual designed to treat all anxiety disorders. (39 pages)

## Videotapes

V2. *Curing Phobias, Shyness, and OCD*

This video, shot at the Commonwealth Club in San Francisco, outlines the origin and the cure of phobias, shyness, and OCD.

*V3. *The Tools to Cure Phobias, Shyness, and OCD*

The full first four Phobease lectures detailing the origins of these disorders and the specific tools needed to overcome these devastating disorders.

*V4. *Phobease Lectures 5 to 10*

Cognitive Restructuring, Conversational and Arguing Skills, Self-Esteem, Co-Dependency, and How To Be Happy

Visit us at www.angelnet.com/fear.html or contact us by e-mail at Phobease@aol.com

---

*Note: Audio 104 and/or videos V3, V4 can be combined with books B1, B2, B3, B4, and B5 for a complete home course.

**Liebro, Co.**
**181 Obsidian Way**
**Hercules, California 94547**
**(707) 651-1044 (ph)**

*Fast, Efficient Service!*

*It's Easy to Order*
Mail your order form to:
Dr. Howard Liebgold
975 Sereno Dr.
Vallejo, CA 94590

| Item No. | Qty. | Item Name | Price | Total |
|---|---|---|---|---|
| **Audio** | | | | |
| 101 | | Self Esteem—two-Tape Set | $20.00 | |
| 102 | | Overcoming Shyness—How to Be a Good Conversationalist | $11.00 | |
| 103 | | How to Be Happy | $11.00 | |
| 104 | | Overcoming Phobias—two-Tape Set | $20.00 | |
| 105 | | Overcoming Stage Fright: Speaking in Public | $11.00 | |
| 106 | | Assertiveness—Getting What You Want | $11.00 | |
| 107 | | Co-Dependency | $11.00 | |
| 108 | | OCD Workshop—four-Tape Set | $34.95 | |
| 109 | | Phobease Relaxation Tape | $11.00 | |
| 110 | | Fearless Flying | $11.00 | |
| **Books** | | | | |
| B1 | | Curing Anxiety, Phobias, Shyness & OCD—the Fifth Edition (175 pages) | $19.95 | |
| B2 | | Phobease Revisited (56 pages) | $6.95 | |
| B3 | | More Phobease Revisited (72 pages) | $6.95 | |
| B4 | | Even More Phobease Revisited (72 pages) | $6.95 | |
| B5 | | The Last Phobease Revisited | $6.95 | |
| B6 | | Children's Manual: Curing Anxiety, Phobias, Shyness, & OCD | $8.95 | |
| **Videos** | | | | |
| V2 | | Curing Anxiety, Phobias, Shyness, and OCD | $29.95 | |
| V3 | | The Tools to Cure Phobias, Shyness, & OCD (Phobease Lectures 1–4; Running time 180 minutes) | $39.95 | |
| V4 | | Cognitive Restructuring, Conversational and Arguing Skills, Self-Esteem, Co-Dependency, How to Be Happy (Phobease Lectures 5–10; Running time 180 minutes) | $39.95 | |
| V3 &V4 | | Special: Both Videos | $75.00 | |

Subtotal _____

(California) Add 8% Sales Tax _____

Shipping & Handling @ $1.00 per item _____

TOTAL COST _____

Paid by: Check _____

Make Checks payable to LIEBRO, CO.

Name _____

Address _____

City, State, Zip _____

Phone _____

Credit Card: Visa _____ MasterCard _____

Credit Card # _____

Exp. Date_____

Name on Card _____

Signature _____

Visit our website at www.angelnet.com/fear.html or e-mail us at Phobease@aol.com

# APPENDIX B

# Phobia and OCD Organizations

**Phobease—Kaiser Hospital**
Dr. Howard Liebgold
975 Sereno Drive
Vallejo, CA 94589
(707) 651-2297

**Phobease—Kaiser Hospital**
Walnut Creek Medical Center
1425 South Main Street
Walnut Creek, CA 94596
(925) 295-4190

**Anxiety Disorders Association of America**
8730 Georgia Avenue, Suite 600
Silver Spring, MD 20910
(240) 485-1001
anxdis@adaa.org

**National Anxiety Foundation**
3134 Custer Drive
Lexington, KY 40517-4001

**The Trichotillomania Learning Center**
1215 Mission Street, Suite 2
Santa Cruz, CA 95060
(408) 457-1004

**International Paruresis Association**
P.O. Box 26225
Baltimore, MD 21210
(800) 247-3864
www.shybladder.org

**Phobease—Kaiser Hospital**
Vacaville Medical Center
1330 Vaca Valley Road
Vacaville, CA 95687
(707) 453-4155

**Obsessive Compulsive Foundation, Inc.**
P.O. Box 70
Milford, CT 06460
(203) 878-5669
www.oc-foundation.org
Hotline For Acute Attacks
National Institute of Mental Health
(800) 647-2642

If you are looking for a program in your area, call your nearest hospital or regional medical center or the ADAA and ask if they offer a cognitive behavioral program for panic attacks, phobias or obsessive compulsive disorder.